1993

THE LAW OF ILLINOIS

VOLUME I
Lincoln's Cases Before the Illinois Supreme Court,
From His Entry Into the Practice of Law
Until His Entry Into Congress

Published by
The Illinois Company
Shiloh, Illinois

Library of Congress Catalog Card Number: 92-97537

ISBN 0-9635192-0-4

Manufactured in the United States of America

Dedicated to

Patsy Miriam Long,
my mother,

and

Kate Knight Patch,
my grandmother,

*who first told me
about Abraham Lincoln*

FOREWORD

by

William D. Beard

Assistant Editor
The Lincoln Legal Papers

Abraham Lincoln practiced law for nearly a quarter century, yet his career before the Illinois and federal courts remains the least studied aspect of the sixteenth President's life. Research by **The Lincoln Legal Papers: A Documentary History of the Law Practice of Abraham Lincoln** has discovered Lincoln had a much larger law practice than previously estimated. Original estimates figured Lincoln handled 3,000 cases, but it now appears the actual total will approach 5,000 cases.

Lincoln was an aggressive and tenacious litigator whose mastery of civil and criminal procedure is evident from existing court records. Popular notions about his carelessness and homespun demeanor tend to obscure a tough streak in Lincoln's pre-trial preparation and courtroom tactics. Indeed, John P. Frank's **Lincoln as a Lawyer** concluded that Lincoln possessed five qualities imperative for being a successful lawyer: (1) a personality that attracted clients and impressed juries, (2) organizational skills that enabled him to grasp the key issue(s) in a case, (3) brilliant verbal expression in written and oral arguments, (4) the mental capacity to retain important information and ideas, and (5) the ambition to manage a substantial workload.

Those qualities were apparent to Lincoln's clients and colleagues as well. Several colleagues referred to Lincoln as the finest trial lawyer in the state. Statistics substantiate the claim as Lincoln and his partners, John Todd Stuart (1837-1841), Stephen T. Logan (1841-1844), and William H. Herndon (1844-1861), especially Herndon in their peak years together, had the largest

i

trial practice among their peers of the Sangamon County bar. For example, during 1853 Lincoln and Herndon were responsible for no less than one-third of all cases brought before the Sangamon Circuit Court. At that time there were over 40 attorneys practicing there, so this share stood well above its closest rivals.

While impressive, Lincoln's trial level caseload pales in relative importance to his practice before the Illinois Supreme Court. Lincoln had a major appellate practice in Illinois during his career. In 1916, John T. Richards identified 177 Lincoln Supreme Court cases. That figure remained unchanged until *Lincoln Legal Papers* research in the Illinois Supreme Court records in the State Archives identified 402 Supreme Court cases managed by Lincoln and/or his partners, including 290 definitely involving Lincoln. In one peak year (1845) the firm had 39 cases. From these results it is clear that Lincoln had the largest appellate practice in central Illinois, and probably the largest statewide.

John Long's fine study of Lincoln early practice before the Illinois Supreme Court confirms that Lincoln "could split hairs as well as he split rails." Long's case-by-case analysis indicates Lincoln's ability as an appellate attorney by showing his meticulous preparation for each appeal. His technique of simplification is portrayed by reducing the case to a few essential points and offering a very limited number of citations to substantiate them. Thus, this self-trained lawyer played an important role in molding the outlines of Illinois' jurisprudence.

Long's analysis also supports Lincoln's definition of the role of law in a republic: "**legislation** and **adjudication** must follow, and conform to, the progress of society." In Lincoln's view the law was the glue holding the fragile American republic together. At the base of Lincoln's political philosophy was the "right to rise" concept. For Lincoln, the Declaration of Independence was the primary statement justifying the American experiment in republican government. The principle "Liberty to All" proved to be an "Apple of Gold," Lincoln wrote in 1861.

"The Union and the Constitution, are the picture of silver, subsequently framed around it. The picture was made, not to conceal or destroy the apple; but to adorn and preserve it. The picture was made for the apple -- not the apple for the picture." Thus, the nation and its laws, expressed in the U.S. Constitution, state constitutions, statutes, and legal decisions, were to enhance the central idea, as Lincoln saw it, of equality, which Lincoln embellished to mean equality of opportunity. Men and women were to have an equal opportunity to rise in society so far as their talents and ambitions allowed. Buttressing the individual's climb up the ladder of prosperity was a system of law that was living, active, and always changing in order that justice keep pace with society.

America's emergence from a subsistence to a market economy during the years of Lincoln's legal career increased the responsibility of the legal system. If Eastern and European capital was to transform Western prairies into prosperous farms and cities, there must be a system of conflict resolution which all participants respected. For ambitious men and women to continue their upward climb they must believe they would receive a fair hearing and judgment in the courts. Therefore, Lincoln believed it imperative that "reverence for the law" must "become the political religion of the nation," because anarchy and ruin for all would occur if the so-called losers in the court shot the judges and burned the courthouses. John Long's study of Lincoln in the Illinois Supreme Court confirms that respect for that court's decisions was maintained by the diligent labor and professional integrity of attorneys such as Abraham Lincoln.

This book contains no footnotes (with the insignificant exception of one at the bottom of page four, concerning the number of appellate cases in which Lincoln appeared before the Illinois Supreme Court), for the reason that my method of composition has not involved drawing upon any pre-existing sources, so as to require attribution, in footnotes, to those sources. Rather, I have worked strictly from the text of the original, reported decisions of the Illinois Supreme Court in Lincoln's cases. The conclusions that I have drawn and the evaluations that I have made, concerning Lincoln's performance in his appellate cases, have been based upon the legal education which I received at St. Louis University School of Law; upon my experience as a law clerk for Justice George J. Moran, Sr., of the Appellate Court of Illinois for the Fifth Judicial District for the period of a year; upon my own writing of appellate briefs, as a practicing lawyer, for submission to the Appellate Court of Illinois for the Fifth Judicial District; and upon my experience in the general practice of law in the small towns of southern Illinois for the past 16 years.

Moreover, the circumstances under which I wrote the chapters of this book prevented me from examining any scholarly works about Lincoln's career as a lawyer, from which I might have been able to draw and repeat observations about Lincoln's performance as an appellate lawyer. I wrote most of these chapters in my law office, while trying to address legal work that waited to be done. In short, I wrote these chapters -- about Lincoln's appellate cases -- in circumstances which I believe were substantially similar to those in which Lincoln himself worked on those appellate cases in the first place.

I trust that the similarity of Lincoln's experience and my own, in the practice of law in Illinois, as well as my own love for the law and the people of Illinois, have given me more insight into Lincoln's performance as an appellate lawyer, and his dealings with his clients, than others might dare to claim for themselves.

Lincoln once said of Henry Clay that he was "my beau ideal of a statesman." Lincoln is my beau ideal of a statesman, lawyer, and man. My hopes for our country's future are buoyed by the knowledge that, in this admiration of Lincoln, I am surely not alone.

John Long

December 2, 1992
Shiloh, Illinois

PROLOGUE

The history of the law of Illinois is, in large part, the record of the heartaches and triumphs of humble, obscure, and ordinary people. The individual who shines forth out of that history, as the most inspiring participant in it, is Abraham Lincoln. This book discusses Abraham Lincoln's work before the Illinois Supreme Court, as revealed by the reported decisions of that Court, during the first half of his legal career: that is, from 1836 through 1847.

Lincoln was admitted to the practice of law by the Illinois Supreme Court on September 9, 1836, when he was 27 years old. He engaged in the practice of law until 1860, when he was 51 years old. The 24 years in between marked his maturation from being merely one of many ambitious, intelligent lawyers to being the "Great Emancipator" and the author of both the Gettysburg Address and the Second Inaugural Address. During those years -- excepting only the two that he was in Congress, from 1847 to 1849 -- he earned his living and supported his family by thinking, writing, and speaking about the law in Illinois. He handled at least 166[1] appeals before the Illinois Supreme Court, a huge number by today's standards. In connection with those appeals, he wrote -- or collaborated on -- 55 briefs which may still be found and read in the printed reports of the decisions of the Illinois Supreme Court.

Of Lincoln's 166 cases before the Illinois Supreme Court, for which decisions of the Illinois Supreme Court are reported, 83 occurred during the first half of his legal career: that is, before his entry into Congress. This book analyzes each case in turn, identifying the legal issues involved therein, setting forth passages from Lincoln's written legal arguments, and commenting upon Lincoln's performance as an appellate lawyer.

The 83 cases, from the first half Lincoln's legal career, are set forth in the following Table of Contents:

1

TABLE OF CONTENTS

CHAPTER	DISCUSSION OF CASE NAMED	CITATION	PAGE NUMBER
Prologue			1
1	Scammon vs. Cline	3 Ill. 456 (1840)	5
2	Cannon vs. Kinney	4 Ill. 9 (1841)	7
3	Maus vs. Worthing	4 Ill. 26 (1841)	10
4	Bailey vs.Cromwell	4 Ill. 71 (1841)	11
5	Ballentine vs. Beall	4 Ill. 203 (1841)	13
6	Elkin vs. People	4 Ill. 208 (1841)	15
7	Benedict vs. Dillehunt	4 Ill. 287 (1841)	17
8	Abrams vs. Camp	4 Ill. 290 (1841)	19
9	Hancock vs. Hodgson	4 Ill. 330 (1841)	21
10	Grable vs. Margrave	4 Ill. 372 (1842)	23
11	Averill vs. Field	4 Ill. 390 (1842)	25
12	Wilson vs. Alexander	4 Ill. 392 (1842)	28
13	Schlenker vs. Risley	4 Ill. 483 (1842)	31
14	Mason vs. Park	4 Ill. 532 (1842)	33
15	Greathouse vs.Smith	4 Ill. 541 (1842)	35
16	Watkins vs. White	4 Ill. 549 (1842)	37
17	Payne vs. Frazier	5 Ill. 55 (1842)	39
18	Fitch vs. Pinckard	5 Ill. 69 (1842)	41
19	Edwards vs. Helm	5 Ill. 142 (1842)	43
20	Grubb vs. Crane	5 Ill. 153 (1842)	45
21	Pentecost vs. Magahee	5 Ill. 326 (1843)	47
22	Robinson vs. Chesseldine	5 Ill. 332 (1843)	48
23	Lazell vs. Francis	5 Ill. 421 (1843)	50
24	Spear vs. Campbell	5 Ill. 424 (1843)	52
25	Bruce vs. Truett	5 Ill. 454 (1843)	54
26	England vs. Clark	5 Ill. 486 (1843)	56
27	Johnson vs. Weedman	5 Ill. 495 (1843)	58
28	Hall vs. Perkins	5 Ill. 549 (1843)	60
29	Lockridge vs. Foster	5 Ill. 570 (1843)	62
30	Dorman vs. Lane	6 Ill. 143 (1844)	64

31	Davis vs. Harkness	6 Ill. 173 (1844)	66
32	Martin vs. Dryden	6 Ill. 187 (1844)	69
33	Warner vs. Helm	6 Ill. 220 (1844)	85
34	McDonald vs. Fithian	6 Ill. 269 (1844)	87
35	Favor vs. Marlett	6 Ill. 385 (1844)	88
36	Parker vs. Smith	6 Ill. 411 (1844)	90
37	Stickney vs. Cassell	6 Ill. 418 (1844)	92
38	Kimball vs. Cook	6 Ill. 423 (1844)	94
39	Morgan vs. Griffin	6 Ill. 565 (1844)	97
40	Cook vs. Hall	6 Ill. 575 (1844)	100
41	Field vs. Rawlings	6 Ill. 581 (1844)	104
42	Broadwell vs. Broadwell	6 Ill. 599 (1844)	106
43	Rogers vs. Dickey	6 Ill. 636 (1844)	110
44	Kelly vs. Garrett	6 Ill. 649 (1844)	113
45	McCall vs. Lesher	7 Ill. 46-7 (1845)	115
46	Wren vs. Moss	7 Ill. 72 (1845)	118
47	Risinger vs. Cheney	7 Ill. 84 (1845)	120
48	Eldridge vs. Rowe	7 Ill. 91 (1845)	122
49	Frisby vs. Ballance	7 Ill. 141 (1845)	124
50	Hall vs. Irwin	7 Ill. 176 (1845)	126
51	City of Springfield vs. Hickox	7 Ill. 241 (1845)	129
52	Ross vs. Nesbit	7 Ill. 252 (1845)	132
53	Simpson vs. Ranlett	7 Ill. 312 (1845)	134
54	Murphy vs. Summerville	7 Ill. 361 (1845)	136
55	Trailor vs. Hill	7 Ill. 364 (1845)	138
56	Chase vs. Debolt	7 Ill. 371 (1845)	141
57	Smith vs. Byrd	7 Ill. 412 (1845)	144
58	Moore vs. Hamilton	7 Ill. 429 (1845)	146
59	McNamara vs. King	7 Ill. 432 (1845)	148
60	Ellis vs. Locke	7 Ill. 459 (1845)	150
61	Bryan vs. Wash	7 Ill. 557 (1845)	152
62	Wright vs. Bennett	7 Ill. 587 (1845)	155
63	Kincaid vs. Turner	7 Ill. 618 (1845)	158
64	Cunningham vs. Fithian	7 Ill. 650 (1845)	160

65	Wilson vs. Van Winkle	7 Ill. 684 (1845)	163
66	Patterson vs. Edwards	7 Ill. 720 (1845)	166
67	Griggs vs. Gear	8 Ill. 2 (1845)	168
68	Edgar County vs. Mayo	8 Ill. 82 (1846)	171
69	Roney vs. Monaghan	8 Ill. 85 (1846)	174
70	People ex rel. Harris vs. Browne	8 Ill. 87 (1846)	175
71	Munsell vs. Temple	8 Ill. 93 (1846)	177
72	Fell vs. Price	8 Ill. 186 (1846)	180
73	Wright vs. Taylor	8 Ill. 193 (1846)	183
74	Welch vs. Sykes	8 Ill. 197 (1846)	186
75	Hawks vs. Lands	8 Ill. 227 (1846)	189
76	Garrett vs. Stevenson	8 Ill. 261 (1846)	192
77	Henderson vs. Welch	8 Ill. 340 (1846)	195
78	Cowls vs. Cowls	8 Ill. 435 (1846)	198
79	Wilcoxen vs. Roby	8 Ill. 475 (1846)	201
80	Trumbull vs Campbell	8 Ill. 502 (1846)	203
81	Cooper vs. Crosby	8 Ill. 506 (1846)	206
82	Shaeffer vs. Weed	8 Ill. 511 (1846)	211
83	Anderson vs. Ryan	8 Ill. 583 (1846)	214

A Retrospection on the First Half of Lincoln's
Career before the Illinois Supreme Court 217
Notes on Indices 219
Index A Names of People and Organizations 221
Index B Names of Places 241
Index C Legal Topics, Listed Case by Case 245
Index D Legal Topics, in Alphabetical Order 269
Index E Authorities Cited in Lincoln's Briefs 291

[1] The figure 166, as the number of appellate cases in which Lincoln was involved before the Illinois Supreme Court, is based upon the list published at 400 Ill. 616 - 619. The Lincoln Legal Papers project has determined, however, that Lincoln was involved in even more appellate cases before the Illinois Supreme Court.

Lincoln's first appellate case, to be included in the reports of the Illinois Supreme Court's decisions, was *Scammon vs. Cline,* 3 Ill. 456 (1840). The case arose in Boone County, which was about 180 miles north of Lincoln's home in Springfield. A lawyer named J. L. Loop obviously had handled the trial of the case in Boone County, and had referred it to Lincoln to represent his client, Cornelius Cline, in defending against the appeal which the other party had taken to the Illinois Supreme Court in Springfield. Lincoln's presence in Springfield, and his access there to one of the few law libraries in the State -- namely, the Illinois Supreme Court's law library -- put him in a position to gain such business, if he performed his appellate duties well. That Lincoln was similarly retained on appeal in other cases throughout his legal career, indicates that his appellate work earned the respect of his fellow lawyers around the State of Illinois.

The lot of an appellate lawyer is sometimes to be stuck with a hair-splitting argument made by his client's trial lawyer in the trial court. This happened to Lincoln in his defense against the appeal in *Scammon vs. Cline.* It is also true, however, that a young, eager lawyer -- as Lincoln was in 1840 -- is typically more willing to make a hair-splitting argument in behalf of his client, perhaps mistaking his willingness to make the argument for either brilliance or zeal.

Scammon had sued Cline before a justice of the peace of Boone County in 1839. Cline won a judgment in his favor, and Scammon sought to appeal to the local circuit court for a completely new trial, known as a trial *de novo.* About that time, the Illinois legislature removed Boone County from the jurisdiction of the Circuit Court of Jo Daviess County, and created a separate Circuit Court of Boone County. The circuit clerk had already been appointed for Boone County before March 2, 1839, but the statute setting the time for the commencement of the sessions of the Circuit Court of Boone County was not passed until March 2, 1839. Scammon filed his appeal papers with the Circuit Clerk of Boone County on March 1, 1839. Cline's trial lawyer argued to the Circuit Court of Boone County that Scammon's appeal should be dismissed on the ground that -- as of March 1, 1839 -- Scammon should have filed his appeal papers with the Circuit Clerk of Jo Daviess County because the Circuit Court of Boone County was not then legally in existence. The Circuit Court of Boone County agreed, and dismissed Scammon's appeal, whereupon Scammon appealed to the Illinois Supreme Court.

Lincoln then presented the same argument to the Illinois Supreme Court that Cline's trial lawyer had made to the Circuit Court of Boone County: namely, that Scammon had filed his appeal papers one day too early with the Circuit Clerk of Boone County.

The Illinois Supreme Court rejected this argument, and held that the Circuit Court of Boone County was in existence, for the purpose of taking an appeal to it, from the time of the appointment of the circuit clerk, which had occurred before March 2, 1839. The Illinois Supreme Court reversed the judgment in favor of Cline and remanded the case to the Circuit Court of Boone County for trial.

Thus Lincoln lost his first appellate case, and it must be said -- in view of the strained character of his only argument -- rightly so. Lincoln afterward rarely made an argument on appeal as tenuous.

If a man were to lend an item of personal property to a friend, and a third person then stole that item out of the possession of the friend, it seems sensible to us that the owner should be able to sue the thief for damages. Whether the owner could, in fact, sue the thief, was an open question in Illinois until Lincoln won his appeal to the Illinois Supreme Court in the case of *Cannon vs. Kinney,* 4 Ill. 9 (1841).

Lincoln represented Manly Cannon, the owner of a horse, both at trial and on appeal. Cannon had loaned a horse to John Harris, so that John Harris could ride from an area known as "the Lead Mines" to Sangamon County. After arriving in Sangamon County, Harris placed the horse in the hands of his brother, James Harris, for feeding and safekeeping throughout the winter. The brother, James Harris, experienced a shortage of horse feed and, so, delivered the horse to yet another brother, Robert Harris, for feeding and safekeeping throughout the winter. When the grass began to grow in the spring, Robert Harris turned the horse out on to the prairie with his own horses. The defendant, Matthew Kinney, stole the horse from off the prairie. Cannon sued Kinney for the value of the horse, $65.

In the trial court, Kinney moved for a directed verdict on the ground that there was no evidence that he had taken the horse from Cannon's *possession.* Kinney asserted that the basis of Cannon's action, for trespass to personal property, was a violation of his possession of the horse. Thus Kinney argued, in essence, that the last person to possess the horse -- namely, Robert Harris -- was the only one who could sue him for damages for trespass to personal property.

The trial court agreed with Kinney, and directed a verdict against Lincoln's client, Cannon. Lincoln appealed to the Illinois Supreme Court for Cannon.

In that appeal, Lincoln filed his first brief which was printed in the reports of the decisions of the Illinois Supreme Court. The term "bailee," as used in the brief, refers to one who has borrowed, or who otherwise rightfully holds possession of, an item of personal property for another.

The brief read as follows:

"A. Lincoln, for the plaintiff in error, relied upon the following points and authorities:

I. If the plaintiff showed himself to be the general owner of the horse, and also entitled to the immediate possession of him, at the time the defendant seized him, he showed a constructive possession, which is sufficient: 1 Chit. Plead., 153.

1. The general owner of personal property may maintain trespass against a third person who takes such property from the bailee, by gratuitous loan, of such general owner: Ibid, 154; 3 Johns. Dig., 575.

2. The general owner of personal property, who deposits such property with a bailee, and such bailee places the property in the hands of a third person for safe keeping, may maintain trespass against a stranger who takes such property from such safekeeper: 6 Bac. Abr., 577; 1 Chit. Plead., 153, note 2; 1 Pick., 232.

NOTE. -- Property in the hands of a naked bailee is not changed by the gift and delivery of the same, by such bailee, to a third person: 6 Bac. Abr., title Trespass, E. 577; 6 Bac. Abr., title Trover, C 684

In this case, the keeper had no lien upon the horse for the keeping:

1st: Because there was a special undertaking to pay;

2d: Because the facts of the case do not raise a lien under the law: Montagu on Lien, 29, and note (f); Esp. N.P., 584.

If there were a lien in favor of Harris, Kinney could not avail himself of it in defense: 3 Stark Ev., 1504, note 2; 2 N.H. Rep. 319; 3 T.R., 606; 7 East, 5, 6, 7.

The doctrine of possession, in the action of trespass and trover, is precisely the same, except as to time. In trespass it must be at the time of the taking: 1 Chit. Plead., 153. In trover it must be at the time of the conversion: Chit. Plead., 138."

The Illinois Supreme Court agreed with Lincoln, and indicated that Cannon's ownership of the horse gave him a "constructive possession" or "legal possession" (as distinguished from actual, physical possession) sufficient to allow him to sue the thief for damages equal to the value of the horse. The Illinois Supreme Court remanded the case to the trial court for a new trial.

Lincoln's brief is admirable, first, for its having expressed complicated legal arguments clearly in few words, and, second, for the balanced, dignified tone of the writing style. Lincoln's growth as a speaker was marked by his movement toward expression which was, at once, simpler and more dignified. Lincoln's scratching, with his quill pen, the words of his numerous legal briefs in the quiet of his law office may have first shown him the way toward that paradoxical combination of greater simplicity and greater dignity of expression.

It is difficult to imagine an argument more persnickety than that which Lincoln made in defending against the appeal in the case of *Maus vs. Worthing,* 4 Ill. 26 (1841).

In that case, Jacob Maus had lost to Amos Worthing in the Circuit Court of Tazewell County. Maus sought to appeal to the Illinois Supreme Court. In order to take the appeal, Maus had to file an appeal bond with the Illinois Supreme Court, guaranteeing his payment of a sum of money to Worthing if he lost the appeal. The appeal bond had to be signed both by Jacob Maus himself and by another person as a surety.

Pursuant to a power of attorney from W. S. Maus (whom we might imagine to have been the father or brother of Jacob Maus), a John A. Jones signed the name of W.S. Maus on the appeal bond as the surety.

Lincoln argued that Jones' signing of W. S. Maus' name was void, and that the appeal bond was invalid, because the power of attorney -- by which W.S. Maus purported to give Jones authority to sign for him -- was not "under seal."

Centuries before Lincoln's time, a seal on a legal document meant a drop of wax on that legal document, bearing the impression of a signet ring. By 1841, however, a legal document was considered to be under seal if the signer merely made a circular pen scrawl after his name, resembling perhaps a child's drawing of a fluffy cloud. Lincoln's argument was thus that -- in the absence of the pen scrawl after W.S. Maus' signature on the power of attorney -- Jacob Maus' appeal should be dismissed.

The Illinois Supreme Court agreed and dismissed the appeal, to the consternation of a dissenting Justice Sidney Breese. Justice Breese wrote, in his dissent, "The rule, as laid down, seems to me to be destitute of any good reason on which to base it, and altogether too technical for this age. How a scrawl made with pen and ink, and affixed to the name of the writer of the letter, which is the authority to execute the appeal bond, could give it any additional validity, I cannot discover."

Lincoln's first recorded encounter with the issue of slavery, as a practicing lawyer, occurred in the case of *Bailey vs. Cromwell,* 4 Ill. 71(1841). In that case, Lincoln had represented David Bailey at trial in the Circuit Court of Tazewell County, Illinois. Bailey had attempted to purchase a black girl, named Nance, from Nathan Cromwell.

Cromwell had assured Bailey, at the time of the purported purchase, that Nance was his property -- that is, his slave -- whom he could sell at will. Bailey gave Cromwell a promissory note for the sale price of the girl. Bailey contended at the trial of the case that Cromwell had agreed that -- whenever he should demand payment of the note from Bailey -- he would first supply to Bailey the necessary papers to prove that the girl was a slave.

Immediately after making the purported sale, Cromwell left on a journey for Texas, but died in St. Louis while on his way there. The girl, Nance, remained in the possession of Bailey for about six months, insisting all the while that she was a free person. She then left Bailey's service, and did not return to him.

The administrators of the Estate of Nathan Cromwell, Deceased, sued Bailey on the promissory note. Lincoln argued, for Bailey, in the trial court, that Congress' Ordinance of 1787 (which applied to the Northwest Territory, out of which the State of Illinois was formed) prohibited slavery throughout the Northwest Territory and, so, made the consideration given by Cromwell in exchange for the promissory note -- namely, the purported transfer of the slave girl -- illegal in the State of Illinois. Consequently, Lincoln argued that Bailey's promissory note, having been based upon an illegal consideration, was void and uncollectible. Lincoln also made passing reference to article VI of the Illinois Constitution of 1818 as support for his argument that the consideration given for the promissory note -- the purported transfer of a slave girl -- was illegal. The Illinois Constitution of 1818 was unclear, however, as to whether some form of slavery or indentured servitude was then permitted in the State of Illinois. Article VI of the Illinois Constitution of 1818 attempted to ratify the continued servitude of persons who had been held as slaves in Illinois while Illinois was still a territory.

The circuit court disagreed with Lincoln and entered a judgment in favor of Cromwell's administrators, on Bailey's promissory note, for the amount of $431.97. Lincoln appealed, for Bailey, to the Illinois Supreme Court.

Rather than seize upon the obvious and large question, of whether slavery in any form could then exist in the State of Illinois, the Illinois Supreme Court ruled in Lincoln's favor by discussing evidentiary presumptions. The Illinois Supreme Court, noted, first, that every person in Illinois was presumed to be free, without regard to color. It then held that Cromwell's administrators had the burden of rebutting this presumption, and of proving that the girl, Nance, was in fact Cromwell's slave at the time of the transfer. The Illinois Supreme Court held, finally, that Cromwell's administrators had not proved that the girl had been Cromwell's slave or that Cromwell had a right to sell her. The Illinois Supreme Court stated, at the conclusion of its opinion, that "The sale of a free person is illegal, and that being the consideration of the note, that is illegal also, and consequently no recovery can be had upon the note."

It is jarring for us today to read this decision of the Illinois Supreme Court, in which it calmly discussed whether the sale of a particular person was legal. This is because we read the decision through a lens poured out of mighty historical events, which involved the subsequent life and work of Abraham Lincoln.

We cherish the image that we have of Lincoln as one who always fought for the downtrodden. In at least one case -- *Ballentine vs. Beall,* 4 Ill. 203 (1841) -- however, Lincoln seemed to be cast in the role of one who was attempting to tread down further an already downtrodden party.

In 1832, an individual named Hays Taylor had incurred a debt to Joseph Wilson for the amount of $64.67. Wilson sued Taylor, obtained a judgment against him for the amount of the debt, and had attempted to collect the judgment by having two different writs of execution issued, under which the Sheriff of Wabash County, Illinois, was authorized to levy upon and seize Hays Taylor's land, for the purpose of selling it and then paying the judgment with the proceeds of the sale. The writs of execution were returned unsatisfied, because Taylor was deep in debt as a result of his failed investment in a steamboat.

Although Taylor owned no land in his own name, he had, in fact, paid the purchase money for a tract of land to Andrew Correll, and he had directed Andrew Correll to convey the legal title to the land to Taylor's brother-in-law, Harvey Ballentine, in trust for Taylor. Taylor had stated to Andrew Correll, as the reason for his desiring to have the legal title to the land conveyed to his brother-in-law, that "if everything else went [as a result of his investment in the steamboat], he wished to have the land."

Wilson then sued the brother-in-law, Harvey Ballentine, to have the conveyance to him set aside as fraudulent, and to have the land sold to pay the debt which Taylor owed to Wilson. (A conveyance of assets which a debtor makes to another person, in order to get assets out of his name and thereby frustrate the efforts of his creditor to collect a debt which he owes to him, is a fraudulent conveyance, which can be set aside for the purpose of enabling the creditor to seize and sell the assets for the payment of the debt.)

In the course of the litigation, the plaintiff, Joseph Wilson, died, and he was replaced by the administrator of his estate, Joshua Beall.

The Circuit Court of Wabash County, Illinois, after hearing the evidence, concluded that the conveyance of the tract of land -- which Taylor had arranged from Andrew Correll to his brother-in-law, Harvey Ballentine -- was indeed fraudulent. The circuit court entered a decree in equity setting aside the conveyance, and ordering that the land be sold to pay the debt which Taylor owed to Wilson.

Harvey Ballentine, the ostensible owner of the legal title to the land, then appealed to the Illinois Supreme Court. Lincoln represented the creditor -- Joshua Beall, as the administrator of Joseph Wilson's estate -- in defending against the appeal.

The Illinois Supreme Court agreed with Lincoln, and the creditor whom he represented, and affirmed the decree of the Circuit Court of Wabash County, Illinois. The creditor was thus authorized to have the land, which Harvey Ballentine held in his name, sold to pay the debt which Taylor owed.

In the case of *Elkin vs. the People,* 4 Ill. 208 (1841), Lincoln represented a man on appeal who had disregarded the advice in the Book of Proverbs, chapter 11, verse 15: "He that is surety for a stranger shall smart for it."

Garret Elkin, and others who are not named in the case's title, had agreed to act as sureties on a bond posted by the Sheriff of Sangamon County, Illinois. The sheriff had been required to post a bond in connection with his having seized and sold land, which apparently belonged to Fleming F. McIntire and others, to pay a judgment debt which they owed.

The sheriff's bond -- the payment of which Garret Elkin and others assured -- guaranteed that the sheriff would receive and handle properly any redemption money that a judgment debtor paid to him, after the sale of his land, in order to redeem his land. In this particular case, it appears that the sheriff who had sold the land received judgment debtors' redemption money, but misappropriated it for his own use. The judgment debtors then sued Garret Elkin and the other sureties on the suretyship contract guaranteeing payment under the sheriff's bond.

Elkin and his associates argued that the bond, and their suretyship contract, had lapsed because the sheriff had left office before he received and misappropriated the redemption money. The Circuit Court of Sangamon County, Illinois, disagreed, however, and entered a judgment against Elkin and his associates for the amount of $1,492.83 on their suretyship contract guaranteeing the performance of the sheriff's bond. They then appealed to the Illinois Supreme Court, and Lincoln represented them on the appeal.

The Illinois Supreme Court held that -- for the purposes of interpreting the Illinois statute in question, on the subject of sheriff's sales -- the individual who had sold the land continued to be the individual to whom the judgment debtor could pay his redemption money after the sale, even if that individual had ceased to be the sheriff officially between the time of the sale and the time of the payment of the redemption money. Consequently, the Illinois Supreme Court concluded -- adversely to Lincoln and his clients -- that the sheriff's bond and the suretyship contract which Elkin and his associates had made were both enforceable. Lincoln's clients were thus required to refund, to the judgment debtors, the redemption money which the judgment debtors had paid to the sheriff.

In *Benedict vs. Dillehunt,* 4 Ill. 287 (1841), Lincoln defended against an argument on appeal which seems particularly trivial.

Benjamin Dillehunt had brought an action before a justice of the peace of Macon County, Illinois, against Kirby Benedict, and had recovered a judgment for $33.53. Benedict appealed from that judgment to the Circuit Court of Macon County, Illinois, for a completely new trial known as a trial *de novo.* (The system -- of allowing justices of the peace to hear a case in the first instance, and then allowing the defeated party to appeal from the judgment of a justice of the peace, to the local circuit court, for a trial *de novo* -- continued intact in Illinois until 1964.)

The Circuit Court of Macon County heard the case again, and affirmed the judgment of the justice of the peace in the following words: "This day came the parties, and, by consent, the cause is tried by the court, and the court having heard the same, it is ordered, that the judgment of the court below be affirmed, and that the appellee have execution against the appellant for the amount of said judgment, and also his costs in this court, and the court below expended."

Still disappointed with the adverse judgment for the amount of $33.53 (which was probably more than a month's wages for an average worker in 1841), Benedict appealed to the Illinois Supreme Court. A Belleville lawyer named Lyman Trumbull -- who, 24 years later, would be the author of the Thirteenth Amendment to the United States Constitution, which abolished slavery in our country -- represented the appellant, Kirby Benedict. Lincoln represented the appellee, Benjamin Dillehunt.

On appeal, Benedict argued that the judgment of the circuit court was defective, because it did not state a precise amount for the judgment. The Illinois Supreme Court pointed out that the appeal bond which Benedict had posted recited that the judgment of the justice of the peace was for "$33.53 debt, and $8.08 costs." The Illinois Supreme Court quoted a Latin maxim to the effect that that which can be made certain is considered to be certain, and held that the judgment of the Circuit Court of Macon County, Illinois, affirming the earlier judgment of the justice of the peace, was precise enough. The Illinois Supreme Court affirmed the judgment of the Circuit Court of Macon County, and Lincoln's client was then presumably able to collect his $33.53, plus costs.

In *Abrams vs. Camp,* 4 Ill. 290 (1841), Lincoln won a case on appeal which enabled his clients to seek to collect a debt which may have been incurred in a card game.

William Camp had given a promissory note to William Abrams. Abrams assigned the note to Klein. Klein obtained a judgment *at law* against Camp, on the note, for the amount of $191.43. (A distinction has traditionally existed in common law jurisdictions, such as Illinois, between actions at law and actions in equity. This traditional distinction, which arose out of centuries of litigation in England, is not susceptible to any short explanation.)

In the action at law, Camp had tried to defend himself by alleging that he had given the promissory note to Abrams to cover a gambling debt which he had incurred to Abrams in a card game. He asserted that -- because the promissory note represented a gambling debt -- it was void and unenforceable under Illinois law. (This continues to be the law in Illinois.)

Camp failed to prove the character of the promissory note as a gambling debt, in the action at law, because Abrams refused to testify about the matter on the ground that his testimony might incriminate him. For perhaps the same reason, Camp also failed to testify himself, in the action at law, about the character of the promissory note as a gambling debt. In the absence of proof on this point, the circuit court entered a judgment, in the action at law, against Camp for the amount of $191.43.

Camp then filed an action for an injunction, in a court of equity, to prohibit Klein and Abrams from enforcing the judgment at law for $191.43 against him, on the ground that the promissory note constituted a gambling debt. The Circuit Court of Sangamon County agreed with Camp and entered the injunction.

Klein and Abrams appealed to the Illinois Supreme Court, and were there represented by Lincoln and Stephen T.

Logan. Logan was an older, established lawyer who, about that time, took Lincoln on as his partner.

Lincoln and Logan argued that the doctrine of *res judicata* barred Camp from relitigating a matter which had already been resolved against him in the court of law: namely, the character of the debt for which the promissory note had been given. The Illinois Supreme Court agreed with Lincoln and Logan, and reversed the decree of the Circuit Court of Sangamon County which entered the injunction, thereby allowing Klein and Abrams to seek to collect the judgment on the promissory note from Camp.

The case of *Hancock vs. Hodgson,* 4 Ill. 330 (1841), involved a promissory note for $1,000.00 which Lincoln's clients -- John Hancock, Peter Menard, Benjamin Greely, and Benjamin Briggs -- had given to Daniel Milnor.

Lincoln's clients had owned land in Tazewell County, on which Daniel Milnor held a mortgage. In May, 1840, Milnor obtained a decree foreclosing the mortgage against Lincoln's clients, and an order for the sale of the land, for the purpose of paying the mortgage indebtedness of $4,644.87. Hancock and the others gave Milnor a promissory note on July 31, 1840, for the amount of $1,000.00, in return for Milnor's agreement to delay the foreclosure sale for four months. Hancock and his associates evidently thought that -- within those four months -- they could raise the money to pay the mortgage indebtedness and thereby avoid the mortgage sale.

Hancock and the others apparently did not pay the mortgage indebtedness. Milnor completed the mortgage sale, apparently after having waited four months. Milnor died, and his executor, Hodgson, sued Hancock and the others on the $1,000.00 promissory note.

Hancock and the others resisted paying the promissory note on a variety of grounds, including the argument that Milnor had given them nothing of value (that is, no consideration) for the promissory note, in consequence of which the promissory note should be considered to be void. They also argued that the interest rate provided by the promissory note on the face amount of the note after the maturity date -- that is, 12 percent per year -- was usurious because it exceeded the limit then set on interest rates by an Illinois statute.

The trial court upheld the validity of the promissory note, and entered a judgment in favor of Daniel Milnor's executor. Hancock and the others then appealed to the Illinois Supreme Court. Lincoln and Stephen Logan represented Hancock and his associates on the appeal.

The Illinois Supreme Court affirmed the judgment of the trial court. Consequently, Lincoln's clients had to pay on the promissory note which they had unwisely given to Daniel Milnor.

The most interesting aspect of this case is the identity of one of the lawyers who opposed Lincoln on appeal: namely, Edward Baker. Baker either was, or became, one of Lincoln's best friends. Lincoln named his second son Edward Baker Lincoln after him, and he was the godfather to that child. This child died in 1850, when he was almost four years of age, and was the child of whom Lincoln spoke in his Farewell Address in Springfield when he said, "Here my children have been born, and one is buried."

On October 21, 1861, Edward Baker was killed, while fighting for the Union, at the Battle of Ball's Bluff in northern Virginia. The loss of this old friend caused Lincoln much grief.

In the case of *Grable vs. Margrave,* 4 Ill. 372 (1842), Lincoln represented on appeal a man named Thomas Margrave. Thomas Margrave was the father of a girl who had been seduced by William Grable.

Margrave had sued Grable in the Circuit Court of Gallatin County for damages because of the seduction of his daughter. At trial, the Circuit Court of Gallatin County had permitted Margrave to prove that he was a poor man and that the defendant, William Grable, was a man of considerable means. Ordinarily, the financial circumstances of either party to a case are not deemed to be relevant to the issues to be decided. The jury rendered a verdict against Grable, and the circuit court entered a judgment upon the verdict. Grable appealed to the Illinois Supreme Court.

On the appeal, the Illinois Supreme Court indicated that the purpose of such an action was not only to allow the injured family to obtain compensatory damages from the wrongdoer -- for the payment of necessary expenses, and for the dishonor and disgrace cast upon the family -- but also for punitive damages, which are intended to teach the defendant, and others who might be tempted to do the same thing, a lesson. The Illinois Supreme Court indicated that, in a case where punitive damages are appropriate, the "pecuniary ability of the defendant is peculiarly the proper subject of inquiry," so that the jury will know how great an award of punitive damages must be in order to make the defendant wince and in order to teach him a lesson which he will remember. It was appropriate, therefore, for Margrave to have proved at trial the wealth of the defendant, William Grable.

As to the issue whether Margrave should also have been able to prove his poverty at trial, the Illinois Supreme Court's reasoning was less convincing. The Court stated that evidence of Margrave's poverty was relevant to enable the jury "to understand fully the effect of the injury upon him, and to give him such damages as his peculiar condition in life and circumstances entitle him to receive. It is easily perceived how a poor man would be more seriously injured by the loss of the service of his daughter, and the payment of expenses necessarily incurred in consequence of the seduction, than the individual more favorably circumstanced as to property." The Illinois Supreme Court upheld the circuit court's decision to admit evidence of Margrave's poverty at the trial of the case, and affirmed the circuit court's judgment.

Lincoln's client, Thomas Margrave, thus won the case on appeal and retained his judgment for damages against the defendant, William Grable, for the seduction of Thomas Margrave's daughter.

The business of subdividing land into lots, and selling the lots, and thereby contributing to the growth of a city, has been flourishing in Illinois for more than a century and a half, as indicated by the facts in the case of *Averill vs. Field,* 4 Ill. 390 (1842).

Lincoln and his partner, Stephen Logan, represented Riley Averill and Alfred Lowell on appeal to the Illinois Supreme Court, in a case that involved their execution of a promissory note -- payable to Spencer Field -- for their purchase of subdivision lots in an addition to the town of Pekin, Illinois.

Field had apparently laid out lots in a subdivision which he called Field's addition to the town of Pekin. Fields sold half of the lots in the subdivision to Averill and Lowell in return for a promissory note in the amount of $364.50, which was to become due upon a satisfaction of an unusual condition: namely, that both the seller, Field, and the purchasers, Averill and Lowell, should proceed to sell the lots held by them respectively; that, as such sales were made, each party would pay to the other one half of the proceeds of the sales; and that Fields should wait for the payment of the amount of the promissory note until the amount of all the sales should equal the amount of the note. Field sued Averill and Lowell for the amount of the promissory note before they had sold any of the lots which they held. The defense which they raised in the circuit court, to Field's action for the amount of the promissory note, was that the promissory note was not yet due because they had not yet sold any lots, in consequence of which the amount of their sales had not yet equalled the amount of the promissory note. Field demurred -- that is, objected -- to this defense, and the Circuit Court of Tazewell County upheld the demurrer and struck the defense. After having struck this defense, which was the only defense raised by Averill and Lowell, the circuit court entered a judgment against Averill and Lowell for the amount of the

148,498

promissory note: that is, $364.50. From that judgment, Averill and Lowell appealed to the Illinois Supreme Court.

On appeal, the Illinois Supreme Court held that the condition contained in the note -- as to when the note should become payable to Field -- could have been satisfied by *Field's* having sold enough lots to give rise to sale proceeds which equalled the amount of the promissory note. The Illinois Supreme Court further held that Averill and Lowell's pleading in the circuit court, which raised their defense, was defective because it did not allege that Field himself had not sold any lots in the subdivision.

Lincoln and Logan argued in behalf of Averill and Lowell that, if Field had sold any lots in the subdivision, it was more appropriate to require him to allege, in his pleadings, that he had sold enough lots to cause the promissory note to become due, rather than to require them to allege that Field had not sold any lots in the subdivision.

The Illinois Supreme Court was unmoved by this argument, however, and concluded that Averill and Lowell -- as the makers of the promissory note -- had the burden, in the circuit court, of pleading and proving all the facts necessary to demonstrate the non-occurrence of the condition in question. The Illinois Supreme Court affirmed the judgment of the Circuit Court of Tazewell County, against Averill and Lowell, and in favor of Field.

The argument made by Lincoln and Logan in behalf of Averill and Lowell -- that Fields should have pleaded his sale of lots, if he had sold any -- strongly suggests that Fields had not succeeded in selling any of his lots either. Consequently, the judgment of the circuit court and of the Illinois Supreme Court went against Averill and Fields simply because of their trial lawyer's error in failing to plead their one defense properly. The decision does not indicate whether Lincoln and Logan had represented Averill and Lowell at trial.

A final, noteworthy aspect of the Illinois Supreme Court's decision is that Justice Stephen Douglas wrote it. This was the same Stephen Douglas whom Lincoln debated in the summer of 1858, during the campaign for the office of United States Senator from the State of Illinois. In those debates, Lincoln commented at least once, with some asperity, upon Douglas' career on the Illinois Supreme Court.

Lincoln won the case of *Wilson vs. Alexander,* 4 Ill. 392 (1842), on the strength of his legal research, which he probably conducted in the law library of the Illinois Supreme Court in Springfield.

In that case, Samuel Wilson had died intestate: that is, without a will. James Wilson acted as the administrator of Samuel Wilson's estate. In his capacity as administrator, James Wilson brought an action against David Alexander to recover $150.00, which was the amount of a forged promissory note -- ostensibly executed by Samuel Wilson during his life -- which David Alexander had passed to the administrator, without knowledge of the forgery, in partial payment of another promissory note which David Alexander had made to Samuel Wilson.

The forged note for $150.00 purported to be executed by Samuel Wilson in favor of Isaac Krieder, who then supposedly assigned it to Joseph Allen, and who, in turn, assigned it to David Alexander. When the administrator of Samuel Wilson's estate demanded payment of the promissory note which David Alexander had himself executed in favor of Samuel Wilson, David Alexander paid off his own note by giving the administrator a combination of money and the forged $150.00 note which he held. The administrator conceded at trial that David Alexander did not know that the $150.00 note, bearing the name of Samuel Wilson as its maker, was forged.

After the administrator discovered that the $150.00 note was a forgery, he sought a judgment against David Alexander to require him to pay Samuel Wilson's estate an additional $150.00 in money, in place of the forged note.

The Circuit Court of Tazewell County instructed the jury that -- if they believed that David Alexander had passed the note innocently, in ignorance of its character as a forgery -- they should find in favor of David Alexander. The administrator objected to this instruction, to no avail, in the circuit court. Having thus been instructed, the jury had to return a verdict in favor of David Alexander, because the administrator had admitted that David Alexander did not know that the note was a forgery when he delivered it to the administrator. The circuit court entered a judgment in favor of David Alexander on the jury's verdict, and the administrator appealed to the Illinois Supreme Court.

Lincoln represented the administrator on appeal.

Lincoln's opponent cited to the Illinois Supreme Court the rule that -- if an individual or institution accepted and cashed, as valid, a promissory note or other negotiable instrument bearing a forgery of its signature -- the individual or institution could not, upon later discovering the forgery, cancel the transaction and recover its money from an innocent party who had delivered the forged document to it. The reason for this rule was that -- as between the innocent party who delivered the forged document, and the individual or institution who should have recognized that its signature had been forged on the document -- the individual or institution who negligently accepted and cashed the document should bear the loss.

Lincoln, in his legal research, however, had discovered, and cited to the Illinois Supreme Court, cases from the courts of three other States   to the effect that -- as between an innocent party who innocently delivered a forged note, and another innocent party who accepted and cashed it -- the party who delivered the note should bear the loss, and the party who accepted and cashed it should be able to recover from him the amount of the money previously credited or paid on the strength of the forged note. The reason for this second rule was that the party who delivered the note implicitly warranted it as genuine.

Lincoln's opponent argued that James Wilson, as the administrator of Samuel Wilson's estate, stood in the same position as Samuel Wilson himself, had Samuel Wilson been alive and accepted the forged note from David Alexander. Lincoln's opponent thus argued that the first rule should apply to the case, and that the administrator should bear the loss.

The Illinois Supreme Court agreed with Lincoln, however, and concluded that the administrator of a decedent's estate should not be charged with knowing that the purported signature of the decedent on a negotiable instrument was a forgery. Consequently, the Illinois Supreme Court reversed the judgment of the Circuit Court of Tazewell County, and remanded the case to that circuit court for a new trial, which Lincoln's client undoubtedly won.

The result in this case attested Lincoln's power as a legal researcher.

The case of *Schlencker vs. Risley,* 4 Ill. 483 (1842), is a difficult one to understand thoroughly. Lincoln represented Joshua Risley in defending against the appeal taken to the Illinois Supreme Court by a man named Gideon Schlencker and another named Wallace.

Williams was apparently a justice of the peace of Wabash County, Illinois. He had issued, in his capacity as justice of the peace, a warrant for the arrest of Joshua Risley. Wallace, who was a constable in Wabash County, formed a posse to hunt down Joshua Risley. In forming that posse, Wallace ordered Gideon Schlencker to aid him in arresting Joshua Risley. Schlencker objected to going with the posse, and offered to pay Wallace a dollar if he would leave Schlencker off the posse, but Wallace refused and threatened to prosecute Schlencker if he did not go with Wallace and the posse to arrest Joshua Risley. Wallace and his posse, including Schlencker, succeeded in arresting Joshua Risley. The arrest of Joshua Risley, proved to be false and invalid, because Joshua Risley had committed no offense.

Joshua Risley sued Williams, Wallace, Schlencker, and two other individuals in the Circuit Court of Wabash County. The jury returned a verdict of guilty against Wallace and Schlencker, but not guilty as to the other defendants, and awarded Joshua Risley damages in the amount of $333.00.

After the return of this verdict, Wallace and Schlencker moved for a new trial, but the Circuit Court of Wabash County denied the motion, and entered a judgment against them on the verdict. Wallace and Schlencker then appealed to the Illinois Supreme Court.

The Illinois Supreme Court, in its decision, discussed the bases of the defendants' motion for a new trial. Wallace wanted a new trial in order to prove, by offering evidence of the general reputation of Williams' character as a justice of the peace, that Williams had issued the arrest warrant to Wallace in Williams' official capacity as a justice of the peace. The Illinois Supreme Court observed that Williams' official capacity as a justice of the peace had already been demonstrated at the trial of the case, and that further evidence on that point could not alter the result against Wallace.

Gideon Schlencker sought a new trial in order to bring forward a new witness, Mary Wise, who had been present when Wallace had ordered Schlencker to join the posse. Schlencker had apparently discovered Mary Wise's knowledge of that event only after the trial of the case.

The Illinois Supreme Court recited the rule that "Before a new trial could be granted on the ground of newly discovered evidence, it must appear that the evidence shall only have been discovered since the former trial, as material to the issue; that it is not cumulative; and that the party has not been guilty of negligence in not discovering and producing it on the former trial." The Illinois Supreme Court concluded that the testimony of Mary Wise, which Schlencker sought to offer at a new trial, met all these requirements, but that, as evidence, it was entirely unnecessary because Schlencker had satisfactorily proved at the first trial that he went with the posse only under Wallace's compulsion.

The Illinois Supreme Court denied Wallace's and Schlencker's motion for a new trial, and affirmed the judgment against them -- and in favor of Lincoln's client, Joshua Risley -- for the amount of $333.00.

The Illinois Supreme Court ruled against Lincoln's client -- incorrectly, by today's standards -- in the case of *Mason vs. Park,* 4 Ill. 532 (1842).

Benjamin F. Park, Lincoln's client on appeal, apparently owned land in Richland County, Illinois, which had timber growing on it. An Illinois statute permitted an owner of timberland to recover damages from any individual who cut timber on that owner's land without his permission.

George Mason cut and removed two trees from Park's land, without Park's permission. Mason later admitted to another individual that he had cut those two trees on Park's land.

Park sued Mason, under the Illinois statute which prohibited the unauthorized cutting of timber upon another's land, in the Circuit Court of Richland County. At the trial, Park called, as a witness, the individual to whom Mason had admitted that he had cut two trees on Park's land. Park did not introduce any other evidence to prove that the land, from which the trees had been removed, belonged to him.

Mason essentially requested the circuit court to direct a verdict in his favor, by instructing the jury that Mason's verbal admission -- as to Park's ownership of the land -- was not sufficient proof of Park's ownership of the land to permit him to bring his action against Mason under the Illinois statute. The circuit court refused to give this instruction, and instructed the jury instead, that Park was not required to introduce his deed to the land into evidence, in order to prove his ownership of the land, if Mason had admitted he had cut the trees on Park's land.

The jury returned a verdict for Park for the amount of $48.00, and the circuit court entered a judgment upon the verdict. Mason appealed to the Illinois Supreme Court. Lincoln represented Park in defending against the appeal.

The Illinois Supreme Court referred to an imagined "best evidence rule," which has been dying a slow death in Illinois for the past 150 years, and which is still sometimes solemnly invoked by lawyers and judges alike.

The true "best evidence rule" -- to the extent one exists in Illinois -- is that, when documentary evidence is relevant, the originals of the documents must be introduced into evidence rather than copies thereof, unless there is a satisfactory explanation for the absence of the originals. The spurious "best evidence rule," which led the Illinois Supreme Court astray in this case, is supposedly to the effect that, on any issue, a party "must produce the best evidence which the nature of the case will admit of." The exasperating quality of this spurious "best evidence rule" is that no one can ever know in advance what the other party to a case will deem to be the best evidence on a point, except for the certainty that it will be something other than what the first party has introduced to prove the point.

The Illinois Supreme Court concluded that Park had to introduce the best evidence of his title to the land, that the best evidence of that title was his deed to the land, and that Park failed to introduce the best evidence of his ownership of the land when he neglected to place his deed in evidence. Lincoln pointed out, for Park, that there should be no need to prove Park's ownership of the land when Mason himself had expressly admitted that he cut the trees on Park's land. The Illinois Supreme Court essentially held that this verbal admission by Mason was not the best evidence of Park's ownership of the land, and should not have even been allowed into evidence.

If Mason's verbal admission were disregarded, there was no other evidence in the case of Park's ownership of the land, and Park did not establish his right to sue Mason for damages under the Illinois statute. The Illinois Supreme Court thus reversed the judgment of the circuit court in favor of Lincoln's client, Benjamin F. Park. To his credit, the chief justice of the Illinois Supreme Court dissented from this decision based upon reasoning which was contorted, to say the least.

The decision of the Illinois Supreme Court in *Greathouse vs. Smith,* 4 Ill. 541 (1842), is short, but not easy to explain.

David A. Smith had obtained a judgment in the Circuit Court of Macoupin County in September, 1841, against the firm of Greathouse & Chestnut for the amount of $852.02. A statute had been passed by the Illinois legislature on February 27, 1841, however, which regulated the sale of property for the purpose of enforcing judgments. The existence of this statute apparently hindered Smith, in some manner, from having property, that was owned by Greathouse & Chestnut, seized and sold in order to pay the judgment.

Rather than attempting to execute (that is, to take the legal actions necessary to collect) on that first judgment, therefore, David Smith brought a second action against Greathouse & Chestnut in the Circuit Court of Macoupin County, known as "an action of debt," based upon the first judgment which he had obtained against Greathouse & Chestnut. By bringing this second action, Smith apparently sought greater freedom to have Greathouse & Chestnut's property seized and sold.

Greathouse & Chestnut argued at the trial of the second case that it was unfair for Smith to be allowed to bring the second action in order to circumvent whatever restrictions had been imposed upon him by the Illinois statute regulating the sale of a judgment debtor's property. The circuit court disregarded this argument, however, and entered a judgment in the second case for David Smith, again apparently for the amount of $852.02. Greathouse & Chestnut appealed to the Illinois Supreme Court.

Lincoln represented Smith in defending against the appeal.

The Illinois Supreme Court stated, "We know of no principle which inhibits the creditor, on a judgment which is in force and unsatisfied, from recovering in an action brought on it, although he may, at the time of bringing the suit, be entitled to an execution on his judgment. He is at liberty to proceed by execution to collect the judgment, or institute a new action on it." The Illinois Supreme Court affirmed the judgment in favor of Lincoln's client, Smith.

The law in Illinois today is to the contrary: namely, after a creditor has once obtained a judgment against a debtor, he can certainly seek to enforce that judgment, but he is not at liberty to seek a second judgment based upon the same cause of action. The principle of *res judicata* would prohibit the creditor from obtaining a second judgment against the debtor based upon the same cause of action.

The case of *Watkins vs. White,* 4 Ill. 549 (1842), involved, among other things, the story of a dispute between a father and a son.

Thomas Watkins had a son, who is not named in the decision. He also owned a mare. An argument occurred between the father and the son. Although he was a minor, the son resolved to leave his father's home. The son stole his father's mare, and sold it to James Maxey in Springfield for "ten dollars in money, and forty dollars in county orders." About eight or nine months after the son had run away from his father's home, he was returned to his father in a gravely ill condition, and he died about two or three days later.

Meanwhile, Maxey had sold the mare to John Constant, and Constant had sold the mare to John White. John White apparently kept the mare at a public livery stable in Springfield, from which members of the public could rent the mare for their own transportation about Springfield.

Thomas Watkins sued John White, in an action of replevin, which was the old form of action for recovering specific personal property which had been wrongfully taken from a plaintiff.

The defense which John White sought to make was that Thomas Watkins had visited the race track in Springfield in the fall of 1840, and had seen the mare being ridden to the race track by a patron of the races; that Thomas Watkins thereafter delayed an unreasonable length of time in claiming the mare; and that, because of his delay, Thomas Watkins ratified his son's sale of the mare. The Circuit Court of Sangamon County agreed with the defendant and instructed the jury "That if they believed from the evidence that the plaintiff knew the mare was in Springfield, in the possession of other persons, who are exercising acts of ownership over her, and that, with that knowledge, he forbore for more than a reasonable time, to be judged of by the jury, to claim her, they might infer from that, that he had ratified the sale of the mare by his son, and find a verdict for the defendant, although the action might not be within the statute of limitations."

After having been thus instructed, the jury returned a verdict in favor of the defendant, John White. The Circuit Court of Sangamon County entered a judgment on the verdict, in favor of John White and against Thomas Watkins. Thomas Watkins then appealed from the judgment to the Illinois Supreme Court, and Lincoln represented him on the appeal.

Lincoln cited a treatise on the law of sales, and a volume of Blackstone's Commentaries on the Laws of England. He argued that -- because Thomas Watkins had brought his action of replevin within the period of the applicable statute of limitations -- any delay on his part in bringing the action should not be taken as a ratification, by him, of his son's theft and sale of the mare. The Illinois Supreme Court agreed with Lincoln, and reversed the judgment of the Circuit Court of Sangamon County, and remanded the case to the circuit court for a new trial.

17

The case of *Payne vs. Frazier,* 5 Ill. 55 (1842), affords an example of an individual's having sought a remedy too late to do himself any good.

Morgan Payne owned land in Vermilion County. The State of Illinois had located a railroad across Payne's land, in consequence of which Payne obtained a judgment against the State of Illinois for $150.00 as just compensation for the land which it had taken.

Samuel Frazier purchased Payne's land. One of the terms of the sale of the land, from Payne to Frazier, was that the $150.00 judgment which the State of Illinois owed to Payne was to be paid instead to Frazier.

After having sold the land to Frazier, Payne approached a commissioner of the state board of public works, named Alexander, and offered to accept $50.00 from Alexander as a full settlement of the amount which the State of Illinois owed Payne on the $150.00 judgment. Frazier became aware of Payne's effort wrongly to collect this money from Alexander. Frazier filed an action against both Payne and Alexander, praying for an injunction which would prohibit Alexander from paying any part of the $150.00 judgment to Payne, and, further, which would require Alexander to pay that judgment to Frazier. An injunction (apparently a temporary restraining order, obtained without notice to the defendant) was obtained, and service thereof was made on Payne on June 8, 1839.

Within a few days -- on June 27, 1839 -- Payne was able to persuade Alexander to pay him $50.00 in full satisfaction of the $150.00 judgment which Payne had against the State of Illinois. Four days later, on July 1, 1839, Frazier finally had the injunction served on Alexander, which purported to prohibit him from paying anything to Payne.

Alexander filed an answer in which he alleged that the injunction had been served on him too late, and that he had already satisfied Payne's judgment by paying $50.00 to Payne. For some reason, the Circuit Court of Vermilion County ignored

Alexander's answer, and ultimately ordered Alexander to pay Frazier the amount of the $150.00 judgment within thirty days. Alexander appealed from this judgment to the Illinois Supreme Court.

Lincoln represented Frazier in defending against the appeal.

The Illinois Supreme Court simply concluded that the facts -- as alleged by Alexander in his answer -- furnished him a complete defense, if they were true. The Illinois Supreme Court reversed the judgment of the Circuit Court of Vermilion County, and remanded the case to that circuit court, with instructions to permit Frazier to file whatever reply he desired to Alexander's answer, and thereafter to proceed to a determination of the merits. Unless Frazier were able, on the remand, to allege facts in reply which demonstrated that Alexander knew of the injunction before he paid the $50.00 to Payne, Alexander undoubtedly won the case on the merits, and Lincoln's client had to bear the consequences of having served the injunction too late on Alexander.

18

The case of *Fitch vs. Pinckard,* 5 Ill. 69 (1842), was the first case, in which Lincoln was involved on appeal, which arose in Madison County, Illinois.

A man named Fitch and the heirs of another man named Thomas Fay brought an action of ejectment against William Pinckard, in order to evict him from the possession of parts of lots numbered "ten (10) and eleven (11) on the penitentiary plat" concerning land in the City of Alton. The tract of land in question extended 25 feet along State Street, and 50 feet along Second Street, in Alton, and a brick building "partially occupied by the drugstore of Marsh, Hankinson & Co." stood on that tract of land.

The plaintiffs -- Fitch and the heirs of Thomas Fay -- claimed to have a title to the land which was superior to William Pinckard's on two bases: namely, a tax deed to the land obtained from the City of Alton, by reason of a sale for the payment of the real estate taxes levied upon the land in 1837, and a sheriff's deed to the land obtained by Thomas Fay at an execution sale of the land which was held to pay a judgment which Thomas Fay had obtained against William Pinckard. The jury found in favor of Pinckard. The Circuit Court of Madison County denied the plaintiffs' motion for a new trial, and entered a judgment upon the jury's verdict in favor of Pinckard. The plaintiffs -- Fitch and the heirs of Thomas Fay -- appealed to the Illinois Supreme Court.

Lincoln was one of five lawyers who represented Pinckard in defending against the appeal.

Lincoln argued that the tax sale was void because it was not certain that the real estate tax, for which the land had been sold, had accrued upon that particular land. He further argued that the execution sale was void because of the uncertainty as to what portion of the land had been included in that execution sale.

The Illinois Supreme Court agreed with Lincoln on both points. It noted that the sheriff's certificate of levy indicated that he had levied upon, and sold, "a certain lot situated on the angle of State and Second streets," which description might have been satisfied by any of four different tracts of land at the intersection of State and Second streets. Because of such uncertainty, the execution sale, based upon the sheriff's levy upon the land, was void.

The Illinois Supreme Court, therefore, affirmed the judgment of the Circuit Court of Madison County, Illinois, in favor of Lincoln's client, Pinckard.

19

The case of *Edwards vs. Helm,* 5 Ill. 142 (1842), was the second case from Madison County, in which Lincoln was involved on appeal.

The facts of the case are somewhat confusing. Benjamin F. Edwards had executed a promissory note payable to N. A. Ware on July 6, 1836, for the amount of $6,000.00 for the purchase of land in Alton described as "an undivided fourth part of Block 49," which was apparently located at the intersection of Second Street and Piasa Street in Alton. John Helm signed on the promissory note as a surety: that is, he guaranteed payment of the note if Edwards failed to pay.

On July 14, 1836, Edwards then also gave Helm a second promissory note for $7,000.00, to cover a debt which Edwards owed directly to Helm. Edwards also gave Helm a mortgage to secure (that is, to guarantee) Edwards' payment of both promissory notes.

The seller of the land, Ware, assigned Edwards' promissory note for $6,000.00 to Warner, who then assigned the promissory note to two individuals, Craig and Warner. Edwards did not pay the $6,000.00 note, and Craig and Warner sued Edwards and Helm, and obtained a judgment against them for a total of $7,613.27. To collect their judgment, Craig and Warner then had the Sheriff of Madison County twice levy upon, and conduct execution sales of, portions of Edwards' land. Craig and Warner were the purchasers of those portions of Edwards' land at the two execution sales.

Helm sought to collect the amount that Edwards owed to him by filing an action to foreclose upon the mortgage which Edwards had given him on Edwards' land. The Circuit Court of Madison County entered a decree in favor of Helm, and against Edwards, for the amount of $12,224.30. The decree also gave Helm a "strict foreclosure" of the mortgage: that is, it gave the mortgaged land to Helm in payment of the debt which Edwards owed to him. The decree further provided that Edwards' other creditors -- Craig and Warner -- could recover the land for themselves if they redeemed the land by paying Helm the amount of $12,224.30. From that decree, Craig and Warner appealed to the Illinois Supreme Court.

Lincoln, with two other lawyers, represented Craig and Warner on appeal.

Lincoln apparently argued that, from the record of the trial, it was impossible to determine whether the portions of Edwards' land, upon which Craig and Warner twice levied, and which they purchased themselves at the execution sales, were included within the premises which Edwards had mortgaged to Helm. The Illinois Supreme Court agreed, and held that -- in the absence of information on that point -- it had to reverse the decree, and remand the case for further pleadings by Craig and Warner.

Lincoln's client, Craig and Warner, thus won the appeal.

20

The numerous cases concerning the sale of land to pay judgment debts -- in which Lincoln was involved on appeal -- demonstrate that such sales were common in Lincoln's time. The case of *Grubb vs. Crane,* 5 Ill. 153 (1842), is yet another example.

William B. Crane owned two tracts of land. He sold both tracts to Samuel Grubb for the amount of $1,800.00. Grubb gave Crane two promissory notes for the tracts of land. One promissory note was for $800.00, payable on July 1, 1839, and the other promissory note was for $1,000.00, payable on November 1, 1839. Crane signed a "bond for a deed," whereby he promised to deliver deeds to the tracts of land to Grubb upon Grubb's payment of the notes.

Grubb paid the first promissory note when it was due, and a small portion of the second promissory note. Crane then sought, and recovered, a judgment against Grubb for the balance of the second note, in the amount of $964.25. A writ of execution was issued, for the enforcement of that judgment, but Grubb apparently had no property -- beside the tracts of land -- with which to pay the judgment.

Crane then filed an action in the court of equity, in order to have the two tracts of land sold to pay the amount of the judgment. Grubb failed to respond to the action, and a decree *pro confesso* was entered against him, requiring the sale of the two tracts of land.

After the tracts of land had been sold under the decree, and the commissioner's report of the sale filed with the Circuit Court of Sangamon County, Grubb belatedly entered his appearance and moved to set aside the commissioner's report, and asked for leave to file his answer to the original pleading which Crane had filed in the equity action. The Circuit Court of Sangamon County denied the motion, and approved the commissioner's report.

Grubb then filed, as a separate proceeding, his bill of review, for the purpose of obtaining a further review of the results in Crane's initial equity action. Crane appeared in that second action, and moved to dismiss Grubb's bill of review. The circuit court granted the motion, and dismissed Grubb's bill of review.

The debtor, Grubb, then appealed from that dismissal to the Illinois Supreme Court. Lincoln and his partner, Stephen Logan, represented Crane in defending against the appeal. James Shields (a man whom Lincoln almost fought in a duel across the Mississippi River from Alton, Illinois) represented Grubb in prosecuting the appeal. Justice Stephen Douglas authored the Illinois Supreme Court's opinion in the case.

Crane made thirteen assignments of error, all of which involved dry technicalities, and none of which merit an attempt to explain them. Judge Stephen Douglas' opinion for the Illinois Supreme Court affirmed the circuit court's decree in favor of Lincoln's client, Crane.

The case of *Pentecost vs. Magahee,* 5 Ill. 326 (1843), involved the application of a rule of law which remains in effect: namely, that the judgment of a trial court must become final before a disappointed litigant may take an appeal from that judgment.

In that case, Hugh Pentecost and another man, named Pickering, had filed a bill (that is, a complaint) in the Circuit Court of Edwards County, Illinois, in which they sought an injunction against Magahee to prohibit him from enforcing a judgment at law which he obtained against them. The circuit court initially issued the injunction.

Magahee had then filed his answer, to the bill for an injunction, and then moved for a dissolution of the injunction against him. The circuit court dissolved the injunction -- and thereby permitted Magahee to enforce his judgment at law -- but did not dismiss Pentecost's and Pickering's bill for an injunction. Pentecost and Pickering then sought to appeal, from the order dissolving the injunction, to the Illinois Supreme Court.

Lincoln represented Magahee in defending against the appeal. Lincoln's friend, Edward Baker, for whom Lincoln named his second son, was one of two lawyers who represented the appellants, Pentecost and Pickering.

The Illinois Supreme Court concluded that a party could not appeal from an order of a circuit court which merely dissolved an injunction. The Court's reasoning was that the entry of a final judgment is a prerequisite to the taking of an appeal, that the mere dissolving of an injunction (as distinguished from a dismissal of plaintiff's entire case) is interlocutory rather than final, and that, in consequence, an appeal from an order which only dissolved an injunction is premature. The Illinois Supreme Court affirmed the circuit court's dissolution of the injunction, and thereby permitted Lincoln's client, Magahee to proceed to enforce his judgment at law against Pentecost and Pickering.

The case of *Robinson vs. Chesseldine,* 5 Ill. 332 (1843), is yet another case concerning one party's action to collect the amount of a promissory note from another party. The number of these cases in the old reports of the Illinois Supreme Court indicates the difficulty that people of that day had in borrowing money from an established bank. This was simply because there were few banks. Consequently, any person who desired to borrow money to finance a business venture was forced to approach another person, who had money, and to ask to borrow it from him. The borrower would then give a promissory note, for the amount of the loan, to the lender.

In this particular case, Greenleaf C. Robinson had signed a promissory note for the amount of $680.85, payable to Henry Chesseldine, on November 9, 1840, which was to be payable one year after that date. Robinson did not pay, and Chesseldine brought an action in the Circuit Court of Brown County against Robinson. Chesseldine obtained a judgment against Robinson for the amount of the note, and had a writ of execution issued to the Sheriff of Brown County. The Sheriff levied that writ upon Robinson's lands, and advertised those lands for sale on July 18, 1842.

Robinson apparently filed an equitable action in the Circuit Court of Brown County, for the purpose of obtaining an injunction which would prevent the Sheriff from selling Robinson's lands. The Circuit Court of Brown County refused to issue the injunction. Robinson then appealed, from that refusal, to the Illinois Supreme Court.

Lincoln and his partner, Stephen Logan, represented Chesseldine in defending against the appeal.

The Illinois Supreme Court concluded that -- if there had been any irregularities in the procedure followed by Chesseldine for having the lands sold -- Robinson would have had a complete remedy therefor in the original proceeding at law. The Court stated that Robinson could have sought, in the original proceeding at law against him, to have obtained a stay of the sale of his lands until a hearing could be held upon his motion questioning the propriety of the procedures that had been followed. Because Robinson could have sought relief in the original action at law, the Illinois Supreme Court concluded that the Circuit Court of Brown County had no jurisdiction to entertain the second, equitable action which Robinson had brought, and that the Circuit Court of Brown County was correct in denying Robinson the injunction which he had requested. The Illinois Supreme Court thus affirmed the denial of the injunction, and the lands of Robinson were apparently sold to pay his debt, under his promissory note, to Chesseldine.

23

The case of *Lazell vs. Francis,* 5 Ill. 421 (1843), was yet another of the many cases, concerning promissory notes, in which Lincoln was involved as an appellate lawyer.

Simeon Francis had executed a promissory note for the amount of $202.06, payable to John A. Lazell or to his order, on June 16, 1829. The promissory note was to be payable one day after the date of its execution.

John A. Lazell assigned the note to George Lazell after it had become due. George Lazell did not take any action on the note until 1842, when he commenced an action against Simeon Francis in the Circuit Court of Sangamon County.

Francis demurred to the complaint (that is, raised a defense or otherwise questioned the sufficiency of the complaint) by asserting that he had had an agreement with John A. Lazell to the following effect: that John A. Lazell and Simeon Francis were jointly liable to the firm of Collins & Hannay for an amount in excess of $600.00; that Francis and John A. Lazell had agreed that Francis' liability on the promissory note, to John A. Lazell, would be discharged if Francis would pay the indebtedness which they jointly owed to the firm of Collins & Hannay; that Francis did pay the entire indebtedness due to the firm of Collins & Hannay; and that, in consequence, Francis' liability to John A. Lazell on the promissory note had been discharged.

The Circuit Court of Sangamon County sustained Francis' demurrer, and entered a judgment in his favor. George Lazell appealed to the Illinois Supreme Court from that judgment.

Lincoln and his partner, Stephen Logan, represented Francis in defending against the appeal.

George Lazell contended, on appeal, that the defendant Francis' defense was invalid because it alleged an agreement which varied the terms of the promissory note itself, and that the terms of the promissory note should be held to govern. Lazell thus essentially argued that the "parol evidence rule" should have prohibited Francis from introducing evidence to demonstrate that the agreement, between Francis and John A. Lazell, was anything other than that expressed in the promissory note which Francis had executed.

The Illinois Supreme Court disagreed, and held that Francis had asserted what was, in substance, the affirmative defense of payment of the note. The Illinois Supreme Court further concluded that Francis' defense was valid, and, so, affirmed the judgment of the circuit court in his favor.

Lincoln was, once again, on the winning side in an appeal concerning a promissory note.

24

Lincoln and his partner, Stephen Logan, lost the case of *Spear vs. Campbell,* 5 Ill. 424 (1843), on appeal, because of their having failed to join a "necessary party" to the proceedings in the Circuit Court of Sangamon County.

Isaac Spear had become indebted to James Campbell and another man named Dabney. Campbell and Dabney had begun actions at law against Isaac Spear, for the purpose of obtaining judgments against him which would allow them to collect the debts which he owed them. Before Campbell and Dabney were able to obtain their judgments against Isaac Spear, he conveyed certain land that he owned to David Spear, who was apparently a relative of his, without receiving any payment from David Spear for the land. Campbell and Dabney finally obtained judgments against Isaac Spear, and then sought to enforce their judgments against the land which Isaac Spear had conveyed to David Spear. In the Circuit Court of Sangamon County, Campbell and Dabney -- who were there apparently represented by Lincoln and Stephen Logan -- argued that the conveyance from Isaac Spear to David Spear had been fraudulent, and for the purpose of avoiding the payment of the debts which Isaac Spear owed to Campbell and Dabney. Campbell and Dabney sued only the present owner of the land, David Spear, in the circuit court, and did not join the judgment debtor, Isaac Spear, to the proceeding. The Circuit Court of Sangamon County found in favor of Campbell and Dabney and entered a judgment which would have allowed them to collect the amount of their judgments at law, against Isaac Spear, out of the value of the land held by David Spear.

David Spear appealed from that judgment to the Illinois Supreme Court. Lincoln and Stephen Logan continued to represent Campbell and Dabney in defending against the appeal.

David Spear argued, on appeal, that the judgment debtor, Isaac Spear, had been a necessary party to the proceedings in the circuit court and that -- in the absence of such a necessary party -- the circuit court should have refused to have entered a judgment in the case.

Lincoln and Logan argued that the judgment debtor, Isaac Spear, was not a necessary party and that -- even if he were -- the defendant, David Spear, had failed to raise this objection in the circuit court and, so, had waived it.

The Illinois Supreme Court held that the judgment debtor, Isaac Spear, was not only a necessary party, but an indispensable party to the proceedings in the circuit court. The Illinois Supreme Court stated that, if the judgment debtor had only been a necessary party, but not absolutely indispensable to a disposition of the proceedings in the circuit court -- the defendant's failure to object in the circuit court, to the absence of the judgment debtor from the proceedings, would have effectively been a waiver of that objection. Because the judgment debtor was indispensable to the proceedings in the circuit court, however, the Illinois Supreme Court concluded that the defendant's failure to make the objection in the circuit court was not a waiver of that objection. The Illinois Supreme Court, therefore, considered the defendant's objection -- to the absence of the judgment debtor from the proceedings before the circuit court -- and reversed the judgment that the circuit court had entered in favor of Campbell and Dabney. Lincoln and Stephen Logan thus lost this particular case and probably resolved that, in the future, they would join the judgment debtor as a party to any similar actions.

25

Lincoln and his partner, Stephen Logan, were again on the winning side in the case of *Bruce vs. Truett,* 5 Ill. 454 (1843).

The parties involved in the case were Green Bruce and Miers Truett. It is not clear, from a reading of the decision in the case, which of these individuals was the plaintiff, and which was the defendant, at trial.

The plaintiff had sued the defendant in the Circuit Court of Jo Daviess County, on an account that the defendant had maintained with the plaintiff. This suggests that the plaintiff may have operated a retail business of some sort, from which the defendant had purchased goods.

The defendant did not make a motion for a continuance of the trial of the case, on the ground that he was unable to locate a witness having knowledge of significant facts relevant to the issues of the case. The case was tried to a jury, and the jury returned a verdict in favor of the plaintiff for the amount of $452.00. The circuit court entered a judgment on that verdict in favor of the plaintiff and against the defendant.

After having suffered an adverse judgment, the defendant filed a motion for a new trial on the ground that he had supposedly just located a witness -- named O. Ellers -- who had previously been employed by the plaintiff, and to whom the plaintiff had owed a promissory note of $300.00. This witness, O. Ellers, supposedly would testify that he had released the plaintiff's $300.00 indebtedness to him in discharge of part of the $452.00 balance which the defendant owed to the plaintiff. The defendant asserted, in an affidavit attached to his motion for a new trial, that the witness, O. Ellers, had moved to the State of Delaware; that the defendant had been looking for the witness for a period of two years; and that the defendant had been able to locate the witness only upon the same day that the jury had returned the verdict against him in this case.

The circuit court denied the defendant's motion for a new trial. The defendant appealed to the Illinois Supreme Court from this denial of his motion for a new trial.

Lincoln and Logan represented the plaintiff in defending against the appeal.

In considering the defendant's appeal, the Illinois Supreme Court remarked, first, that the defendant had failed to set forth all the testimony given at the trial of the case in his "bill of exceptions." (In those days, the attorneys themselves had to write out, in longhand, all the relevant testimony given at the trial of the case. One or more such longhand reports of testimony at trial, in Lincoln's own handwriting, may be seen in the Library of Congress' microfilm of the Herndon-Weik Papers. Viewing that microfilm compels one to wonder how Lincoln, or any lawyer in that day, found the time to perform the laborious work involved in writing out the transcript of the testimony at a trial in longhand.) The Illinois Supreme Court stated that, in the absence of a complete transcript of the testimony given at trial, it was unable to determine how significant the missing testimony, of O. Ellers, would have been.

The Court remarked also that -- if the defendant had considered the testimony of O. Ellers to be so important -- the defendant should have made a motion for a continuance of the case to permit him to obtain the testimony of that witness by means of a deposition. The Court indicated, finally, that the defendant's assertion in his affidavit -- that he had located the witness O. Ellers, after two years of searching for him, only upon the day that the jury returned the verdict against him -- was less than convincing.

The Illinois Supreme Court affirmed the circuit court's denial of the defendant's motion for new trial. Lincoln and Logan had thus won another case on appeal for one of their clients.

26

Lincoln was involved, on the losing side, in the case of *England vs. Clark,* 5 Ill. 486 (1843), which is still a leading case on the subject of the application of the doctrine of *caveat emptor* to execution sales.

An "execution," in this context, means those steps taken by a sheriff -- after a judgment has been entered against a debtor -- to seize the debtor's personal property or land, for the purpose of selling it, and using the proceeds of the sale to pay the amount of the judgment to the creditor. The sale conducted by a sheriff, under an execution, is known as an execution sale.

In *England vs. Clark,* Clark had obtained a judgment against Ferguson and Lukins. Clark then had the sheriff -- of Menard County, apparently -- seize a mare which Clark thought belonged to Ferguson and Lukins. The sheriff conducted an execution sale, at which England bid on, and purchased, the mare. England paid his money for the mare over to the sheriff, who, in turn, paid the net amount remaining, after the payment of the sheriff's costs, over to Clark.

After England had paid his money, and obtained possession of the mare, a third party, who is not named in the decision, came forward and began an action of replevin against England for possession of the mare. That third party successfully proved that the mare was his, rather than Ferguson and Lukin's. England had to deliver the mare to that third party.

Because England was then out the money that he had paid to the sheriff, for the mare, he brought an action in the Circuit Court of Menard County, Illinois, against the original judgment creditor, Clark, who had received the benefit of England's payment of his money for the mare. In the circuit court, Clark made a motion to dismiss England's complaint, on the ground that the doctrine of *caveat emptor* applied to the execution sale, and that England was not entitled to recover anything from Clark. The circuit court agreed with Clark, and dismissed England's complaint. England appealed from the dismissal of this complaint to the Illinois Supreme Court.

On the appeal, England was represented by Lincoln. Lincoln's good friend, Edward Baker, was one of three lawyers who represented Clark.

Lincoln filed a brief, which was printed with the opinion in the case. Lincoln argued essentially that, in equity and good conscience, the original judgment creditor, Clark, ought to be required to refund to England the money which he had received from the execution sale, because there had been "a total failure of the consideration on which the money was paid." Lincoln also apparently asserted -- perhaps at the oral argument of the case -- that, although the doctrine of *caveat emptor* applied at judicial sales (that is, court-supervised sales such as mortgage foreclosure sales), the doctrine should not apply to execution sales.

The Illinois Supreme Court disagreed with Lincoln, and held that the doctrine of *caveat emptor* applies to execution sales. The Court affirmed the circuit court's judgment dismissing the complaint filed by Lincoln's client, England.

Consequently, any purchaser at an execution sale purchases at his own risk. If the property which he purchases at the execution sale proves to have been owned by some third party, rather than by the judgment debtor, that third party will be able to reclaim the property, and the purchaser at the execution sale will not be able to obtain a refund of his money from the judgment creditor who received the benefit of the execution sale.

This is still the law in Illinois, as was demonstrated by the Illinois Supreme Court's decision in *Dixon vs. City National Bank of Metropolis,* 81 Ill. 2d 429, 410 N.E. 2d 1983, 43 Ill. Dec. 710 (1980), in which the Illinois Supreme Court cited and followed its decision in *England vs. Clark.* In *Dixon vs. City National Bank of Metropolis,* the Illinois Supreme Court further noted that it is not entirely clear, in Illinois, whether the purchaser at an execution sale, who is deprived of the property which he purchased, can even sue the original judgment debtor -- whose debt was discharged by the purchaser's payment of his money -- in order to recover the amount which he paid.

Anyone who purchases property at an execution sale in Illinois, therefore, does so strictly at his own risk.

27

A bailment exists when the owner of an item of personal property entrusts it to another. The owner is known as the bailor, and the person to whom the item is entrusted is known as the bailee.

Agistment -- a word not even found in some contemporary dictionaries -- was "the taking in of cattle or livestock to feed at a rate of so much per head" (Oxford English Dictionary).

Conversion is a civil wrong, known as a tort, that arises when an individual wrongfully exercises dominion over another's item of personal property. That individual, who has been guilty of conversion, can be forced to pay to the owner of the item the fair market value of the item at the time of the conversion.

In the case of *Johnson vs. Weedman,* 5 Ill. 495 (1843), Andrew Johnson had bailed his horse with John Weedman for the special purpose of agistment: that is, John Weedman was merely to keep and pasture Andrew Johnson's horse.

For some reason, not disclosed by the opinion in the case, Weedman rode the horse on a 15-mile journey, which action was hardly consistent with the special purpose for which he had possession of the horse. Perhaps Johnson would never have learned of Weedman's misuse of the horse, except that the horse died within a few hours after the completion of the journey. The opinion in the case indicates that the horse's death was "not in consequence of the riding."

Johnson sued Weedman in the Ciruit Court of De Witt County, Illinois, and alleged that Weedman had converted the horse. The jury returned a verdict in favor of Weedman. Johnson made a motion for a new trial, which the circuit court denied. Johnson appealed, from the denial of his motion for a new trial, to the Illinois Supreme Court.

Lincoln represented Weedman in defending against the appeal. Lincoln filed a brief which set forth the following three points:

"1. The riding of the horse was not such an abuse of the lawful possession as amounts to a conversion.

2. If the riding was a conversion, the injury done by the riding, and not the value of the horse, is the measure of damages. . . .

3. Though the riding of the horse may be a conversion, still, as it did no injury to the horse, the damage can but be nominal; and after verdict, a new trial is never allowed to enable a plaintiff, to recover nominal damages merely."

The Illinois Supreme Court agreed with Lincoln's first point, that Weedman's unauthorized riding of the horse was not a conversion. The Court explicitly stated that it was not saying that Weedman had the right to use the horse, but only that forcing Weedman to pay the fair market value of the horse, by characterizing his unauthorized use of the horse as a conversion, was too drastic a remedy, and that Johnson was entitled at most to the damages which he actually suffered because of the wrongful use of the horse. The Illinois Supreme Court also stated, in further agreement with Lincoln, that Johnson could only recover nominal damages for the wrongful use of the horse, and that he would not be granted a new trial merely for the purpose of allowing him to seek nominal damages. The Illinois Supreme Court affirmed the judgment of the Circuit Court of De Witt County in favor of Lincoln's client, Weedman.

Not much of Lincoln's writing or speeches from the year 1843, or before, exists. What does exist typically is marked by Lincoln's self-conscious striving after humor or somewhat florid eloquence. In Lincoln's brief in this case -- which he wrote at age 34 -- can be seen the characteristics of Lincoln as a mature public speaker and writer: that is, a seriousness which causes him to address the point immediately, and a simple, yet precise, mode of expression. It is not saying too much to assert that Lincoln's surprising growth as a speaker and writer late in his life involved -- at least in part -- his realization that he could address and persuade the public with the same directness and simplicity with which he had addressed and persuaded the Illinois Supreme Court in his appellate cases over the years.

28

It is somewhat difficult to discern exactly to what extent Lincoln contributed to the results in the case of *Hall vs. Perkins,* 5 Ill. 549 (1843).

In that case, the plaintiff had executed and delivered to the defendant a "title bond," by which he promised to convey to the defendant, by warranty deed, certain tracts of land in Tazewell County on or before December 25, 1839. In consideration for his receipt of that "title bond," the defendant had signed and delivered to the plaintiff two promissory notes. The parties to the case were named Samuel Hall and Elisah Perkins, but the decision in the case does not reveal which of these men was the plaintiff and which was the defendant.

The plaintiff sued the defendant in the Circuit Court of Tazewell County, seeking to recover a judgment for the amount of the two promissory notes. The defendant asserted, in his defense, that the plaintiff had never conveyed the tracts of land to him by means of a warranty deed, as required by the title bond which the plaintiff had executed. The circuit court apparently viewed the plaintiff's title bond and the defendant's promissory notes as constituting two separate transactions, because it rendered a judgment in favor of the plaintiff, on the defendant's promissory notes, for the amount of $46.00 and costs.

The defendant appealed from that judgment to the Illinois Supreme Court.

Lincoln represented the plaintiff on appeal.

Justice James Shields of the Illinois Supreme Court wrote, in the Court's opinion in the case, that the promissory notes and the title bond constituted one agreement, and that the plaintiff's failure to perform as required by the title bond barred him from recovering any damages on the defendant's promissory notes. The Illinois Supreme Court thus reversed the judgment of the circuit court, and Lincoln lost this particular appeal.

Although the decision of the Illinois Supreme Court was correct, it is interesting to note that the author of that decision, Justice James Shields, was the individual against whom Lincoln almost fought a duel, with cavalry broadswords on an island in the Mississippi River near Alton, Illinois, in 1842. Shields was thereafter appointed to the Illinois Supreme Court, by the Governor of the State of Illinois, on August 16, 1843. Shields and Lincoln were never friends, and Shields presumably had no regrets at finding that the law required him to rule against Lincoln in this case.

29

The case of *Lockridge vs. Foster,* 5 Ill. 570 (1843), reveals that a party may lose some of his rights by delaying his assertion of them.

In that case, an individual named George Foster had sold a 240-acre farm, and an additional 128-acre tract of land, to John Lockridge for the amount of $2,400 on December 19, 1836. Foster had assured Lockridge that he, Foster, had good title to the entire farm. Lockridge, who was then a resident of Indiana, took Foster at his word, and gave him two promissory notes, for $1,200 apiece, to pay the purchase price of the tracts of land. One of the promissory notes was due on May 1, 1837, and the other promissory note was due on December 25, 1837.

After Lockridge moved from Indiana to his new farm in 1837, he discovered that his seller, George Foster, had not had title to four-elevenths of 58 acres in the farm. The heirs of a deceased individual named Abram Miller owned the four-elevenths interest in those 58 acres.

After discovering the defect in the title which Foster had conveyed to him, Lockridge did nothing immediately either to correct the defect or to sue Foster in order to rescind the contract. Rather, Lockridge built a house and made other valuable improvements on the land. In addition, Lockridge paid in full the first $1,200 promissory note that became due.

George Foster died in the spring of 1837, and Peyton Foster was appointed administrator of his estate. In March, 1842, the administrator obtained a default judgment against Lockridge for the amount of $1,221.86, which was the balance then due on the second promissory note. Lockridge proceeded to pay about half of that judgment to the administrator.

Lockridge then belatedly filed a bill (that is, a complaint) in the equity division of the Circuit Court of Sangamon County, in which he asked that his contract with George Foster be rescinded and that his money be returned to him. The circuit court refused to rescind the contract, but did issue an injunction which restrained Peyton Foster, the administrator of George

Foster's estate, from collecting the last $200 which Lockridge owed on the judgment on the second promissory note.

Lockridge was dissatisfied with this result and appealed from the judgment to the Illinois Supreme Court.

Lincoln and his partner, Stephen Logan, represented Peyton Foster, the administrator of George Foster's estate, in defending against the appeal.

The Illinois Supreme Court concluded that George Foster had indeed been guilty of fraud by having falsely represented to Lockridge that he, George Foster, had good title to the entire farm. The Court held that Lockridge, on discovering the fraud, was free either to rescind the contract and to recover in full the purchase money which he had paid, or to confirm the contract and to sue George Foster, or the administrator of his estate, for damages sufficient to compensate Lockridge for the defect in the title to the farm. The Court stated, "The election rested solely with him, but he was bound to make it within a reasonable time. The whole case, in our opinion, shows most conclusively that he elected to confirm the contract."

The Court pointed out that Lockridge had done nothing to assert his rights until five years after his discovery of the fraud. This was beyond the reasonable time within which Lockridge could have elected to rescind the contract and to recover in full the purchase money which he had paid.

In the Illinois Supreme Court's view, however, Lockridge was still entitled to damages. It regarded the credit of $200 -- which the circuit court's injunction effectively gave Lockridge against the balance due on the judgment on the second promissory note -- as a fair amount of damages to compensate Lockridge for the defect in the title to the farm. This was because the defect in the title caused Lockridge not to own 21 acres which he would otherwise have owned, and the average price of the land was about $7.50 per acre.

Consequently, the Illinois Supreme Court affirmed the judgment of the circuit court in favor of Lockridge, but the true winner was Lincoln's client, the administrator of George Foster's estate.

30

The case of *Dorman vs. Lane,* 6 Ill. 143 (1844), is another which demonstrates that a party may lose his rights by delaying his effort to enforce those rights.

A man named Christopher Robinson had died in Gallatin County, Illinois, apparently about 1826. One of his creditors, John Lane, filed a petition in the Probate Court of Gallatin County to have himself appointed administrator of the Estate of Christopher Robinson, Deceased. The Probate Court of Gallatin County entered an order on November 30, 1826, which appointed John Lane administrator.

The decedent owed John Lane the amount of $1,008.87. In 1826, the Probate Court of Gallatin County also entered an order in favor of John Lane, and against the Estate of Christopher Robinson, Deceased, finding that the estate owed John Lane the amount of $1,008.87. This order was apparently effective in giving Lane a lien on the land of the decedent.

For the next 15 years, John Lane occupied the land of the decedent, Christopher Robinson, in his own right, and not as administrator of the estate, and he received profits from his occupation of the land (referred to in the decision as "mesne profits") during that time. In 1841, Lane finally filed a petition in the Circuit Court of Gallatin County for an order authorizing the sale of the land in order to pay the debt of $1,008.87 which the estate owed to him. This action by Lane was probably prompted by efforts of the only heirs of Christopher Robinson -- William Dorman and his wife -- to call Lane to account for having apparently abused his position of administrator for his own benefit.

The heirs of Christopher Robinson -- William Dorman and his wife -- opposed Lane's petition for an order to sell the real estate on the grounds that Lane had waited too long, and that he had already received "mesne profits" from his occupation of the land more than sufficient to pay the entire amount of the debt. The Circuit Court of Gallatin County disallowed the defenses raised by William Dorman and his wife, and entered an order directing Lane to sell the land for the purpose of paying the debt which the estate owed to him. William Dorman and his wife appealed to the Illinois Supreme Court from that order.

On the appeal, Lincoln represented William Dorman and his wife. His friend, Lyman Trumbull, represented Lane. Justice James Shields of the Illinois Supreme Court -- against whom Lincoln had nearly fought a duel in 1842 -- wrote the opinion in the case.

Lincoln argued, first, that Lane's lien, as a creditor, on the land owned by the decedent's estate had expired, and that Lane's right to have the land sold to pay the debt owed to him had terminated, because of the lapse of time. Lincoln argued, second, that "the value of the mesne profits of the land, together with the legal interest thereon, are assets in Lane's hands; and the amount thereof should have been accurately ascertained by the court below, and deducted from Lane's debt and interest, and the sale ordered to satisfy the balance only, if any such balance should have appeared."

The Illinois Supreme Court agreed with Lincoln. It laid down the rule that -- after the expiration of one year from the final settlement of the accounts of a decedent by the administrator in the probate court -- the administrator could not have the land owned by the estate sold to pay debts. The Court also said, of Lane's inactivity for fifteen years, "this delay, this neglect of duty, this gross *laches,* on his part remaining wholly unaccounted for cuts him off from any right to the benefit of this application." The Court noted, further, that the circuit court should have inquired into the heirs' assertion, that Lane had received more than enough, in the form of mesne profits from the land, to pay off the debt which the estate owed to him.

Consequently, the Illinois Supreme Court reversed the order of the circuit court, and remanded the case to the circuit court for further proceedings. Lincoln thus had won the appeal for William Dorman and his wife.

31

In the case of *Davis vs. Harkness,* 6 Ill. 173 (1844), Lincoln and his partner, Stephen Logan, represented two minor children against the estate of their stepfather, who had defrauded them out of their inheritance from their natural father.

The minor children -- Elisah Harkness, who was born about 1819, and Hannah Harkness, who was born about 1821 -- were the children of Samuel Harkness. Samuel Harkness died in Ohio in 1822 when Elisah was about three years old and Hannah was about one year old. His widow was appointed administratrix of his estate. She then remarried in 1824 to Thomas H. Hains. After her remarriage, Thomas H. Hains essentially took over the administration of Samuel Harkness' estate, and appropriated the estate to his own benefit.

Hains did support and educate Elisah and Hannah. Under Ohio law, however, they were entitled to receive one-third of their natural father's estate, which third would have amounted to approximately $1,000.00.

Thomas H. Hains and this family resided in Ohio until 1833, when he, and they, moved to Illinois. Hains apparently practiced medicine in McLean County, Illinois, until his death in 1838.

At his death, David Davis was appointed administrator of Thomas Hains' estate. In 1838, the boy, Elisah Harkness, was 19 years old. The girl, Hannah, was 17 years old. She had married John McClure.

After the death of Thomas H. Hains, Elisah Harkness, Hannah McClure, and her husband, John McClure, filed a bill (that is, a complaint) in the Circuit Court of McLean County to compel David Davis, the administrator of the Estate of Thomas H. Hains, Deceased, to account to Elisah Harkness and Hannah McClure for their shares of their natural father's estate. The administrator responded that the expenses which Hains had incurred for the maintenance and education of the children, was more than their combined shares of the natural father's estate and that, in consequence, the Estate of Thomas H. Hains, Deceased, owed them nothing.

The circuit court found that the children's share of their natural father's estate had a value of approximately $1,000.00. It then concluded that the stepfather, Thomas H. Hains, was only entitled to use the interest earned by that $1,000.00 in order to provide for the maintenance and education of the children, and that he was not entitled to consume the principal in order to provide for their maintenance and education. The circuit court thus allowed the Estate of Thomas H. Hains, Deceased, a credit, for the expense which he incurred in rearing and educating the children, but only to the extent of the interest which would have been earned on the amount of $1,000.00, apparently calculated at the rate of six percent per year, since the natural father's death in 1822. The circuit court thus apparently required the administrator of the Estate of Thomas H. Hains, Deceased, to pay the children -- Elisah Harkness and Hannah McClure -- the amount of $1,292.50.

The administrator of the Estate of Thomas H. Hains, Deceased, appealed from that order to the Illinois Supreme Court.

Lincoln and his partner, Stephen Logan, represented the children in defending against the appeal. They stated, in their brief which they filed in the case, "The general rule is, that a guardian should not be permitted to break the capital of the ward for education and maintenance . . ."

The Illinois Supreme Court agreed with the views expressed by Lincoln and Logan. The Court stated, in a passage which continues, unfortunately, to ring true, "The inducements for guardians to invent for their wards artificial wants, that they may reap an incidental benefit in the expenditure of their estate, has admonished the courts to guard, with a jealous eye, the estates of infants, who are unable to protect themselves. Without this the ward would but too often become the victim of the guardian, and the most ample estate would, during a protracted minority, become dissipated more to his advantage than that of his ward."

The Illinois Supreme Court concluded that Thomas H. Hains had wrongfully consumed part of the principal amount of $1,000.00, to which the minor children were entitled to receive from their natural father's estate. It affirmed the order of the circuit court, which required the stepfather's estate to pay to the minor children the amount of $1,292.50.

Lincoln and Logan had thus won the appeal for the minor children.

The longest appellate brief (that is, a written argument, citing authorities, which is submitted to an appellate court) bearing Lincoln's name, in the reports of the decisions of the Illinois Supreme Court, appears in the case of *Martin vs. Dryden,* 6 Ill. 187 (1844), which case arose in Madison County. The brief is about 8 1/2 printed pages long, occupying page 197 through page 205 of volume 6 of the Illinois Supreme Court reports.

If Lincoln authored the brief (as this writer believes), the brief constitutes the best example of Lincoln's abilities to perform legal research, to engage in legal reasoning, and to combine his legal research and legal reasoning in a graceful written style. The brief is headed by the following introduction, however:

A. Lincoln and *J. M. Krum,* for the appellees:

The following is a portion of a printed argument, presented by John M. Krum, Esq., who contended, ..."

A history of Madison County contained in the library of the Illinois State Historical Society, below the Old State Capitol in Springfield, states that J. M. Krum, an attorney from Alton, was a learned and able man, who eventually moved to St. Louis and was elected mayor of St. Louis. J. M. Krum thus apparently had the *ability* himself to have written the excellent brief which followed his and Lincoln's names. Whether he had a law library sufficient to permit him to do the necessary research, however, may properly be doubted.

Lincoln's advantage, as a lawyer practicing in Springfield, was that his office was across the street from the then State Capitol building, which housed the law library of the Illinois Supreme Court. The room in which the law library was contained may still be observed in the Old State Capitol building in Springfield. Consequently, it was quite possible for Lincoln in Springfield -- and probably impossible for J. M. Krum in Alton -- to have done the research, into the cases from other States, necessary in the writing of this brief.

The phrasing of the brief, at various points, also bespeaks Lincoln's authorship of the brief. The brief has never before (to this writer's knowledge) been made known to the public as a significant piece of Lincoln's writing.

The case of *Martin vs. Dryden* involved the question whether a creditor's attachment lien on his debtor's land -- obtained after the debtor had executed a deed concerning the land to others, but before the deed had been recorded -- took precedence over the interests which those others acquired in the land by means of that deed.

The facts of the case were as follows:

In May, 1836, 28 residents of Baltimore, Maryland, formed a partnership known as the "Baltimore and Western Land Association," for the purpose of buying, selling, and speculating in lands in the State of Illinois and elsewhere. The partnership was to last for a period of five years.

The partnership employed an agent named Charles A. Warfield. He was to visit the western States and to buy and sell land at his discretion, taking the titles to the tracts that he purchased in his own name. He was to keep a journal of his activities, and to make monthly reports to the partnership. His expenses were to be paid by the partnership.

Warfield was to have one-fourth of the net profits on the sale of the lands when the partnership terminated after a period of five years, or, if the partnership terminated before five years, one-fifth of all the partnership's interest in the land which it had acquired.

The tracts involved in this case were located in Madison County, Illinois. Warfield purchased those tracts of land in his own name, but with the partnership's funds, in 1836 and 1837.

On March 11, 1840, Warfield conveyed those tracts to three of the partners -- namely, Dryden, Gosnell, and Wood -- to be held by them in trust for the partnership. Warfield's deed to the three partners, as trustees, was recorded in Madison County, Illinois, on December 20, 1840.

In the course of his activities in Madison County, Warfield had apparently become indebted to an individual named John Martin. Martin filed a lawsuit against Warfield in Madison County on July 14, 1840, and, on that same day, had an "attachment" levied upon the tracts of land in Madison County which Warfield had purchased in his own name. An "attachment" means that the Sheriff of Madison County effectively seized the tracts of land for the purpose of holding them as security for the payment of any judgment which Martin might ultimately recover against Warfield.

It is important to note that Martin filed his lawsuit against Warfield, and had the tracts of land attached, *after* Warfield had deeded the tracts of land to three partners of the Baltimore and Western Land Association, but *before* that deed was recorded in Madison County.

In September, 1841, the Circuit Court of Madison County entered a judgment for Martin, and against Warfield, for the amount of $1,666.35.

On September 6, 1841, the three partners -- Dryden, Gosnell, and Wood -- filed a bill (that is, a complaint) in the Circuit Court of Madison County, in behalf of all the members of the partnership, against Martin and Warfield, charging that Martin had actual notice that Warfield's name had appeared on the titles to the tracts of land only in his capacity as an agent for the partnership. The partners asked that Martin be prohibited from proceeding with his attachment action against the tracts of land, and that all liens on the lands, arising from the attachment action, be set aside.

Warfield filed an answer in the three partners' injunction proceeding and admitted that Martin had actual notice of his (Warfield's) role as a mere agent of the partnership.

Martin denied that he had actual notice or knowledge of Warfield's role as an agent of the partnership.

The Circuit Court of Madison County found in favor of the partnership, and entered an injunction prohibiting Martin from proceeding with his attachment action against the tracts of land. From that decree, Martin appealed to the Illinois Supreme Court.

Lincoln and a lawyer from Alton, named J. M. Krum, represented the three partners -- Dryden, Gosnell, and Wood -- and the partnership itself in defending against the appeal.

Lincoln's and Krum's brief for the appellees -- Dryden, Gosnell, and Wood -- discussed seven different points.

The first of these was one raised by the attorneys for the appellant, John Martin: namely, that the other 24 partners in the Baltimore and Western Land Association -- none of whom had been joined to the injunction action begun by Dryden, Gosnell, and Wood -- were necessary parties, in whose absence the court of equity should have refused to have issued the injunction.

The second point discussed in Lincoln's and Krum's brief, and the first raised by them, was that the decree issuing the injunction was "warranted from the case made by the pleadings, and the proofs in the case."

The third point was that John Martin had purchased the lands in controversy *pendente lite* (that is, during the pendency of this litigation in the circuit court) and, so, had purchased with full knowledge of the rights of Dryden, Gosnell, and Wood, as revealed by the litigation.

The fourth point was that John Martin's attachment of the lands on July 14, 1840, did not give him a *lien* on the lands which he could enforce by means of a sale of the lands.

The fifth point was that -- at the time of Martin's attachment of the lands -- the legal title to the lands was no longer in the partnership's agent, Charles Warfield, but had been conveyed to Dryden, Gosnell, and Wood for the Baltimore Western Land Association. The argument was that Martin had no interest in the lands which could then be attached by the Sheriff of Madison County, Illinois.

The sixth point was that the attachment process specified by the Illinois statute was intended only as a means to compel a defendant to enter his appearance in a case personally, to answer the complaint against him; that this purpose had been served when the partnership's agent, Charles Warfield, had entered his appearance in Martin's attachment action; that Charles Warfield's appearance in the case should have caused the lands to be released from the attachment; and that, in consequence, Martin's remedy, if any, should have been to collect his debt from Charles Warfield personally, rather than from the value of the lands in question.

The seventh point appeared to be in the alternative to the fifth point. Lincoln and Krum conceded that, pursuant to the partnership agreement, Charles Warfield might be deemed to have *some* interest in the lands -- perhaps as much as a one-fifth interest -- under some circumstances. They asserted, however, that Warfield's potential interest in the lands was too vague and uncertain to be the subject of an attachment.

Lincoln's and Krum's brief for the appellees in *Martin vs. Dryden* began by reciting the six points that Lincoln and Krum desired to make in behalf of the appellees, and, in addition, one issue that the attorneys for the appellant, John Martin, had raised in his brief. That issue, raised in Martin's brief, was whether the action for an injunction -- brought by three of the partners of the Baltimore and Western Land Association in behalf of all 28 partners, to prohibit Martin's proceeding with the attachment action against lands in Madison County to collect a debt for $1,666.35 which the partnership's agent, Warfield, personally owed to Martin -- should have been dismissed on the ground that the remaining 24 partners, who had not joined in bringing the injunction action, were *necessary parties*. The portion of Lincoln's and Krum's brief, devoted to discussing that issue, follows:

"Before entering into the consideration of the points made in behalf of the complainants, the question raised under the fifth error assigned, as to the right of the complainants to maintain their suit, will first be disposed of. The objection, *it is supposed,* is based on the ground that all the persons, materially interested in the *subject* of the suit, are not parties to it. The general principle, that every person materially interested in the *subject of the suit,* should be joined in it, is not denied. '*Subject of suit,*' *may mean either the estate,* respecting which the question has arisen, or the *question* itself. Calvert on parties to suits in equity, 15 Law Lib. 6, 9; 3 Ves. 75; 16 do. 326, 1808. But a person only consequentially interested, need not be made a party. Calvert, 5. There is, also, another well established rule in regard to parties, viz: that although a person has an interest in the object of a suit, he need not be made a party, if he has a representative, &c. Story's Eq. Pl. 97, 135, 145, 414.

It is stated in the bill, that the 'complainants sue in behalf of themselves and the subscribers,' &c., of the said association, and it is apparent that the relief sought, is, in its nature beneficial to all whom the complainants undertook to represent. Calvert, 58; 13 Ves. 397, 526.

The complainants represent the interests of the *cestui que trust,* and this, from the nature of the trust, as shown by the bill; the latter, therefore, is not a necessary party. Story's Eq. Jur. 138; 2 Johns. Ch. R 197; 11 Ves. 4, 29; 16 do. 321.

It seems clear, therefore, on principle, that the complainants, representing not only their own, but the interest of all the subscribers to the association, have an undoubted right to sue as they have done. But again, waiving the right of complainants to sue, on the principle of representation, the bill shows the legal title of the subject of the suit, to be in complainants. This title is sustained at the hearing, by the reading in evidence, (without objection on the part of Martin), the deed of Warfield to complainants, by which the lands in controversy are absolutely conveyed to the complainants. On two grounds, therefore, is the objection met, and fully answered."

The six points which Lincoln and Krum themselves made and argued in their brief in that case are presented below:

"I. That the decree of the Court is supported by the record, there cannot exist a rational doubt. All the material allegations on the part of the complainants, on which a material issue depended, were substantially proved at the hearing. No objection appears to have been made, or exception taken to any part of the evidence. Every fact, and every conclusion which the evidence conduced to prove, or which might reasonably be inferred, cannot now be called in question. If any objection existed as to the competency or legality of the testimony, the objection should have been made at the hearing. The defendant is now concluded. It was incumbent on the complainants to establish their title to, or interest in, the lands in question. *Secondly,* to show that the free and uninterrupted enjoyment of their right in the lands had been invaded by the defendants. The production of the deed from Warfield to complainants was sufficient to establish their right, title, and interest in and to the property in controversy. This deed bears date, March 11, 1840. As between the complainants and Warfield, nothing further was necessary to perfect the complainants' right. The defendant, Martin, does not pretend that he had any title or interest in the property at the date of this deed -- whatever claim or right Martin does set up, is of a date subsequent to the deed, and is derived from the same source, not by voluntary conveyance from Warfield, but by process of law. It cannot be contended that Martin, in virtue of his levy under his attachment, acquired any title or interest in the lands in controversy. The levy under the attachment gave no rights to Martin, which he could assert and maintain, either at law or in equity. In the most favorable view, it can only be said that Martin acquired the only tangible interest he has in the lands in question, by purchase at sheriff's sale, which was subsequent to the recording of the deed from Warfield to complainants, and subsequent to the filing of complainants' bill. But it may be said, that in the finding of the Court, as recited in the decree, certain facts are found as true, which finding is not warranted by the proofs in the case. Suppose such were the case, (which, however, is not admitted), if there appear upon the record sufficient to sustain the decree, would the recital of a fact, not warranted by the proof, vitiate the final order of the Court? No one will contend for such an absurdity. The Court will now look through the whole record, and if sufficient appear to sustain the judgment of the Court below, no matter what is stated by way of recital, the decree, if in conformity to equity, will not be disturbed.

Again, *how* and *through whom,* does defendant, Martin, claim? Certainly, if any claim he has, it is derived through his co-defendant, Warfield, If Martin asserts no *right* or *title* in the lands in question, the matter is at an end -- but if a *right* or *title* is set up, it becomes material to inquire *when, how, and through* whom, his right or title is derived. Whether his right or title accrued at the date of the levy under his attachment, or at the date of the sheriff's sale, is not important, in the view now presented; it cannot be denied that *however,* or *whenever* his right or title *did accrue,* it is derived through his co-defendant, Warfield. If Martin claims as purchaser at sheriff's sale, I take it, he stands affected like any other purchaser. No difference exists between a purchaser at private sale and one at sheriff's sale. 2 Sug. on Ven. 254, 336, 9 Johns. 168; 10 do. 456; 2 Scam. 499.

This position leads to the consideration of an important point in the evidence in this case, viz: Is the answer of defendant, Warfield, evidence against his co-defendant, Martin?

It is true, the answer of one defendant in Chancery cannot, in general, be read in evidence against his co-defendant. But this rule does not apply to cases where the other defendant claims through him, whose answer is sought to be made evidence. 1 Greenl. Ev. 210; 6 Cranch, 8, 24; 1 Gall 630, 635. The answer of Warfield is therefore competent evidence against his co-defendant. Applying this rule to the case at bar, the facts stated in Warfield's answer confirm in proof, beyond all doubt, every material allegation in the complainants' bill. No objection was made, nor exception taken at the hearing to the competency of this proof. The answer of Warfield is in evidence, and it is now too late to question its competency. All objections to it are tacitly waived. The defendant, whose right it was to object to this evidence at the hearing, is now concluded by his silence.

II.   The general principle, that all who claim as purchasers, *pendente lite,* though they are not parties to the suit, they and their interests, are nevertheless bound by the decree, is too well settled to be called in question. *Preston vs. Tubbin,* 1 Vern. 286; 1 Johns. Ch. R. 565, 579.

The pendency of complainants' bill, at the time of Martin's purchase at sheriff's sale, was notice to the world. It is a *lis pendens* as to him. The record shows that he had actual notice of complainants' rights, long before his purchase at sheriff's sale. If Martin sought to defend himself on the ground that he is a *bona fide* purchaser for a valuable consideration, without notice, he was bound to deny every circumstance from which notice could be inferred. 2 Ves. jr. 458; 3 P. Wms. 244 n.; 1 Johns. Ch. R 574. At law, the old rule was, that a purchase of land pending a suit concerning it, was *champerty;*

and it is a maxim of the common law, the *pendente lite, nihil innovetur.*

No principle is better established, nor one founded on more indispensable necessity, than that the purchase of the subject matter in controversy, *pendente lite,* does not change the rights of the parties. 2 Johns. Ch. R. 441; 4 do. 46.

III. Had defendant, Martin, a lien on the lands in controversy in virtue of the levy made under his attachment? It is contended, on the part of the complainants, that a levy upon lands under an attachment, creates no lien, in the proper sense of the term.

1. If a lien, it is so by statute. The proceeding by attachment being against common right, the statute and all proceedings and rights acquired thereby, will be construed *stricti juris.* 1 Scam. 476; 2 do. 17.

2. Because the manifest object of the statute is, to compel the appearance of a party in the jurisdiction where his property may be located. By the appearance of the defendant, the great object of the statute is sustained. The statute no where declares, that the real estate attached shall stand as security for the payment of the attaching creditor's debt, nor that such creditor shall have a lien.

It is essential to a lien at law, *first,* that the claimant should be in possession; *secondly,* that he should have some claim unsatisfied; *thirdly,* that he should have a right to hold until his claim shall be satisfied. 2 East, 27; 1 Story's Eq. Jur. 483.

3. Because the attaching creditor has no interest or estate whatever in the lands attached. 9 Mass. 104; Ib. 265, 112; 14 do. 217.

In some States, where attachments on mesne process are authorized, the statutes expressly provide that the property attached shall stand as security to satisfy whatever judgments &c. the creditor may recover; *vide* attachment law of Mass. The statute of Illinois has no such provision. For a full *expose* of the reasoning and authorities upon this question, the following references are made; Cushings's Trustee Process, 25, 47, 51.

Story on Bail. 197, 204; but more particularly to the elaborate and discriminating opinion of Mr. Justice Story, in the matter of *John S. Foster,* in the Circuit Court of the United States, for Mass. reported in 5 Law Reporter, 55.

IV. The question, whether the lands seized under an attachment are discharged therefrom, on the appearance and pleading of the defendant at the return term of the attachment, is now probably for the first time raised in this Court.

The record shows that the action, in which the attachment against Warfield issued, was in assumpsit, to which at the return term of the process, the defendant entered his appearance and filed his plea of non assumpsit to the said account. Such appearance and plea, it is contended, under the provision of the 12th and 29th sections of the Act concerning Attachments, R.L. 87, 93, operates to discharge or liberate the defendant's estate from the attachment. By the 12th Sec. it is provided, that, 'if the defendant (at the return term), appear, put in sufficient bail and plead, &c., his estate so attached, shall be liberated,' &c.

The twenty ninth section provides that 'any defendant in an attachment may appear and plead, without giving any bail or entering into any bond.'

It is conceded that the bail contemplated in the twelfth section means *special bail,* and of course in order to liberate the property attached in virtue of this section, it would be incumbent on a defendant to appear, give special bail and plead. But the 29th section had so far modified, or repealed the 12th, as to allow a defendant to release his property, by appearing and pleading to the action, without being required to 'give bail, or enter into any bond.' On the appearance, giving bail and pleading by the defendant, it is expressly declared by the 12th section 'his estate so attached, shall be liberated.' Liberated, in the common acceptation, discharged, released, from the attachment.

The 29th section does not change the effect of such appearance, etc., but its provisions relieve the defendant from one of the conditions imposed by the 12th section, a compliance with which, entitled the defendant to have his estate liberated.

There is a conflict between the two sections. If the well established rule of constructing statutes is applied, the provisions of the 29th section control what is inconsistent with them in the 12th section. Bacon's Abr. title Stat.; 1 Kent's Com. 432-3. No good reason can be shown, in view of the act concerning attachments, and the objects of its creation, why this rule of construction should not be applied to the case at bar. The construction contended for, is according to the letter of the law. In what does this construction conflict with the spirit of the law? If the process of attachment, authorized by statute, is resorted to, for the purpose of compelling the appearance of a debtor in a jurisdiction where his estate may be located, the main purpose and objects of the statute are attained, when the debtor submits himself to such jurisdiction by entering his appearance and pleading to such action. In the case at bar, the defendant in the attachment, at the return term thereof (August term, 1840), entered his appearance and filed his plea to the action. This is admitted upon the record. Now if the construction contended for be correct, then the effect of such appearance and plea is expressly declared by the statute itself, viz: that the debtor's 'state so attached shall be liberated.'

If the estate was liberated from the attachment, it follows, that the defendant, Martin, has no lien on the land attached, even though a lien did exist in his favor prior to such appearance. The defendant in the attachment, pending that suit had full power to alien his title to the lands seized, and the subsequent recovery of a judgment against him under the attachment created no lien on the lands. 9 Cowen 121.

V. Whether the levy under the attachment be regarded as a lien proper, in the sense of that term, or merely a *quasi* lien from analogy, yet nothing more than the actual right, title or interest of the defendant in the lands in controversy could be seized under it.

This is not a question of superior diligence between creditors. The attaching creditor can not put himself in a better position in regard to the lands attached, than the debtor himself occupied at the time of the levy. In short the creditor attaches the property of his debtor, the real, not the apparent interest, nothing more. The interest of Warfield in the lands in controversy, was so indefinite, uncertain and contingent, that there was nothing in fact on which the attachment could be levied. By the terms of the second section of the articles of the association, Warfield was to receive as a compensation for his services, 'one-fourth of the net profits upon a sale of his property,' etc. No sale had taken place; the net profits had not been ascertained.

Whatever sum of money might accrue to Warfield, on a sale, and ascertaining the net profits, the complainants would hold the same in trust for Warfield or his creditors. Such sum could not be seized under the attachment and reduced to the possession of the officer; at best, the amount could only be secured, by trustee or garnishee process.

The complainants and their associates, as to the lands in controversy, must be regarded as *quasi* tenants in common, and their rights, touching their common property, may be likened to the business, property, and liability of a co-partnership of several persons.

The partnership property must be applied to the partnership debts. The interest of the individual partners depends upon the ascertainment of the condition of the firm. The practical result, in this and all analogous cases is, that the actual interest only of the individual partners (or tenant in common) can be seized under an attachment. 2 P. Wms. 500; 3 do. 25, 182; 16 Johns. 102; Story on Partn. 373.

The right of the agent, under the second section of the articles of association, to have one fifth of the lands, depended upon the choice and election of such agent. It was the option of the agent to elect to take one fifth of the lands; creditors could not make the election for him.

VI. It may be said, on the part of the defendant, that the deed from Warfield to complainants is void as to creditors, etc., in other words, that the deed took effect only from the time of filing the same for record. The provisions of the fifth section of the act abolishing the office of State Recorder, R.L. 587, has reference to judgment creditors, and not creditors at large. The policy of the statute doubtless is, to compel the purchaser of land to record his deed, so that the vendor could not perpetrate a fraud by selling a second time. There must be a vigilance required of a purchaser. A purchaser could not be expected to know, nor possess the power to discover all the creditors of his vendor. Judgments are matters of record, public, and subject to the inspection of all. A judgment in fact is the best evidence of the existence of a debt. In law, and in the sense in which the term creditor is used in the act now under consideration, a judgment creditor only is contemplated. 9 Cowen 120; 4 Johns. 216; 13 do. 471; 2 Scam. 499.

The complainants, therefore, contend that their rights are not affected by the provisions of this statute. Martin was not a judgment creditor, nor did he acquire any right or title in the lands in controversy, prior to the recording of Warfield's deed to the complainants."

In ruling on the appeal brought by John Martin from the injunction entered in favor of Abraham Lincoln's and J. M. Krum's clients -- Joshua Dryden, Samuel Gosnell, and Nicholas Wood -- in the case of *Martin vs. Dryden,* the Illinois Supreme Court first addressed the question whether the answer of Charles Warfield (the agent of the partnership known as the Baltimore and Western Land Association), which admitted that John Martin had actual notice of his role as an agent of the partnership in handling the lands in question, should have been binding on John Martin as one who claimed his interest in the lands through Charles Warfield. If that admission were binding, John Martin (the creditor of Charles Warfield who had attached the lands which Charles Warfield held for the partnership) could not have been an innocent *bona fide* purchaser of the lands without notice, and, so, would not have been able to take the lands away from the partnership. The Court concluded that Warfield's interests were obviously allied with the partnership's and that, in consequence, no admission in his answer could bind Martin. Lincoln and his co-counsel, J. M. Krum, thus lost this point.

The Court next considered whether the injunction action brought by the three partners -- Dryden, Gosnell, and Wood -- should have been dismissed because of the absence of the other 24 partners from the action: that is, for lack of necessary parties. It decided that the three partners who began the injunction action fully represented the interest of all the other partners, that any decree concerning the interest of the three partners would bind all of the partners, and that the other 24 partners were not necessary parties. Lincoln and Krum thus gained this point.

The Court then took up the sixth point addressed by Lincoln and Krum: namely, that Warfield's personally entering his appearance in the attachment action begun by the creditor, Martin, was sufficient, under the Illinois attachment statute, to cause the attached lands to be released from the attachment. After considering the various provisions in the attachment statute, concerning the seizing of land and the posting of a bond by the sheriff to guarantee his proper handling of the land, the Court concluded that the statute would be essentially reduced to meaninglessness if a defendant could defeat an attachment simply by personally entering his appearance in the attachment action. Lincoln and Krum, therefore, lost this point.

As to whether the creditor, Martin, gained a lien on the lands by attaching them, the Court held that "the attachment is a lien from the date of the levy, when followed by a judgment, and which will have relation back to it." This holding was against Lincoln and Krum on the fourth point that they discussed in their brief.

As to whether the creditor, Martin, should have had priority over the partnership, with respect to the ownership of the lands, the Court held that the then existing Illinois recording act required that a creditor who -- without actual or constructive notice of his debtor's having conveyed away the land -- obtained a valid lien on the land before the debtor's deed of conveyance was *recorded,* be given preference over persons claiming the land by virtue of a subsequently recorded deed. This was the crucial point in the case, and the Court resolved it against Lincoln and Krum.

The Illinois Supreme Court concluded, finally, that the creditor, Martin, could not be restricted to taking merely a one-fifth interest in the land (Warfield's maximum interest in the land under his agreement with the partnership) because Warfield was ostensibly the owner of the entire fee simple interest in the land and Martin had no notice of any limitation on Warfield's interest. The Court thereby ruled against Lincoln and Krum on the last point that they raised in their brief.

The Illinois Supreme Court reversed the decree entered by the Circuit Court of Madison County, which had awarded an injunction to the three partners -- Dryden, Gosnell, and Wood -- to enable them to prevent John Martin from selling the partnership's land. An impressive effort by Abraham Lincoln and J. M. Krum, in their brief for the appellees, came to nothing.

Concerning Lincoln's abilities as an appellate lawyer, as revealed by his brief in the case of *Martin vs. Dryden,* the present writer can comment on the bases of his having worked as a law clerk for the Appellate Court, Fifth District, for the period of one year, and his having written numerous appellate briefs himself, and having read numerous appellate briefs prepared by other attorneys, over the past 14 years. The quality of Lincoln's brief in *Martin vs. Dryden* -- if such a brief were to be filed today -- would put him in the front ranks of accomplished appellate lawyers.

Lincoln was able to handle, in his brief, a series of exceedingly technical points of law in a style that was graceful and lucid. The difficulty which an appellate attorney always faces, in discussing complicated, technical questions, is that the difficulty of the questions tends to make his exposition of them convoluted and impenetrable. It is fair to say, of Lincoln's writing in his brief, that he made it as easy as possible for a reader thereof to follow his discussion, from point to point, with a full comprehension of the several issues and his argument on each issue.

As lengthy as Lincoln's brief was, it possessed an admirable succinctness. In addressing each of the many issues in turn, Lincoln spoke to the issue and then moved on. There is a temptation -- at least for attorneys to whom writing comes easily -- to belabor a point. It is undoubtedly more persuasive to take up a point, then to discuss it fully, but in as few words as reasonably possible, and, so, to move to the next point.

Lincoln's abilities as a legal researcher are revealed by the brief, because the brief contains numerous references to relevant passages in both treatises and decisions of courts from other states. Lincoln could have obtained these references from the law library of the Illinois Supreme Court only by knowing how to proceed with his legal research, and by committing himself to the long hours of research necessary to obtain references to the most appropriate sources.

That which is most impressive about Lincoln's brief, however, is its balanced, eloquent style. Few briefs submitted to the Appellate Court of Illinois or the Illinois Supreme Court today are written in a style which would compare favorably with the style in Lincoln's brief.

Despite these admirable qualities of Lincoln's brief, he still lost the case on appeal. This demonstrates that an appellate lawyer's abilities as a legal researcher and writer can only do so much, and that he cannot change the facts of his case, and that the facts will ordinarily prove more persuasive than any legal argument he can make.

33

The case of *Warner vs. Helm,* 6 Ill. 220 (1844), was apparently another which the Alton attorney, J. M. Krum, had referred to Lincoln on appeal.

In that case, J. M. Krum, had represented partners doing business under the firm name of Craig & Warner. Craig & Warner had acquired from Nathaniel Ware, by assignment, a promissory note for $6,000.00 which B. F. Edwards had executed to Nathaniel Ware on July 6, 1836.

B. F. Edwards had defaulted on that $6,000.00 promissory note, and Craig & Warner sued him in the municipal court of the City of Alton in 1838, and recovered a judgment against him for the amount of the promissory note.

B. F. Edwards then apparently told the attorneys for Craig & Warner that a particular farm, which he owned in Madison County, had no liens on it and could be taken by Craig & Warner in discharge of the debt which B. F. Edwards owed to them. This representation by B. F. Edwards, concerning the unencumbered state of his title to the farm, was false because he had given a mortgage on that farm to John B. Helm to secure B. F. Edwards' payment of a promissory note for $7,000.00 which he had executed to John B. Helm on May 29, 1837. The opinion of the Illinois Supreme Court in this case indicates, although does not explicitly state, that the mortgage on the farm -- which B. F. Edwards had delivered to John B. Helm -- had been recorded in the Recorder's Office of Madison County.

The attorneys for Craig & Warner -- including J. M. Krum -- took B. F. Edwards at his word concerning the unencumbered state of his title to the farm, and did not search the records in the Recorder's Office to determine whether anyone else had a mortgage on the farm.

Craig & Warner sought to enforce their judgment by having a writ of execution levied upon the farm, and then having the farm sold at an execution sale. They purchased the farm at that execution sale.

John B. Helm then filed an action in the Circuit Court of Madison County to foreclose his mortgage on the same farm. He sought a "strict foreclosure," which means that he sought to have the farm simply turned over to him, without having it put up for public sale.

Craig & Warner filed a cross-bill against Helm's bill (that is, complaint) seeking a strict foreclosure against the farm. The Circuit Court of Madison County dismissed the cross-bill of Craig & Warner, and awarded the farm to Helm by way of strict foreclosure.

Craig & Warner then appealed from that decree of the Circuit Court of Madison County to the Illinois Supreme Court. Lincoln represented Craig & Warner on appeal.

Justice James Shields of the Illinois Supreme Court (who was never friendly with Lincoln, and who had once challenged him to a duel which almost took place on an island in the Mississippi River opposite Alton, Illinois) held that the mortgage, obtained by Helm on the farm, was "a prior incumbrance to the judgment lien; and the recording of it is deemed notice in law to all subsequent incumbrancers by judgment . . . " Justice Shields wrote that Helms was entitled to a decree of foreclosure against the farm, although he did not permit him simply to take over the farm by way of a strict foreclosure. Rather, the Illinois Supreme Court ordered that Helm's mortgage be foreclosed, but that the farm be sold at a public sale, and that the proceeds of the sale be applied first to pay to Helm his debt, interest, and court costs, and that the surplus, if any, should then be paid to Craig & Warner.

Lincoln thus lost another case -- which had been referred to him by J. M. Krum of Alton, Illinois -- on appeal. The fault lay with Krum, rather than with Lincoln, however, for not having searched the records in the Recorder's Office before arranging, in behalf of Craig & Warner, to purchase B. F. Edwards' supposedly unencumbered farm at the execution sale in discharge of their claim against B. F. Edwards.

The next of Lincoln's cases before the Illinois Supreme Court was *McDonald vs. Fithian,* 6 Ill. 269 (1844). The decision in the case does not mention Lincoln's name, but the Illinois Supreme Court's decision -- in the later, related case of *Cunningham vs. Fithian,* 7 Ill. 650 (1845) -- indicates that Abraham Lincoln had been an attorney for the appellees in *McDonald vs. Fithian,* 6 Ill. 269 (1844), and that his name had been accidently omitted from the reported decision in the case. Lincoln's involvement in both of these related cases -- that is, *McDonald vs. Fithian,* 6 Ill. 269 (1844), and *Cunningham vs. Fithian,* 7 Ill. 650 (1845) -- will be considered together in a subsequent discussion of the latter case.

After *McDonald vs. Fithian,* 6 Ill. 269 (1844), the next case before the Illinois Supreme Court, in which Lincoln participated, was that of *Favor vs. Marlett,* 6 Ill. 385 (1844), which arose out of Kane County, in northeastern Illinois.

This case involved an ancient procedure known as "distress for rent," by which procedure a landlord seizes personal property of a tenant, who is delinquent in the payment of his rent, for the purpose of selling that personal property and thereby recovering the amount of the rent due. This procedure still exists in Illinois (735 ILCS 5/9-301 to 9-321), but it is risky for a landlord to rely upon it.

An individual named Kimball Favor, and other persons not named in the decision, owned a shop in Aurora, Illinois. They rented the shop to Franklin M. Grant, who fell behind in the rent that he owed to them. Kimball Favor and his associates then had some unfinished furniture, which was apparently in the possession of Isaac Marlett and which supposedly belonged to Franklin M. Grant, "distrained": that is, seized and sold for the payment of the past due rent. Marlett sued Favor and his associates for damages, and claimed that the unfinished furniture had previously belonged to Grant, but that Grant had assigned it to Marlett, for the purpose of having it finished and sold so that Grant could pay a debt which he owed to Marlett. Marlett called Grant as a witness, to testify as to the value of the personal property which had been taken. Favor and his associates objected to the trial court's permitting Grant to testify concerning the value of the personal property, on the ground that he "was interested in enhancing the damages" and should be regarded as incompetent to testify. (This objection -- that a witness is rendered incompetent to testify because of his financial interest in the subject of the case -- is no longer valid in Illinois.) The trial court allowed Grant's testimony, found the issues in favor of Marlett, and awarded him $92 in damages. Kimball Favor and his associates made a motion for a new trial, which the trial court denied. Kimball Favor and the other defendants appealed from the adverse judgment of the trial court to the Illinois Supreme Court.

Lincoln and another attorney named T. L. Dickey (with whom Lincoln was to work on several other cases) represented Kimball Favor and his associates on appeal.

Lincoln and Dickey argued simply that Grant was an incompetent witness, because of his financial interest in the matter, and should not have been allowed to testify about the value of the personal property that had been distrained and sold.

The Illinois Supreme Court agreed with Lincoln's argument, reversed the trial court's judgment in favor of Marlett, and remanded the case to the trial court for a new trial, at which Grant presumably was not allowed to testify concerning the value of the unfinished furniture

36

The case of *Parker vs. Smith,* 6 Ill. 411 (1844), nearly defies efforts to decipher its facts.

A man named James Parker had obtained a judgment against Norman Smith for the amount of $14.12 1/4, plus court costs in the amount of $19.61 1/2. The name of the justice of the peace who entered that judgment was E. Z. Allen. Parker then had a constable, named D. Warren, levy a writ of execution on two steers, owned by Smith, on March 10, 1842: that is, the constable, Warren, seized Smith's two steers and delivered them to Parker.

Smith then filed an action for damages, in the Circuit Court of LaSalle County, Illinois, against Parker, and the constable, Warren, and the justice of the peace, Allen. Smith apparently asserted that the judgment -- which Allen had entered against him -- was void and that, in consequence, the seizure of his two steers, pursuant to that void judgment, was a trespass to his personal property.

All three defendants filed a "demurrer" (that is, a motion to dismiss Smith's complaint). The Circuit Court of LaSalle County entered a judgment dismissing the complaint of Smith against the three defendants.

Smith appealed from that judgment to the Illinois Supreme Court. Lincoln and another attorney named T.L. Dickey represented Smith on appeal.

Lincoln and Dickey filed a brief in the case in which they argued that the judgment -- which Allen had entered in favor of Parker and against Smith -- was void because it had been entered without ever notifying Smith of the proceeding against him. Lincoln and Dickey further argued that the constable, Warren, knew that the judgment was void for lack of notice to Smith.

The Illinois Supreme Court apparently agreed with Lincoln and Dickey, at least in part, because it reversed the judgment of the Circuit Court of LaSalle County, and remanded the case to the circuit court for further proceedings. The Illinois

Supreme Court thus gave Lincoln's client another chance to make his case against, and to recover damages from, Parker, the justice of the peace, Allen, and the constable, Warren.

37

The case of *Stickney vs. Cassell,* 6 Ill. 418 (1844), involved a carpenter's contract. The case arose out of Gallatin County, Illinois, which borders the Ohio and Wabash Rivers in southeastern Illinois. Because the distance of Gallatin County from Springfield is great, Lincoln obviously did not handle the trial of the case, but, rather, was simply retained to defend against the appeal.

Jacob Cassell was the carpenter. A partnership known as Stickney and Company desired to construct a building. Stickney and Company entered into a contract with Jacob Cassell to the effect "that Cassell is to put all his hands upon Stickney's building at $2.50 per day, and then to put all his hands at work to complete any carpenter's work that said Stickney and Company wishes," at prices specified in the contract, "including the work on said building, being the making of a number of window and door panels."

Jacob Cassell sued the two partners doing business as Stickney and Company for damages, but he did not allege that his damages consisted of the partners' refusing to pay him for work that he had done. Rather, he alleged that the partners had deprived him of a profit by refusing to permit him to complete the building.

A jury returned a verdict in favor of one of the two defendant partners, but a verdict for $500.00 in damages against the other of the defendant partners. The defendant partners then filed a motion in the circuit court for a new trial, which the circuit court denied. The circuit court entered a judgment upon the verdicts, and the defendant partners appealed to the Illinois Supreme Court from that judgment.

Lincoln represented the carpenter, Jacob Cassell, in defending against the appeal.

Lincoln advanced only a procedural argument in favor of his client, Cassell. He asserted that the defendant partners' motion for a new trial had been properly denied because the "bill of exceptions," accompanying the motion, did not aver "that it contains all the evidence." In those days, it was apparently necessary for a party to file -- in connection with a motion for a new trial -- a summary of the evidence presented at the trial.

The Illinois Supreme Court noted, in its opinion, "[A]ll the proceedings in the Court below, as they are presented by the record, appear to have been so irregular and confused, as to render it exceedingly doubtful upon what issues or questions the Court below adjudicated." The Illinois Supreme Court then brushed aside Lincoln's procedural objection, and concluded that -- despite the bill of exceptions' lack of an express averment that it contained all of the evidence -- it was apparent that all of the evidence necessary, for the trial court to consider the propriety of its judgment in ruling upon the motion for a new trial, was included in the bill of exceptions.

The Illinois Supreme Court considered, finally, the nature of the contract between the carpenter, Jacob Cassell, and the partners doing business as Stickney and Company. It stated that there was no testimony introduced at the trial which indicated that the partners prevented or hindered the carpenter from completing the building. Instead, the partners, after a certain point, simply exercised the discretion which they possessed under the contract, and chose not to have the carpenter, Cassell, do any more work on the building. The Court held that the carpenter, Cassell, could not hold the partners, doing business as Stickney and Company, liable in damages for their having chosen not to have him complete the building.

Consequently, the Court reversed the judgment of the Circuit Court of Gallatin County, and remanded the case for a new trial.

38

A mechanic's lien is a lien which a workman, who has participated in the construction of a building on land, or which a supplier of materials (known as a "materialman"), who has supplied materials for the construction of a building on land, can claim against the land itself. The right of a workman or materialman to claim a mechanic's lien against land helps to ensure that he will be paid for his labor or materials. The distinguishing feature of a mechanic's lien is that a workman or materialman may file his claim for a lien on land *after* other interests in the land have become of record in the Recorder's Office, but his claim for a lien may still take priority over those other interests if he filed it within a specified time following his last work on, or last delivery of material to, the land.

The case of *Kimball vs. Cook,* 6 Ill. 423 (1844), reveals that mechanic's liens have been part of the law of Illinois for more than 150 years. Lincoln represented the "mechanic" -- that is, the workman -- in that case who had claimed a lien on land in Marseilles, Illinois, on which he had constructed a flour mill.

A millwright, Amasa Cook, entered into a contract on June 3, 1838, with Lovell Kimball by which he (Cook) was "to do the millwright work of a flouring mill, in a particular manner . . . for which he was to receive four thousand eight hundred dollars, the one-half as the work progressed." Cook completed the flour mill, but Kimball paid him only $2,400.

Cook filed a "bill" (that is, a complaint) in the Circuit Court of LaSalle County, Illinois, by which he sought to enforce his mechanic's lien against the land and thereby to collect the $2,400 remaining due to him. Kimball filed an answer denying that Cook had done the work in accordance with the parties' contract. The venue of the case was then changed to the Circuit Court of Kendall County, Illinois.

At the trial of the case, a point of procedure and a point of evidence arose.

The procedural point concerned Cook's reading into evidence a witness' deposition which he had taken before trial.

The deposition testimony of the witness -- a man named Miller -+- was to the effect that Cook had essentially performed his work in accordance with his contract with Kimball. Kimball made two objections to the deposition, at trial, which he had never previously made. The circuit court overruled Kimball's objections, and allowed Kimball to read the deposition into evidence.

The evidentiary point concerned Kimball's effort to read to the jury his sworn answer, denying the allegations in Cook's "bill," as evidence in his defense. The circuit court refused to allow Kimball to read his sworn answer into evidence or otherwise to testify in his own defense.

The jury returned a verdict of $2,400 in favor of Cook and against Kimball. The circuit court entered a judgment on the verdict, and Kimball appealed from that judgment to the Illinois Supreme Court.

Lincoln and two other lawyers -- O. Peters and T. L. Dickey -- represented Amasa Cook in defending against the appeal.

As to the procedural point involved in the trial, the Illinois Supreme Court held that the circuit court properly overruled Kimball's objections to Cook's use of the deposition, and stated that "All objections which might be obviated by a re-examination of the witness must be considered as waived, if not taken before the trial."

The disposition of the evidentiary point -- concerning whether Kimball could testify in his own defense -- turned on whether the proceeding to enforce the mechanic's lien should be considered to be one "at law" or "in chancery." (Actions at law typically involved a plaintiff's request for money damages only, whereas actions "in chancery" typically involved a plaintiff's request either for an order which compelled a defendant personally to perform some task, an order which declared a party's status, or an order which affected the title to property. Actions "in chancery" were also known as proceedings in "equity.")

In Lincoln's time, Illinois apparently administered "law" separately from "equity," at least to the extent of having different rules of evidence applicable to actions at law and actions in chancery. "By the rules of the courts of law," the Illinois Supreme Court stated, "no party to the record can be a witness without the consent of all the other parties." (This rule, disqualifying parties from testifying in their own legal actions, was long ago abandoned.) In "equity" actions, however, a party was apparently permitted to testify in his own behalf to the limited extent of reading into evidence the sworn answer that he had filed in the case.

After a somewhat tedious discussion of the mechanic's lien statute, the Illinois Supreme Court concluded that Cook's proceeding, to enforce his mechanic's lien on the land, should be deemed to be an "equity" action. Consequently, the Illinois Supreme Court ruled that the circuit court should have permitted Kimball to read his sworn answer into evidence at the trial of the case, as part of his defense. It reversed the judgment of the Circuit Court of Kendall County in favor of Lincoln's client, Amasa Cook, and remanded the case for further proceedings.

Lincoln thus suffered a defeat in his effort to defend against this appeal.

39

A "judgment debtor" is the person against whom a judgment has been rendered in a civil proceeding. A "judgment creditor" is the person in whose favor the judgment has been rendered.

An "execution," in the context of a civil proceeding, is a sheriff's seizure of a judgment debtor's property -- at the request of a judgment creditor -- for the purpose of selling that property and thereby paying the amount of the judgment obtained by the judgment creditor. When a sheriff makes an execution on personal property which he believes belongs to a judgment debtor, however, the possibility always exists that the sheriff will seize property which actually belongs to a third party, rather than to the judgment debtor. The Illinois statutes have always provided a procedure for a third party to assert his ownership of personal property which a sheriff has seized as part an "execution."

The case of *Morgan vs. Griffin,* 6 Ill. 565 (1844), involved an execution sale, and a third party's claim that the property seized, and sold at the execution sale, belonged to him rather than to the judgment debtor.

An individual named Young Griffin had obtained a judgment against two other individuals named Gunn and Fox in the Circuit Court of Scott County, Illinois. The circuit court issued a writ of execution on the judgment, and the sheriff of Scott County levied that writ of execution on (that is, seized) certain items of personal property which appeared to be owned by Gunn and Fox, but which were claimed by Thomas Morgan. Thomas Morgan initiated the procedure, provided by statute, to have a "trial of the right of property," in an effort to obtain a determination that he was the owner of the items of personal property. The sheriff of Scott County apparently was required, by the statute existing at that time, to impanel a jury and to preside over the trial. (The current version of the statute would require the circuit court to conduct the "trial of the right of property.") The jury impanelled by the sheriff determined that Thomas Morgan did not own the items of property which the sheriff had seized, and that, in consequence, the sheriff could proceed to dispose of those items at the execution sale.

Thomas Morgan appealed from that verdict to the Circuit Court of Scott County. Some party (apparently the judgment creditor, Young Griffin) filed an affidavit of the sheriff in the circuit court, in which the sheriff stated that -- after Morgan had taken the appeal to the circuit court -- Morgan had consented that the execution sale should be held. Morgan did not contradict the sheriff's affidavit in the circuit court. Some party (apparently the judgment creditor, Young Griffin) made a motion to dismiss Morgan's appeal, and the circuit court both dismissed the appeal and rendered a judgment against Morgan for the amount of the sheriff's court costs. (The curious feature of the decision in this case was that it indicated that the agreement, reached by Thomas Morgan with the judgment creditor, Young Griffin, provided that the proceeds of the sheriff's execution sale should be paid over to Thomas Morgan. If that were so, it is impossible to determine why Thomas Morgan should have continued to prosecute his appeal to the circuit court. To make sense of this decision, this writer assumes that the agreement between Morgan and Griffin actually provided that the proceeds of the execution sale should be paid to Griffin, and that the decision erroneously indicates that, pursuant to the agreement, the proceeds of the execution sale were to be paid to Morgan.)

Morgan then appealed from that judgment of the Circuit Court of Scott County to the Illinois Supreme Court.

Lincoln and another lawyer named D. A. Smith represented the "defendant in error" on appeal, who was apparently the judgment creditor: namely, Young Griffin.

The Illinois Supreme Court held that -- because the affidavit of the sheriff was uncontradicted -- it must be considered as true. The Illinois Supreme Court then stated, "It is evident from it [the sheriff's affidavit], that the matter in dispute was settled by the parties, after the trial before the sheriff, and before the dismissal of the appeal. By such settlement, the plaintiff in execution abandoned his claim on the property, and the same was sold, and the proceeds received by the sheriff for the benefit of Morgan [or, as this writer believes was actually the case, Griffin]. A further trial of the right of property was out of the question. There was no subject matter left to be tried."

As to the circuit court's judgment against Morgan for court costs, the Illinois Supreme Court held that -- when a case is settled without any understanding as to the payment of the costs already incurred -- the lawsuit simply should be discontinued on the record, without the rendition of any judgment for costs against either party.

The Illinois Supreme Court, therefore, affirmed the circuit court's dismissal of Thomas Morgan's appeal, concerning the trial of the right of property, but reversed the circuit court's judgment for court costs against Thomas Morgan. Lincoln thus won the major part of this case, and apparently succeeded in defending Griffin's right to retain the proceeds of the execution sale.

40

The Illinois recording statute -- which establishes a system for recording deeds, mortgages, and other liens which affect land -- provides a means for a purchaser of land to give notice to the rest of the public that he has purchased a particular tract of land. If the purchaser of a tract of land files his deed "for record" with the recorder of the county in which the land is located, his interest in the land will take priority over any other sale or mortgage of the land which its seller purports to make thereafter. If, for example, a seller sells a land to one person, and then purports to sell it a second time to another person, the first person's interest in the land will be fully protected if he has caused his deed to be filed for record before the occurrence of the second, purported sale.

What should happen, though, if the purchaser of land has filed his deed for record with the recorder in a timely manner, but the recorder misplaces the deed and fails to enter it into his books properly until *after* another person obtains an interest in the land? This was the question that was involved in the case of *Cook vs. Hall,* 6 Ill. 575 (1844).

An individual named Jacob Slentz owned land in Clay County, Illinois, as of March, 1840. On October 3, 1840, Slentz conveyed the land "in fee" (that is, his fee simple interest in the land, which constitutes a complete ownership of the land itself, as opposed to having merely a lien on the land) to Anderson and Flanders. Flanders gave the deed to John Jefferds, and requested that he have it filed for record on the morning of October 5, 1840. John Jefferds went to the county seat of Clay County (which was apparently Louisville, Illinois) and asked for the recorder. An individual named David Sweezy was then the Recorder of Clay County, but, for some reason, he had requested James Hogue to perform the duties of the office of recorder. Jefferds gave Flanders' deed to James Hogue on October 5, 1840, and saw him take the deed into "a room attached to the courthouse" and begin to write upon it. James Hogue, however, mislaid the deed and did not enter it into the records in the Recorder's Office. The actual recorder, David Sweezy, later requested another individual, Palemon Schooley, to perform the duties of the office of recorder. On December 20, 1840, James Hogue brought Flanders' deed from Slentz, into Schooley and remarked that he had mislaid or overlooked it. Palemon Schooley entered the deed onto the records in the Recorder's Office on December 20, 1840.

In the meanwhile, however, other individuals named Seymour and Cook obtained a judgment against Jacob Slentz in the Circuit Court of Clay County on October 8, 1840. Under the law in effect in that day, the judgment against Jacob Slentz immediately became a lien on the land that he owned in Clay County. An execution was issued on the judgment, by virtue of which the land in question was sold to one of the judgment creditors, Edward C. Cook, on March 6, 1841. The Sheriff of Clay County gave Cook a sheriff's deed to the land on August 26, 1842, which Cook recorded on November 2, 1842.

On March 13, 1841, Anderson and Flanders had conveyed their fee simple interest in the land -- which they had received from Jacob Slentz -- to Bryant Hall. Hall recorded his deed on March 15, 1841.

Edward C. Cook then brought an action of ejectment against Bryant Hall, in order to establish (as he thought) his superior claim to the land, by virtue of the judgment lien obtained on October 8, 1840, which led to his purchase of the land at the execution sale on March 6, 1841.

Bryant Hall defended his interest in the land by asserting that the deed -- from Jacob Slentz to Anderson and Flanders -- was effectively recorded on October 5, 1840, the day on which John Jefferds had delivered the deed to the *de facto* recorder, James Hogue. If that were so, then that deed, from Slentz to Anderson and Flanders, on which Hall's title was based, took priority over the judgment lien which attached on October 8, 1840.

The judgment creditor, Edward C. Cook, argued in the Circuit Court of Clay County, Illinois, that the deed -- from Jacob Slentz to Anderson and Flanders -- was not effectively recorded until it was actually entered on the records in the Recorder's Office on December 20, 1840.

The circuit court found the issues for the defendant, Bryant Hall, and entered a judgment in his favor. Edward C. Cook appealed from that judgment to the Illinois Supreme Court.

Lincoln and another lawyer, C. H. Constable, represented Edward C. Cook on the appeal.

In its opinion on the case, the Illinois Supreme Court noted that Illinois had had a State Recorder until 1833, and that only then did Illinois establish the offices of County Recorders. The Illinois Supreme Court reproached the Recorder of Clay County for handling the documents in his office in such a haphazard fashion, and for generally disregarding the duties laid upon him by the statute.

The Illinois Supreme Court then concluded that the deed was effectively recorded, in the office of the Recorder of Clay County, Illinois, when it had been presented to the *de facto* recorder for filing. It said, "The deed ought not to be invalidated, and the title defeated, by the mere omission of the recorder to perform the ministerial duty of making the entry of the filing of the deed for record." It stated, finally, that "If purchasers or creditors are deceived and injured by the neglect of the recorder, they have their remedy against him. They can recover of him all such damages as they may sustain, in consequence of his dereliction of duty." These statements, made 146 years ago, appear to remain the law in the State of Illinois.

Consequently, the Illinois Supreme Court affirmed the

judgment of the Circuit Court of Clay County, Illinois, in favor of the defendant, Bryant Hall. Lincoln lost another appeal, and may, by this time, have begun to wonder when, if ever, he would more consistently experience success in the Illinois Supreme Court.

41

In the case of *Field vs. Rawlings,* 6 Ill. 581 (1844), Lincoln represented, on appeal, the Secretary of the State of Illinois and sureties on a bond which he had given another state official.

The Secretary of State at the time was Alexander P. Field. He had affixed the seal of his office, in the course of the performance of his duties, to "one thousand state bonds." The decision in the case does not make plain the nature of these bonds.

Field, as Secretary of State, had presented to Moses M. Rawlings, who was the "fund commissioner" of the State of Illinois, a bill -- for having affixed the seal of his office to the thousand state bonds -- in the amount of 75 cents per bond: that is, a bill which totaled $750.00. (It was not unusual in those days for public officials to be paid on a kind of piecework basis so much money for each official act performed. An office for which the pay was calculated on this basis was known as a "fee office." Fee offices have now been abolished in Illinois.)

Rawlings apparently had some doubts as to whether this particular charge was authorized by the Illinois statutes, because he required Field to execute and deliver to him -- as a condition of his paying the $750.00 to Field -- a bond guaranteeing Field's repayment of the money to Rawlings, as fund commissioner, if "it should be decided by the legislature or the supreme court that the fees were not legally chargeable to the fund commissioner." Field's bond was also signed by several sureties, who guaranteed Field's repayment of the money if the specified event -- the ruling of the fees to be illegal -- should occur.

On January 9, 1841, the Senate of the Illinois General Assembly (but not the House of Representatives) adopted a resolution to the effect that the fees in question were not legally chargeable to the fund commissioner, Rawlings.

Rawlings then brought an "action of debt" on Field's bond in the Circuit Court of Gallatin County, Illinois, against both Field and the sureties on his bond to require the repayment of the $750.00. (The Bank of Shawneetown was located in Gallatin County, and, so, Rawlings may have been connected with that bank.)

The Circuit Court of Gallatin County entered a judgment on the bond against Field and his sureties. Field and his sureties appealed from that judgment to the Illinois Supreme Court.

Lincoln and another lawyer, named H. Eddy, represented the Secretary of State, Field, and his sureties in making the appeal.

The Illinois Supreme Court concluded, at Lincoln's urging, that a decision by the Illinois Senate alone was not a decision by the legislature, because a decision by the legislature required action by both the Senate and the House of Representatives. The Court stated that sureties on a bond could be held liable only strictly in accordance with their undertaking on the bond, and that a condition precedent to the sureties' liability -- an adverse decision of the legislature -- had not yet occurred. The Court reversed the $750.00 judgment against Field and the sureties and remanded the case for further proceedings. In doing so, the Court pointed out that it should be an easy matter for the fund commissioner, Rawlings, to obtain a joint resolution of both houses of the legislature, to the effect that the fees were improper, which would enable him to recover a judgment against the sureties.

Lincoln prevailed in this appeal in behalf of the Secretary of State and his sureties.

42

In the case of *Broadwell vs. Broadwell,* 6 Ill. 599 (1844), can be seen the effort of a grandfather, Moses Broadwell, to provide for two of his infant and orphaned grandchildren -- Mary Jane Sweat and William Broadwell -- in the year 1827, when Illinois was still essentially a wilderness.

Moses Broadwell, who apparently resided in Sangamon County, Illinois, desired to make some provision for his two grandchildren before his death, to assure that they would both receive a one-half interest in his tract of land when they became adults. Because the grandchildren were then minors, they could not readily take the title to the land in their own names. Rather than have someone appointed guardian of the granchildren -- who could have taken the title to the land for them -- Moses Broadwell simply deeded the land to his son, John Broadwell, in exchange for a $1,000 bond executed by John Broadwell on January 4, 1827. The bond mentioned John Broadwell's brother and sister, David Broadwell and Sarah Broadwell, and contained the following condition:

> "The condition of this obligation is, that if the said John B. shall make unto the said David Broadwell and Sarah Broadwell, and others a deed for certain land (*describing it*). It is agreed and understood that if Mary Jane Sweat and William Broadwell, or either of them shall live to lawful age, and the said John B. shall make a deed to them, or either of them, to the one equal half of the above described land, then this obligation to be void and of no more effect than as though the deed had been made to the first parties named -- the true intent and meaning of this obligation being, that if Mary Jane Sweat and William Broadwell shall live to lawful age, they are to have the land equally divided between them; and if either or both of them should die before they arrive at lawful age, their parts are to go to the persons first named."

John Broadwell apparently kept the land and never willingly deeded any part of it to the grandchildren when they became adults. The granddaughter, Mary Jane Sweat, who had married Michael Thompson, brought an action (with her husband, because a married woman could not sue in her own name alone in those days) in the Circuit Court of Sangamon County, Illinois, against her uncle, John Broadwell. She sought "specific performance" of his contractual promise to convey a one-half interest in the land to her. ("Specific performance" involves the compelling of a party to do exactly what he has promised to do, rather than assessing damages against him for having breached his promise. It is ordinarily more difficult to obtain the remedy of specific performance of a contractual promise, than to obtain damages for a breach of that contractual promise.)

John Broadwell argued at trial that the bond permitted him to take his choice of deeding a one-half interest in the land to the granddaughter, or of paying her one half of the $1,000 bond: that is the amount of $500. The circuit court agreed with John Broadwell, and entered a decree which ordered John Broadwell to pay the granddaughter, Mary Jane Thompson, $500.

The granddaughter and her husband appealed from that decree to the Illinois Supreme Court, because she desired to receive her interest in the land instead of the $500. Lincoln and his close fried, E. D. Baker, defended John Broadwell on appeal.

Lincoln and Baker filed a brief in the case which made three points, and which read as follows:

"1.   It requires a much less strength of case, on the part of a defendant to resist a bill to perform a contract, than it does on the part of the plaintiff to maintain a bill to enforce a specific performance. 2 Story's Eq. Jr. sections 692, 693, 742, 750, 751, 769.

2.   Where a party applies to a court of equity to enforce a specific performance of a written contract, the

adverse party is allowed to show by parol [that is, evidence outside the contract itself], that the instrument relied on does not express the true agreement of the parties. 2 Story's Eq. Jur. section 770; Bradbury v. White, 4 Greenl. 391; Dwight v. Pomeroy, 17 Mass. 328.

3. A defendant may show by parol, that by mistake of law, a written instrument is executed in such form and terms as to be, in legal effect, different from what the parties supposed and intended and thereby defeat a specific performance of such instrument. Cathcart v. Robinson, 5 Peters 276, 277."

Lincoln and Baker argued primarily that Moses Broadwell -- in requiring the bond from John Broadwell -- had intended to give John Broadwell the option of deeding a one-half interest in the land to each of the grandchildren, or of paying $500 to each of the grandchildren, as each became an adult. They asserted that Moses Broadwell and John Broadwell had made a mutual mistake by believing that the bond, as worded, legally gave John Broadwell such an option. They argued, further, that the Illinois Supreme Court should rely upon the parol evidence (that is, evidence of Moses Broadwell's intention outside the writing of the bond itself) to interpret the bond as giving John Broadwell that option.

The Illinois Supreme Court decided, however, that the bond was "remarkably explicit, that the conveyance of the land was the primary object." It expressed surprise that, in view of the explicitness of the provisions of the bond, John Broadwell ever should have ventured to argue that he should be allowed to discharge the bond merely by paying $500 to the granddaughter, Mary Jane Thompson.

The Illinois Supreme Court reversed the decree of the circuit court, held that Mary Jane Thompson was entitled to receive a one-half interest in the land, and also held that she was entitled to receive from John Broadwell one half of the rents and profits which he had earned from the land since she had become 18 years of age.

Lincoln and Baker thus suffered defeat in their defense against the appeal.

The case of *Rogers vs. Dickey,* 6 Ill. 636 (1844), was heard by the Illinois Supreme Court during its "December Term" that began in December, 1844. Lincoln and his partner, Stephen T. Logan, appeared before the Court in behalf of the appellees. This was apparently the last case in which Lincoln and Logan appeared before the Illinois Supreme Court as partners. They dissolved their law partnership in December, 1844, so that Logan could take in his son as his new partner. Lincoln then opened his own office, and took in William H. Herndon as his junior partner.

Because Lincoln and his wife, Mary, and his one-year-old son, Robert, had just moved into their own house in Springfield in May, 1844, Lincoln probably worried some about how well he would do in his own law office, and about whether he would be able to support his family properly.

The case of *Rogers vs. Dickey* began in Sangamon County, and Lincoln may have been involved in the case at the trial level.

As of March 18, 1842, Josias T. Betts owed John Dickey the amount of $150.00 for rent on a house. On May 1, 1842, Dickey caused items of Betts' personal property located on the leased premises to be "distrained" (that is, seized) as security for payment of the rent, by a constable of Sangamon County. Dickey obtained a judgment against Betts, for the amount of the rent, in the Circuit Court of Sangamon County, Illinois, at its July term in 1842.

Betts had another creditor, however, named Rogers, who was apparently from Cook County. On March 8, 1842, Rogers delivered to the Sheriff of Sangamon County a writ of execution which had been issued by the Circuit Court of Cook County, Illinois, in favor of Rogers, and against Betts, for the amount of $200.00. On May 26, 1842, the Sheriff of Sangamon County went to the constable -- who had previously distrained the items of Betts' personal property, as security for the payment of the rent owed to Dickey -- and took those items of Betts' personal property out of the constable's possession in order to pay the debt owed to Rogers.

A contest ensued in the Circuit Court of Sangamon County -- between Betts' landlord, Dickey, and Betts' other creditor, Rogers -- as to which of them had the superior claim upon Betts' items of personal property. The circuit court entered a judgment in favor of the landlord, Dickey, which would have permitted him to sell Betts' items of personal property in order to collect the amount of rent due to him.

The other creditor, Rogers, appealed from that judgment to the Illinois Supreme Court. Lincoln and Logan represented the landlord, Dickey, in defending against the appeal.

In its opinion in the case, the Illinois Supreme Court observed that there was no precedent in Illinois which gave a clear answer to the question whether the landlord, as the first creditor to have seized Betts' items of personal property, should be given preference over the second creditor. This absence of Illinois precedent was a recurring problems in the early years of the State. In the absence of Illinois precedent, the Illinois Supreme Court discussed similar statutes, concerning judgments and writs of execution, from the States of Kentucky and New York, and also discussed the common law of England on the subject. (Illinois courts today have almost no occasion to discuss the common law of England.)

The Illinois Supreme Court adopted the rule followed in England, which was to the effect that -- if two or more writs of execution had been delivered at different times, either to the same or to different officers of the law, and if no sale had yet been made of the debtor's goods -- the writ of execution first delivered must be given the priority, even though the seizure under that writ of execution may have occurred after the seizure under the writ of execution delivered second. Because no sale had occurred in this case, under the landlord Dickey's distress for rent, the Illinois Supreme Court concluded that Rogers' writ of execution should be given priority, because he had delivered it to the Sheriff of Sangamon County on March 8, 1842, before the landlord Dickey had distrained Betts' items of personal property on May 1, 1842. The Illinois Supreme Court thus reversed the judgment of the Circuit Court of Sangamon County in favor of the landlord Dickey, and Lincoln and Logan suffered a defeat in the last case which they handled together, as partners, before the Illinois Supreme Court.

44

The case of *Kelly vs. Garrett*, 6 Ill. 649 (1844), involved a bank which apparently had become insolvent, in a county which no longer exists in Illinois: namely, the Berrien County Bank in Niles, Illinois, which city is now part of Cook County, Illinois.

An individual named James Kinzie had made a promissory note payable to Augustus Garrett for the amount of $300.00, plus interest, which was to be paid at the Berrien County Bank in Niles, Illinois. Garrett assigned the promissory note to an individual named Royal T. Kelly. Royal T. Kelly must have further conveyed the promissory note to the Berrien County Bank, which had become insolvent, and for which a receiver had been appointed. The Berrien County Bank brought an action against Augustus Garrett, in the name of Royal T. Kelly, on the basis of Garrett's assignment of the note to Royal T. Kelly. (It is still possible for the holder of a promissory note to sue an individual who has endorsed the promissory note over to him.) The bank commenced the action in the Circuit Court of Cook County, Illinois, in August, 1838.

Garrett pleaded a defense known as a "set-off" (that is, a defense which would give the individual claiming it a reduction of the damages sought by the other party against him). Garrett's set-off defense was that he held promissory notes executed by the Berrien County Bank in June, 1838, for the amount of $424.00. These promissory notes were not made payable to Garrett specifically, but were payable to "bearer": that is, to whatever person held the promissory notes and presented them for payment. Garrett argued that -- in view of his greater claim against the Berrien County Bank -- the bank should not be able to recover anything from him.

The bank asked the trial judge to instruct the jury that Garrett had to have proved that he possessed the promissory notes before the bank's commencement of its case against Garrett in August, 1838, and that, in the absence of such proof, Garrett's set-off defense must fail. The trial judge refused to give this instruction, however, and instructed the jury, instead, that the jury could presume, merely from the date on the bank's promissory notes (June, 1838), that Garrett had held the promissory notes as of the time of the bank's commencement of its case against Garrett.

The jury returned a verdict in favor of Garrett, which found that he had no liability to the bank on the promissory note which he had assigned to Royal T. Kelly. The trial judge entered a judgment on that verdict, and the bank appealed from the judgment to the Illinois Supreme Court.

Lincoln and two other attorneys -- A. O. Beaumont and M. Skinner -- represented the bank in prosecuting the appeal. Lincoln's old partner, Stephen T. Logan, represented Garrett in defending against the appeal.

Lincoln filed a brief with the Illinois Supreme Court in which he argued that Garrett was not entitled to a presumption, merely from the date on the bank's promissory notes, that he had held the bank's promissory notes as of the time of the bank's commencement of its case against Garrett in August, 1838.

The Illinois Supreme Court agreed with Lincoln and stated, "It is a question of fact to be proved by the defendant (Garrett), and not a presumption of the law." The Court further stated, "The first instruction asked by the plaintiff (the bank), ought, therefore, to have been given, for it involved simply the naked and undeniable proposition . . . that the set-off must be a subsisting demand at the commencement of the suit, as contra-distinguished from demands purchased, or acquired afterwards."

The Illinois Supreme Court reversed the judgment of the Circuit Court of Cook County, and remanded the case to that circuit court for a new trial.

Lincoln thus won the first case, in which he appeared before the Illinois Supreme Court, after the dissolution of his partnership with Stephen T. Logan. Moreover, he defeated his old partner, Stephen T. Logan, in that case.

45

A necessary party to an action is an individual who has an interest in the subject matter of the action which would be materially affected by a judgment in that action. All necessary parties should be joined to the action -- that is, brought within the trial court's personal jurisdiction by means of service of a summons and complaint upon them -- before the trial court enters a judgment in the action. If even a single necessary party has not been joined to the action, a trial court should refuse to enter a judgment until that necessary party has been joined to the action.

The case of *McCall vs. Lesher,* 7 Ill. 46 and 47 (1845), involved the question whether certain individuals were necessary parties to an action and whether a decree entered by a circuit court -- before they had been formally joined to the action -- was valid.

In that case, an individual named Henry Vanderbergh, who was the owner of 400 acres of land in Wabash County, Illinois, had died. Jacob Lesher and another individual named Hinde filed a "bill" (that is, a complaint) in the chancery division of the Circuit Court of Wabash County, Illinois, against Henry Vanderbergh's heirs, in order to compel those heirs to convey the 400 acres of land to Jacob Lesher and Hinde. All of the heirs appeared as defendants in that action, and filed their answer to the bill.

Two of the heirs -- Julia McCall and Ferdinand Vanderbergh -- then died. Their deaths were "suggested" to the circuit court: that is, the circuit court was informed, on the record, of the deaths of those two parties.

On the motion of Jacob Lesher and Hinde, the heirs of Julia McCall and the heirs of Ferdinand Vanderbergh were named as defendants to the action, in place of Julia McCall and

Ferdinand Vanderbergh. No "process" (that is, summons) was ever issued against these additional defendants, nor did they voluntarily enter their appearance in the action.

The Circuit Court of Wabash County, Illinois, held a hearing in the case, and entered a decree requiring the defendants to convey the land in question to Jacob Lesher and Hinde.

The heirs of Henry Vanderbergh, who had been served with process, and who were defendants to the action, appealed from that decree to the Illinois Supreme Court.

Stephen T. Logan represented those heirs of Henry Vanderbergh, who were parties to the action, in prosecuting the appeal before the Illinois Supreme Court. Lincoln represented Jacob Lesher and Hinde in defending against the appeal.

The heirs of Henry Vanderbergh argued that the heirs of the two deceased defendants -- Julia McCall and Ferdinand Vanderbergh -- were necessary parties to the action. They asserted that -- because the heirs of the two deceased defendants had not been served with process and had not voluntarily entered their appearance in the action -- the circuit court's decree, ordering the conveyance of the 400 acres of land, was invalid. Lincoln argued, in behalf of Jacob Lesher and Hinde, that the heirs of the two deceased defendants were not necessary parties. Lincoln argued that -- if those individuals were necessary parties -- their appearance toward the circuit court might be inferred. Lincoln seized upon language in the record of the proceedings before the circuit court which stated "the parties came by their solicitors." He argued that this implied that all of the parties -- including the heirs of the two deceased defendants -- had appeared before the court in the persons of their attorneys.

Lincoln's hands were obviously tied by the failure of the complainants' attorney before the circuit court to have done his job properly, and to have served the heirs of the deceased defendants with process. His arguments, in this instance, seemed strained. In any event, the Illinois Supreme Court brushed aside his arguments and stated, first, that the heirs of the two deceased defendants were necessary, and, second, that "The record ought distinctly to show the service of process upon the defendants, or their voluntary appearance to the action. It must not be left to inference or conjecture."

Lincoln also tried, in this case, to have the appeal dismissed on the ground that the appeal bond, which the appellants had to file, was not in proper form. The Illinois Supreme Court dismissed this argument by observing that Lincoln made the argument too late in behalf of the complainants. Only the complainants' attorney before the circuit court had been in a position to make that particular argument, concerning the propriety of the appeal bond, if the argument was to be made at all.

The Illinois Supreme Court reversed the decree of the Circuit Court of Wabash County, Illinois, and remanded the case to that circuit court for further proceedings. Lincoln thus lost his defense against the appeal in this case.

46

The case of *Wren vs. Moss,* 7 Ill. 72 (1845), was the first divorce proceeding in which Lincoln was involved on appeal.

Aquilla Wren and Clarissa Wren were husband and wife. Aquilla Wren brought an action for divorce against his wife, Clarissa Wren, in the Circuit Court of Peoria County, Illinois. The circuit court entered a decree which dissolved the marriage contract between Aquilla Wren and Clarissa Wren.

Clarissa Wren then applied to the circuit court for an award of alimony. The circuit court entered an order requiring a "master in chancery" (that is, an official appointed by the circuit court to hear evidence on a particular matter, for the sake of assisting the circuit court in reaching a decision on the facts) to investigate the value of Aquilla Wren's property, the annual income which he earned from that property, and the amount necessary for the maintenance of Clarissa Wren. Before the master in chancery could complete his work, however, Aquilla Wren died.

Clarissa Wren then filed an affidavit informing the court of the death of Aquilla Wren. Upon her motion, the circuit court ordered that the divorce action should be "abated" (that is, terminated).

The question -- as to who owned certain lands of Aquilla Wren -- was then confused. Clarissa Wren asserted that she had never relinquished her marital right of "dower" (that is, under the traditional common law, the wife's one-third interest, for the duration of her own life, in all of her husband's lands). Aquilla Wren had left a will, however, in which he named, as his beneficiaries, four persons other than his wife. In addition, two other persons -- named William S. Moss and Smith Frye -- had purchased tracts of land from Aquilla Wren during his lifetime, in which tracts of land Clarissa Wren had not relinquished her marital right of dower.

Clarissa Wren sought, and obtained, the issuance of a writ of error from the Circuit Court of Peoria County. The writ of error was a method by which she could appeal from the divorce decree, entered by the Circuit Court of Peoria County, to the Illinois Supreme Court, for the purpose of having her rights in the lands of Aquilla Wren adjudicated. For the Illinois Supreme Court's decision, concerning her rights, to be binding upon the beneficiaries of Aquilla Wren's will and upon the two individuals who had purchased tracts of land from Aquilla Wren during his life, however, all those individuals had to be joined as parties to the appeal proceeding. Clarissa Wren thus filed a motion in the Illinois Supreme Court for a "rule" (that is, an order) directed to those other individuals requiring them to join the proceeding in error.

The other individuals resisted Clarissa Wren's motion.

Lincoln and another lawyer named E.N. Powell represented Clarissa Wren before the Illinois Supreme Court.

The Illinois Supreme Court agreed with Lincoln and his co-counsel, and concluded that -- unless the other individuals were joined as parties to the proceeding in error, and unless Clarissa Wren were permitted to prosecute that proceeding in error -- she might be unjustly deprived of her marital right of dower in her deceased husband's lands. The Illinois Supreme Court allowed Clarissa's motion for a rule upon the other individuals, requiring them to join the proceeding in error as parties.

Lincoln thus won this point -- and the appeal --for the wife, Clarissa Wren.

47

The case of *Risinger vs. Cheney*, 7 Ill. 84 (1845), involved the doctrine, in the law of contracts, that -- if one party to a contract makes the other party's performance of his obligations under the contract impossible -- the first party cannot then seek damages against the other party because of his failure to perform his obligations under the contract.

Daniel Risinger and another individual named Nye made a promissory note, payable to Owen Cheney, for the amount of $100.00, at Bloomington, Illinois, on May 31, 1845, which was to become due in one month. Risinger and Nye then placed the promissory note in the hands of another individual named Zera Patterson, who was to hold the note as a guaranty, to Owen Cheney, that Risinger and Nye would complete their purchase of a mill, machinery, and a steam engine from Owen Cheney.

The steam mill in question was located on land in McLean County, Illinois. Under the contract which Risinger and Nye had with Cheney, they were to remove the steam mill, and all the machinery connected with it, from the land in McLean County, and then deliver it to a nine-acre tract of ground near Pekin in Tazewell County, Illinois. Risinger and Nye apparently sent workmen to the land in McLean County, for the purpose of removing the steam mill from that land. Before they could remove the steam mill, however, an individual named William Thompson -- who may have had some connection with the State Bank of Illinois, which held a mortgage on that land -- obtained an injunction against Owen Cheney which prohibited him from tearing down or removing the steam mill, and the associated machinery, from the land in McLean County until he should have complied with a decree made in a chancery suit, the terms of which are not revealed in the opinion in this case.

Because of the existence of this injunction, Risinger and Nye were not able to remove the steam mill and associated machinery from the land in McLean County, nor to deliver that steam mill and machinery to the new location in Tazewell County.

Nevertheless, when Risinger's and Nye's promissory note became due, the third party, Zera Patterson, who held that promissory note, delivered it to Owen Cheney, and Owen Cheney sued Risinger and Nye on that promissory note in the Circuit Court of McLean County, Illinois. The circuit court entered a judgment against Risinger and Nye, and in favor of Cheney, for the amount of $101.25 in damages, plus costs of suit.

Risinger and Nye appealed from that judgment of the Circuit Court of McLean County, Illinois, to the Illinois Supreme Court. Lincoln filed a brief in their behalf in which he "contended that the main point in the case was, whether the injunction issue was not a sufficient excuse for Risinger and Nye's failure to perform, so as to save the forfeiture of the note." Lincoln argued that -- because the issuance of the injunction against Cheney had made Risinger's and Nye's performance impossible -- the consideration (that is, the benefit) which Risinger and Nye were to receive under the contract had failed, and, so, Risinger and Nye should be excused from performing under the contract and should not be held to have breached the contract.

The Illinois Supreme Court agreed with Lincoln and stated, "The law is well settled, that he who prevents, or dispenses with a performance of a condition, cannot take advantage of the non-performance. And it is equally well settled, that where there are mutual conditions to be performed, and one of the parties has incapacitated himself from a performance on his part, which condition was a consideration of the promise to be performed by the other, that such incapacity will dispense with performance, or an offer to perform, by the other party to the contract."

The Illinois Supreme Court reversed the judgment of the Circuit Court of McLean County, Illinois. Lincoln had won his argument, and the appeal, for his clients, Risinger and Nye.

48

In the case of *Eldridge vs. Rowe,* 7 Ill. 91 (1845), Lincoln represented a farmhand who was denied compensation for four months of labor for a farmer in Kendall County in northeastern Illinois.

The farmhand, Nelson Rowe, had agreed with the farmer, Barnabas Eldridge, to work for the farmer for eight months for the amount of $90.00. Rowe began working for Eldridge in February, 1843.

About the end of June, 1843, an individual named Lake talked to the farmhand, Rowe, and expressed a desire that Rowe would go to the South with him. A day or two after his conversation with Lake, Rowe quit working for the farmer, Eldridge. By then, Rowe had worked for Eldridge for four months, but he had not yet been paid any of his wages. After Rowe left his employment, the farmer Eldridge refused to pay him anything.

Rowe brought an action, against Eldridge, before a justice of the peace in Kendall County, Illinois. He sought the amount of $47.62 for his four months' of labor for Eldridge. The justice of the peace awarded him a judgment for $30.00.

Eldridge appealed from that judgment to the Circuit Court of Kendall County, Illinois. The case was then tried before a jury.

Rowe presented evidence that his labor was worth from $10.00 to $12.00 per month, and that he had worked for Eldridge for four months. The jury returned a verdict in favor of Rowe, and against Eldridge, for the amount of $26.75. The Circuit Court of Kendall County entered a judgment upon that verdict.

Eldridge appealed from the judgment of the Circuit Court of Kendall County to the Illinois Supreme Court.

Lincoln represented the farmhand, Rowe, in defending against the appeal.

Lincoln's argument was apparently that -- even though Rowe had agreed to work for eight months for Eldridge before he should receive any of his pay -- he was entitled to be compensated fairly for the four months which he did work for Eldridge. This was an argument based upon the theory known as *quantum meruit*.

The Illinois Supreme Court held essentially that -- if an employee's contract with his employer expressly required the performance of a certain condition precedent by the employee, before he should receive any of his pay -- the employee had to perform that condition precedent before he was entitled to recover anything from his employer, and the employee could not avoid the necessity of performing the condition precedent by relying upon the theory of *quantum meruit*.

The Court stated that the farmhand, Rowe, by his explicit agreement with the farmer, Eldridge had to work the full eight months before he was entitled to be paid anything. Because Rowe chose to leave Eldridge's employment after only four months, Rowe had not performed the condition precedent, and, so, was not entitled to recover anything from Eldridge under his explicit agreement with Eldridge. Nor would the Court permit Rowe to avoid the necessity of performing that condition precedent by relying upon the *quantum meruit* argument that he should be paid a fair amount for the time which he actually did labor for Eldridge.

The Illinois Supreme Court reversed the judgment in favor of the farmhand, Nelson Rowe. Lincoln lost his defense against the appeal, and the farmhand, Nelson Rowe, had labored for four months on Barnabas Eldridge's farm for nothing.

49

The doctrine of after-acquired title was involved in the case of *Frisby vs. Ballance,* 7 Ill. 141 (1845). The question -- whether the doctrine of after-acquired title applies -- arises whenever an individual purports to convey land to a third party which he does not then own, but which he later acquires by some means. When the doctrine of after-acquired title applies, it causes the good title, which the grantor later acquired to the land, to be automatically transferred from the grantor to the person to whom he purported to convey the land.

An individual named John Bogardus had delivered a quitclaim deed, concerning land in Peoria County, Illinois, to Isaac Underhill. That quitclaim deed was dated August 5, 1834. At the time that John Bogardus made that deed, however, he did not own the land in question. He acquired the title to the land only later, on January 5, 1838, by means of a patent (that is, a deed) from the United States.

John Bogardus then apparently asserted that he -- rather than Isaac Underhill -- was the owner of the land in question, by virtue of his patent from the United States.

Isaac Underhill and another individual named Lewis Bigelow (to whom Underhill had perhaps deeded a partial interest in the land) brought an action of ejectment against John Bogardus in the Circuit Court of Peoria County, Illinois, in May 1838, in order to evict John Bogardus from the land.

At the trial of the case, Underhill and Bigelow sought to introduce into evidence both the patent from the United States to John Bogardus and the quitclaim deed from John Bogardus to Underhill. Bogardus objected that the quitclaim deed should be excluded from evidence on the ground that it was not sufficient to pass an after-acquired title from Bogardus to Underhill. (A quitclaim deed merely conveys whatever interest a grantor has in land to the grantee. A warranty deed, by contrast, not only conveys the grantor's interest in the land to the grantee, but also gives to the grantee various promises or assurances by the grantor, one of which is that the grantor is actually passing good title to the grantee. Bogardus' argument was essentially that --

although a warranty deed would have been sufficient to convey an after-acquired title, and would have been admissible in evidence, a quitclaim deed was not sufficient to do so and should not be admitted into evidence.)

The Circuit Court of Peoria County agreed with the defendant, Bogardus, and excluded the quitclaim deed from evidence. The jury was thereby compelled to return a verdict in favor of the defendant, Bogardus, and the circuit court entered a judgment on that verdict.

Isaac Underhill and the heirs of Lewis Bigelow (who had died during the pendency of the case) appealed from that judgment to the Illinois Supreme Court. A lawyer named E.N. Powell took the lead in representing Underhill and the heirs of Bigelow on the appeal. Lincoln also represented Underhill and the heirs of Bigelow, and presented a rebuttal in their behalf to the argument presented by Bogardus' attorney.

The Illinois Supreme Court referred to an Illinois statute, in its decision, which appears to have been the predecessor to the current Illinois statute on after-acquired title. The Court concluded that the statute had changed the common law rule, and had made a quitclaim deed sufficient to pass an after-acquired title to a grantee. Based upon the present wording of the statute (765 ILCS 5/7), this holding appears to have been correct.

The Illinois Supreme Court reversed the judgment of the Circuit Court of Peoria County, and found in favor of Lincoln's clients, and remanded the case to the circuit court for a new trial.

The Illinois Supreme Court later overruled its decision in this case. The law in Illinois now appears to be -- despite the plain wording of the relevant Illinois statute (765 ILCS 5/7) -- that a quitclaim deed is not sufficient to pass an after-acquired title to a grantee, and that only a warranty deed will pass an after-acquired title to a grantee.

50

An "administrator" is the individual who administers the estate of a decedent if the decedent has died without a will. An "executor" is an individual who is specifically nominated in a will to implement the provisions of the will and who, therefore, handles the estate of a decedent who has died with a will.

If, however, all the individuals nominated by a decedent's will, to serve as the executor, are themselves deceased or otherwise unable to serve as executor -- or if the decedent's will for some reason failed to nominate an executor -- the individual who is appointed to implement the will, and to handle the decedent's estate, is known as an "administrator with the will annexed."

The case of *Hall vs. Irwin*, 7 Ill. 176 (1845), involved the question whether an "administrator with the will annexed" had the power to sell a decedent's land, in view of the decedent's will's having expressly stated that the "executor" should have a power to sell the decedent's land.

Thomas Payne was a resident of Cass County, Illinois, which is northwest of Springfield. He apparently had no wife, but had several small children. He became ill, and expected to die. In his haste to make some provision for his small children, he hurriedly drafted and signed the following will on September 4, 1835:

"My will is, that my land and personal property be sold at such credit, and in such manner as is thought most advisable to my executor, for the interest of my little children, and the proceeds to be put at interest for the support and education, if the interest should prove sufficient, otherwise the principal is to be used. But the land is not to be sold until it will bring eight dollars per acre, and as they arrive at age or marry, that distribution be made of what shall remain in equal proportions, not depriving the younger children of means of education. I mean that my executor shall use some discretion in distributing, so as to retain sufficient to educate the younger children."

Thomas Payne forgot to nominate an executor in his will, however.

Thomas Payne died. Because no executor was nominated in his will, an individual named Benjamin Gatton was appointed by the probate court to serve as administrator with the will annexed. As administrator with the will annexed, Benjamin Gatton purported to rely upon the power of sale of the land, conferred by the terms of the will upon Thomas Payne's nonexistent executor. Benjamin Gatton conveyed the decedent's land to Henry Hall for a price which exceeded eight dollars per acre, as apparently required by the will.

The heirs of Thomas Payne -- who were undoubtedly his children -- then brought an action of ejectment in the Circuit Court of Cass County, Illinois, against Henry Hall, in order to evict him from the land, and to recover the land for themselves. The heirs of Thomas Payne argued that the power of sale conferred by Thomas Payne's will upon the executor whom he failed to nominate, did not run to the administrator with the will annexed and, in consequence, did not authorize him to make the sale of the land to Henry Hall.

After the heirs of Payne had initially filed the case in the Circuit Court of Cass County, there was a change of venue, and the case was brought into the Circuit Court of Sangamon County. The Circuit Court of Sangamon County agreed with the heirs of Payne and concluded that the administrator with the will annexed, Benjamin Gatton, had no authority -- without authorization of the probate court -- to sell the land in question to Henry Hall. Consequently, the circuit court excluded from evidence the deed made by Benjamin Gatton to Henry Hall for the land. In the absence of that deed, the jury was compelled to conclude that Henry Hall had no right to possess the land, and that the heirs of Thomas Payne should be allowed to evict him. The jury thus returned a verdict in favor of the heirs of Thomas Payne, and the circuit court entered a judgment on that verdict.

Henry Hall appealed from that judgment to the Illinois Supreme Court.

Lincoln and another lawyer, named W. Thomas,

represented the heirs of Thomas Payne before the Illinois Supreme Court.

After a lengthy and somewhat minute discussion of cases and statutes -- including even the English statute of wills, passed during the reign of Henry VIII -- the Illinois Supreme Court decided that the circuit court was correct, and that the power of sale expressed in Thomas Payne's will did not confer upon the administrator with the will annexed the authority to sell Thomas Payne's land. Rather, in the view of the Illinois Supreme Court, the administrator with the will annexed should have first petitioned the probate court for the authority to sell the land in question.

The Illinois Supreme Court affirmed the judgment of the Circuit Court of Sangamon County in favor of the heirs of Thomas Payne. Lincoln had won his defense against the appeal.

The decision in *City of Springfield vs. Hickox,* 7 Ill. 241 (1845), provides an interesting glimpse of the operation of the municipal government of the City of Springfield in the 1840s.

In 1844, the mayor and city council of the City of Springfield issued to an individual named V. Hickox what was known as a "city order," which read as follows:

"$50 Receivable for taxes on real estate and personal property
City of Springfield, Ills., Feb'y 21, 1846.
The treasurer of the city of Springfield will pay V. Hickox, or order, the sum of fifty dollars and _____ cents, with six per cent. interest per annum from date until paid, out of any unappropriated monies in the treasury, being in accordance with a resolution of the city council.

Andrew McCormick, Mayor
James C. Conkling, Clerk City Council."

The decision in the case does not make plain why this "city order" bore the date of February 21, 1846. This probably represented a misprint in the report of the Illinois Supreme Court's decision, and the "city order" was probably signed on February 21, 1844.

The payee of the "city order," V. Hickox, endorsed it over to the firm of merchants in the City of Springfield known as Hickox & Brothers. That firm, Hickox & Brothers, presented the "city order" to the treasurer of the City of Springfield for payment on August 28, 1844. The treasurer declined to pay the "city order" for the reason that "there was not then, and had not been for some time previous, any funds in the treasury, either appropriated or otherwise."

The City of Springfield had, at that time, an ordinance which required merchants to obtain a license from the city, in order to engage in their trade. The ordinance further provided that -- if a merchant engaged in trade in the city without such a license -- he should be tried before the mayor and fined the amount of $12, which was a significant amount in that day.

The firm of Hickox & Brothers apparently refused to obtain a license, but nevertheless engaged in trade in the City of Springfield. The mayor issued a summons to Hickox & Brothers, tried that firm under the licensing ordinance, found it guilty, and fined it $12 for having violated the licensing ordinance.

Hickox & Brothers appealed from the mayor's judgment to the Circuit Court of Sangamon County for what appeared to be a completely new trial: that is, a trial *de novo.*

At that new trial, Hickox & Brothers alleged as a counterclaim (somewhat misleadingly referred to as a "setoff" in the decision) that the City of Springfield owed it $50 under the "city order" which V. Hickox had endorsed over to Hickox & Brothers. Hickox & Brothers sought to recover the $38 difference between the $12 fine which it owed to the City of Springfield and the $50 which the City of Springfield owed to it under the "city order."

The parties agreed that the case would be tried as a bench trial: that is, by the judge alone, without a jury. The trial judge ruled in favor of Hickox & Brothers, and awarded it a judgment of $38 against the City of Springfield.

The City of Springfield appealed from that judgment to the Illinois Supreme Court. Lincoln and another lawyer -- named W. I. Ferguson -- represented the City of Springfield on appeal. Lincoln and Ferguson argued that a resolution adopted by the City Council of Springfield -- which the trial judge had refused to admit into evidence -- revealed that the "city order" was to be payable only out of the real estate taxes and personal property taxes which the City of Springfield eventually received. They asserted that the trial judge should not have permitted Hickox & Brothers to collect the amount of the "city order" out of the general funds of the City of Springfield, which did not then contain the proceeds of any real estate taxes or personal property taxes. Lincoln and Ferguson argued, second, that the "city order" could not properly be made the subject of a setoff against the claim of the City of Springfield for the $12 fine.

The Illinois Supreme Court disapproved of the City of Springfield's use of "city orders" in the following language:

"It is against the policy of the law and the interest of the public that these orders should circulate as money. They should, in reality, be what, upon their face they purport to be, drawn upon a real existing fund instead of an imaginary and prospective one."

The Court held, though, that -- if the City of Springfield were going to use "city orders" -- it could expect to be held liable according to the terms of those "city orders." The Court concluded that the terms of the "city order" in question did not indicate that the "city order" was to be payable only out of future real estate taxes or personal property taxes, and that the resolution of the City of Springfield -- purporting so to restrict the "city orders" -- was parol evidence and was properly excluded by the trial judge.

The Illinois Supreme Court affirmed the judgment of the Circuit Court of Sangamon County, for the amount of $38 against the City of Springfield. Lincoln and Ferguson thus lost the appeal.

52

The case of *Ross vs. Nesbit,* 7 Ill. 252 (1845), involved one question which seemed surprisingly modern: that is, whether an agreement between the parties to arbitrate their dispute prevented the circuit court from having jurisdiction to decide their dispute.

An individual named Matthew Nesbit brought an action of trespass *quare clausum fregit* in the Circuit Court of DeKalb County, Illinois, against Joseph Ross and other individuals in 1844. (The Latin phrase means "wherefore he broke the close," and the common law action of trespass *quare clausum fregit* was that form of action traditionally used to recover damages from another for having trespassed on land.) By that action, Nesbit sought damages for the alleged trespasses -- by Ross and the other individuals -- upon land which Nesbit asserted he owned in DeKalb County.

Ross and the other individuals raised five "pleas" -- that is, defenses -- to the complaint brought by Nesbit for trespass.

The plaintiff, Nesbit, demurred (that is, objected) to the third, fourth, and fifth pleas of the defendants, and the circuit court sustained the plaintiff's objections. The case then proceeded to trial on the bases of the plaintiff's complaint and the defendants' first and second pleas. The jury returned a verdict in favor of the plaintiff, Nesbit, for the amount of $92.00 in damages. The circuit court entered a judgment on that verdict in favor of the plaintiff and against the defendants.

The defendants -- Ross and the other individuals -- appealed from that judgment to the Illinois Supreme Court. Lincoln represented the plaintiff, Nesbit, in defending against the appeal.

The third plea raised by the defendants, and argued by them in the Illinois Supreme Court, was that -- after the commencement of the plaintiff's lawsuit on March 14, 1844 -- the plaintiff and defendants entered into an agreement to have their dispute arbitrated and decided by a man named William Olmstead and two other individuals; that the defendants had been ready and willing since that time to have the dispute arbitrated; and that, in view of the parties' agreement to have their dispute arbitrated, the circuit court should have refused to decide the case, and should, instead, have required the parties to proceed to arbitration.

The fourth and fifth pleas raised by the defendants, and argued by them in the Illinois Supreme Court, asserted that the land in question belonged either to the United States or to one of the defendants, named Jones, but, in any event, not to the plaintiff, Nesbit. The defendants argued that whatever had been done on the land in question was done for the sake of permitting Jones to assert his rights to the land.

Lincoln filed a brief which cited a case from New York, and concluded with the paragraph,

"The Court will consider these pleas, and examine the authorities of the plaintiffs in error, and if the Court can then decide that they are good pleas in trespass, we will cheerfully submit."

The Illinois Supreme Court brushed the defendants' fourth and fifth pleas aside as lacking merit. It devoted most of its discussion to the third plea, concerning the alleged agreement of the parties to arbitrate the dispute. The Court concluded that -- although the parties' actual *submission* of the case to an arbitrator might oust the circuit court of jurisdiction to hear the matter -- the parties' mere *agreement* to submit the case to arbitration would not defeat the circuit court's jurisdiction. The plaintiff was thus free to have the dispute resolved by the circuit court, regardless of whatever agreement he might have made to have the case resolved by arbitration.

The Illinois Supreme Court, therefore, affirmed the judgment of the Circuit Court of DeKalb County in favor of Lincoln's client, Matthew Nesbit.

53

The case of *Simpson vs. Ranlett,* 7 Ill. 312 (1845), involved -- on Lincoln's part, as the attorney on appeal for the defendant-appellant -- a rather picayune assertion concerning a supposed defect in the plaintiff-appellee's "declaration." ("Declaration" was formerly the name given to the plaintiff's initial pleading in an action at law, which pleading is now known as a complaint.)

A man named Joshua Simpson had apparently given a promissory note for the amount of $323.64 to Isaac Burnett in St. Louis, Missouri, on December 2, 1841. The note was payable five months after its execution. Burnett endorsed the note over to Seth Ranlett on the day that it was signed.

Seth Ranlett filed his declaration in the Circuit Court of Putnam County, Illinois, against Joshua Simpson to collect the amount of the promissory note. Ranlett's declaration contained the following allegation as to the endorsement of the note, by Isaac Burnett, over to him: "and the said Isaac Burnett then and there indorsed the same to the said plaintiff, whereof the said defendant then and there had notice, etc."

The defendant, Joshua Simpson, demurred to (that is, filed a motion to dismiss) the declaration on the ground that it did not properly allege the endorsement of the note over to Ranlett. The circuit court overruled the demurrer, and held that the declaration properly pleaded the fact of the endorsement.

The defendant, Joshua Simpson, elected to stand on the assertions he had made in his demurrer, rather than raise any other defenses, probably for the reason that he had no other defenses. The circuit court ordered the clerk of the court to assess and report the damages due to Ranlett under the promissory note (a procedure not followed today, and which would likely be an unconstitutional delegation of judicial authority if it were followed). The clerk assessed and reported, and the circuit court entered judgment for, damages for Ranlett in the amount of $391.64.

The defendant, Joshua Simpson, appealed from that judgment to the Illinois Supreme Court. Lincoln represented Joshua Simpson in prosecuting the appeal.

Lincoln made the same argument on appeal that Joshua Simpson had pressed in the circuit court: namely, that Ranlett's declaration did not properly allege that Isaac Burnett had endorsed Joshua Simpson's note over to Ranlett. Lincoln relied on chapter 73 of the Illinois Revised Statutes of 1845, which provided that promissory notes should be "assignable by indorsement thereon, *under the hand or hands of such person or persons . . . . "* (Emphasis added.) Lincoln argued that -- for Ranlett's declaration to have been sufficient -- it should have alleged that the endorsement by Isaac Burnett on the note was under his own hand.

The Illinois Supreme Court disagreed with Lincoln, and found that the declaration properly alleged the endorsement, and affirmed the judgment for $391.64 against Lincoln's client, Joshua Simpson.

54

The subject of "pleading" involves the rules which govern the manner in which a party must allege his cause of action against another party. During Lincoln's life, Illinois observed the rules of "common law pleading," which rules had grown by a process of accretion over decades -- and even centuries -- of decision-making by common law courts in England and in this country. One feature of common law pleading, as enforced by the courts, was the strictness with which a lawyer, drafting a complaint (or declaration, as it was then known), had to comply with its detailed and rather tedious rules. Lincoln was quite familiar with the niceties of common law pleading, and he relied upon them in numerous cases to persuade the Illinois Supreme Court that his opponent had committed a fatal pleading error at trial. The case of *Murphy vs. Summerville*, 7 Ill. 361 (1845), affords an example of just such a success on Lincoln's part.

Some of the events of the case are impossible to reconstruct from the sketchy discussion of them contained in the Illinois Supreme Court's decision.

This much is reasonably certain, however. An individual named John S. Sloan had executed a bail bond as the principal (that is, the person primarily obligated on the bail bond). Another individual -- apparently named James Murphy -- had evidently acted as a surety on the bail bond, who guaranteed the principal's performance of the condition expressed in the bail bond. The bail bond apparently ran in favor of yet another individual named Alexander Summerville, so that -- if the principal, John S. Sloan, failed to perform the condition expressed in the bail bond -- Alexander Summerville could sue both the principal and the surety (James Murphy) for the amount of the penalty stated in the bail bond.

We think today of a bail bond as arising only out of a criminal proceeding. The decision in this case, though, suggests that the bail bond in question was given to guarantee the principal's performance in connection with a civil proceeding.

The condition expressed in the bail bond was that -- if a judgment were entered against the principal, John S. Sloan, in some other case -- he had either to pay the costs and "condemnation money" (whatever that might mean) or to surrender himself (apparently to the sheriff).

Alexander Summerville filed a declaration (that is, a complaint) against the surety, James Murphy, in the Circuit Court of Edgar County, Illinois. He alleged, in his declaration, that the principal, John S. Sloan, had neither paid the costs and condemnation money, nor surrendered himself. For this reason, he sought to hold the surety, James Murphy, liable for the amount of the penalty -- $250 -- set forth in the bail bond.

James Murphy demurred (that is, objected) to the declaration on the ground that it did not allege the facts necessary to state a cause of action against him. The Circuit Court of Edgar County overruled the demurrer, and entered a judgment in favor of Alexander Summerville -- and against James Murphy -- for the amount of the penalty expressed in the bond, $250, which was to be satisfied by James Murphy's payment of $150.62 1/2. Murphy appealed from that judgment to the Illinois Supreme Court.

Lincoln represented James Murphy on appeal. Lincoln's former partner, Stephen Logan, represented Alexander Summerville in defending against the appeal.

Lincoln filed a brief in which his main point was, "The declaration does not show with certainty that any judgment was rendered against the principal." Although the declaration assumed the entry of a judgment against the principal, John S. Sloan, it had not asserted that a judgment actually had been entered against the principal.

The Illinois Supreme Court agreed with Lincoln and reversed the judgment. It remanded the case to the circuit court with instructions that Alexander Summerville should be given leave to amend his declaration to include the necessary allegation. Lincoln thus won the appeal on a point of pleading.

55

The case of *Trailor vs. Hill,* 7 Ill. 364 (1845), involved a misdescription of land, and the unusual question as to which direction represented north on a map drawn by the parties.

Congress, by an old statute, had granted section 16 of every township in Illinois to public authorities for the purpose of funding public schools. Consequently, school commissioners owned section 16 in every township.

An individual named Leroy Hill had purchased 16 acres in section 16 of Township 12 North, Range 3 West of the Principal Meridian, from the school commissioner of Montgomery County, before Christian County was formed out of the northern portion of Montgomery County. He gave the school commissioner of Montgomery County a promissory note for $100.00, to pay for the 60-acre tract, and the school commissioner eventually delivered a deed to Paulina Hill, who was apparently Leroy Hill's wife, on May 31, 1842.

On November 18, 1840, Leroy Hill had entered into a bond for deed contract with Joel Trailor, concerning the sale of a 60-acre tract of land in that same section 16 from Leroy Hill to Joel Trailor. The bond for deed contract both attempted to describe the tract of land in question, and also had attached to it a grid of section 16 -- having the quarter sections and, furthermore, the quarter-quarter sections marked on it -- on which grid the tract of land in question was supposedly indicated by a blackened area. The blackened area shown on the grid consisted of one quarter-quarter section (40 acres) and an adjacent half of a quarter-quarter section (an additional 20 acres). The blackened area on the map, however, did not correspond to the description contained in the bond for deed contract between Hill and Trailor.

Joel Trailor brought an action for specific performance against Leroy Hill in the Circuit Court of Sangamon County, by which he sought to compel Leroy Hill to convey to Joel Trailor what Joel Trailor said was the 60-acre tract of land that was supposedly the subject of the bond for deed contract.

Leroy Hill filed an answer in which he admitted that the bond for deed contract contained an erroneous description, but asserted that the correct description was different from that advanced by Joel Trailor. Leroy Hill apparently contended that the blackened area on the grid of section 16, attached to the bond for deed contract, correctly represented the 60-acre tract in question if it were rotated to the left, so that the long access of the tract ran not vertically, but horizontally. Hill asserted further that this was the same 60-acre tract which he had purchased from the school commissioner of Montgomery County, and that he had agreed to sell that tract to Trailor if Trailor would assume the responsibility for paying off his promissory note for $100.00. Leroy Hill deposited Paulina Hill's deed for that tract of land in the circuit court, and expressed his willingness to deliver the deed to Trailor if Trailor would pay off the $100.00 promissory note.

In contrast, Joel Trailor asserted that the purchase price of the tract was to have been $300.00; that he had already paid $200.00 to Hill; but that the correct 60-acre tract was different from that contended for by Hill, from that described in the bond for deed contract, and from that shown in the blackened area on the grid of section 16.

The Circuit Court of Sangamon County ruled in Hill's favor, and decreed that -- upon Trailor's payment of $100.00 to a court official known as "the master in chancery" -- the deed on file from Paulina Hill would be delivered to Trailor. This satisfied Trailor not at all, because he would be getting a 60-acre tract of land different from the one which he sought to obtain from Hill. Consequently, Trailor appealed from the decree to the Illinois Supreme Court.

Lincoln and his former partner, Stephen Logan, represented Leroy Hill in defending against the appeal. They filed a brief which "contended that the complainant had brought no evidence to sustain his allegations in the bill."

The Illinois Supreme Court entered into a discussion of the testimony presented by several witnesses at the trial of the case. In analyzing Trailor's assertion that the blackened area on the grid of section 16 was incorrect, the Illinois Supreme Court considered the argument that Trailor apparently had made, to the effect that the top of the sheet, on which the grid appeared, should be taken as north because "all scientific men make the top of a map north." The Illinois Supreme Court replied that this would be a somewhat strained, and by no means safe, interpretation.

The Court remarked also that -- if the right side of the map were taken to represent that north -- the map would perfectly describe the land which Leroy Hill contended was the subject of the bond for deed contract.

In some exasperation, the Illinois Supreme Court stated further that "From an examination of the whole case, it would almost seem that both complainant and defendant had studiously avoided furnishing any evidence, except such as would have the strongest tendency to involve the whole affair in doubt and inextricable confusion."

The Illinois Supreme Court affirmed the decree of the Circuit Court of Sangamon County, and, so, Lincoln and Logan won their defense against the appeal, in behalf of their client, Leroy Hill.

A "principal" is one for whom another acts. An "agent" is that other person who acts in behalf of the principal. An individual who acts as an agent for a principal, without revealing that he is acting in the capacity of an agent, rather than in his own behalf, can be held personally liable on the contracts that he enters into in the course of performing his duties as an agent.

The case of *Chase vs. Debolt,* 7 Ill. 371 (1845), involved a claim by a workman that another -- who had hired him to work on a building at a college -- was liable to the workman personally for his pay, because that other person supposedly had not revealed that he was acting in the capacity of an agent.

An individual identified as Bishop Chase was constructing a college in Peoria County, Illinois, known as Jubilee College. Henry J. Chase was the Bishop's agent, who hired the laborers and superintended the work on Jubilee College.

A workman named George Debolt desired to obtain work on the college. He approached Chase, who employed him, but Chase did not tell him specifically that he (Chase) was acting as the agent for the bishop. Debolt frequently received his paycheck directly from the bishop.

For some reason, Debolt believed that he had a claim for additional work, and he brought that claim against the agent, Henry J. Chase, personally. Debolt brought that action before a justice of the peace in Peoria County, Illinois. The justice of the peace apparently entered a judgment in favor of Debolt, and against Henry J. Chase, for the amount of $75.93 3/4 cents. Chase then must have obtained a trial *de novo* of the case in the Circuit Court of Peoria County, Illinois.

The jury entered a verdict in favor of Debolt for the amount of $75.93 3/4 cents, and the circuit court entered a judgment upon the verdict. Chase then appealed to the Illinois Supreme Court.

Lincoln and another lawyer named H. O. Merriman represented Debolt in defending against the appeal. They filed a brief which read as follows:

> "Where substantial justice has been done between the parties, a new trial will not be granted. *Smith vs. Shultz,* 1 Scam. 491.

> The court will not disturb a verdict on account of excessive damages. *Schlenker vs. Risley,* 3 Scam. 487; *Leigh vs. Hodges,* Ib. 18.

> Where an agent holds himself out as principal, without disclosing his agency, he will be personally responsible. Story on Con. section 314; Story on Agency, sections 266, 267.

> If a person contract in his own name, he will be personally responsible, although the fact of his agency be known at the time of the contract. Story on Con. section 315, and the authorities there cited."

It is interesting that Lincoln cited one of his previous cases before the Illinois Supreme Court -- *Schlenker vs. Risley* -- in which he had won. It is a common tendency for appellate lawyers, even today, to cite -- in later arguments to an appellate court -- cases in which they were previously successful before the court.

The Illinois Supreme Court disagreed with Lincoln on this occasion, however. It conceded "Agents may become liable for contracts made for their principals, where they conceal or do not disclose their character of agent, and it is unknown to the party with whom they contract . . . ." The Court concluded, though, that -- if the party with whom the agent has contracted actually knew of his character as an agent for a principal -- the agent could not be held personally liable on the contract.

In this case, the Court thought that the evidence revealed that, regardless of what Chase had specifically stated to Debolt, about his character as an agent for the bishop, Debolt knew that Chase was only an agent and that he was not personally contracting with Debolt to have work done on the building at Jubilee College. The Court ruled that Debolt's knowledge of

Chase's character as an agent discharged Chase from all personal liability on the contract with Debolt.

The Court thus reversed the judgment in favor of Lincoln's client, George Debolt, and remanded the case to the Circuit Court of Peoria County for a new trial.

57

In order for any court to enter a judgment which is binding upon a party, the court must first obtain personal jurisdiction over that party. This is ordinarily accomplished by the service of a summons upon that party. A judgment entered by a court which had no personal jurisdiction over a party is void as to that party.

This principle -- that a court must have personal jurisdiction over a party in order to enter a valid judgment against him -- was involved in the case of *Smith vs. Byrd,* 7 Ill. 412 (1845).

In that case, Adam Byrd had commenced an action against Joseph H. Smith before a justice of the peace in Jo Daviess County, Illinois. The justice of the peace rendered a verdict against the defendant, Joseph H. Smith, for the amount of $100.00. Joseph H. Smith removed the case to the Circuit Court of Jo Daviess County by a writ of *certiorari,* and he was there entitled to receive a new trial on the cause of action against him.

While the action was pending in the circuit court, Adam Byrd and Joseph H. Smith agreed that they would refer the case to arbitrators, and that the arbitrators' award would be entered and enforced as the judgment of the circuit court. The parties submitted their case to arbitrators, who decided that both Joseph H. Smith and George Smith, who had not previously been a party to the action, should pay Adam Byrd the amount of $40.00 plus court costs. The Circuit Court of Jo Daviess County entered a judgment on the arbitrators' award against both Joseph H. Smith and George Smith. Both Joseph H. Smith and George Smith appealed from that judgment to the Illinois Supreme Court.

Lincoln represented Adam Byrd in defending against the appeal.

Lincoln was in an impossible legal position because -- to win the appeal with respect to George Smith -- he had to argue that the circuit court could enter a binding judgment against him without ever having obtained personal jurisdiction over him.

Perhaps Lincoln conceded that the judgment against George Smith was void, but that the judgment against Joseph H. Smith, over whom the circuit court did have personal jurisdiction, should be deemed valid.

The Illinois Supreme Court rejected that argument, however, in the following words: "The judgment was clearly unauthorized as to George F. Smith. He was not originally a party to the case. Nor does the record show that he afterwards became a party, or in any manner assented to the proceeding before the arbitrators, or in the circuit court. The court had no jurisdiction over his person. Although the award may be binding between the original parties, it is a mere nullity as to him. The judgment is a unit, and must be reversed as to both of the Smiths."

Consequently the Illinois Supreme Court reversed the judgment for $40.00 in favor of Lincoln's client, Adam Byrd, and remanded the case for a new trial in the Circuit Court of Jo Daviess County.

58

A court may not enter an order which binds a party unless it first obtains jurisdiction over that party. Jurisdiction may take the form of personal jurisdiction over that party, which means that the party's own person is completely subject to the authority of the court as a result of his having been properly served with "process" (that is, with a summons). If a party cannot be found, however, it will not be possible to serve him with process and thereby to bring him within the personal jurisdiction of the court. If a party cannot be located, but property that he owns can be located, within the State of Illinois, it is possible to "attach" his property, and thereby to give the court jurisdiction over that party's property. An "attachment" of personal property occurs when a sheriff takes that personal property into his possession, pursuant to a writ of attachment. An "attachment" of land effectively occurs when a sheriff records a notice of an attachment lien, concerning the land, in the office of the recorder of the county in which the land is located.

The case of *Moore vs. Hamilton*, 7 Ill. 429 (1845), involved the distinction between a lawsuit based upon the court's personal jurisdiction over the defendant, and a lawsuit based upon merely the court's jurisdiction over the defendant's property, obtained by means of an attachment of the defendant's property.

Although the decision in the case is not clear on this point, it appears that Artois Hamilton sued Joshua Moore in the Circuit Court of Hancock County, Illinois, in an effort to hold Joshua Moore liable to him for a "tort" (that is, a civil wrong allegedly committed by Moore against Hamilton). Hamilton simply may have been complaining that Moore had, in some manner, inflicted a personal injury on Hamilton.

Hamilton apparently thought that Moore was located in Peoria County, because he directed the summons to the Sheriff of Peoria County for attempted service on Moore. The Sheriff of Peoria County, however, returned the summons and indicated thereon that he had not been able to find Moore. Hamilton never was able to obtain personal service on Moore.

Hamilton then had an attachment made upon personal property and land owned by Moore. In connection with the attachment, he apparently published a notice in some newspaper, directed to Moore, indicating that Moore's personal property and land had been seized pursuant to the attachment.

Moore never appeared to defend himself in the case. A jury returned a verdict in favor of Hamilton for the amount of $145.74, and the Circuit Court of Hancock County entered a judgment upon the verdict, and authorized the sale of Moore's property that had been attached.

Moore -- who had finally become aware of the proceeding against him -- appealed from that judgment to the Illinois Supreme Court. Lincoln represented Moore in taking the appeal.

Lincoln argued that the Illinois statute concerning attachment did not allow the court's jurisdiction in a personal injury case to be founded merely upon the attachment of the defendant's personal property or land. Rather, a personal injury action had to be founded upon personal jurisdiction over the defendant himself, or else the personal injury action had to be dismissed.

The brief which Lincoln filed read as follows:

"In this case, a personal service was necessary. Rev. Stat. Ch. IX, section 3.
The certificate of publication did not authorize a judgment. Constructive notice is insufficient."

The Illinois Supreme Court agreed with Lincoln, and concluded that the attachment statute had been misused in this case to permit a personal injury action to be brought against the defendant, in the absence of personal jurisdiction over the defendant. It reversed the judgment and remanded the case to the Circuit Court of Hancock County for further proceedings.

Lincoln had thus won his appeal for Joshua Moore.

59

A large percentage of the litigation in Illinois courts today concerns personal injuries. It is interesting to note -- while reading decisions of the Illinois Supreme Court from Lincoln's era -- that comparatively few of those decisions concerned personal injury actions. This is because tort law -- which is that branch of the law which permits injured persons to seek compensatory damages from those persons who have negligently or intentionally injured them -- gained increasing significance as the State of Illinois became industrialized.

The case of *McNamara vs. King,* 7 Ill. 432 (1845), was a personal injury action for assault and battery.

Charles McNamara apparently had attacked George King with a deadly weapon and had severely wounded him. As a result of the injuries which he suffered, George King was dangerously ill for several weeks.

George King brought an action of trespass -- which was the old form of action which had to be used if one desired to complain of an assault and battery -- against Charles McNamara in the Circuit Court of Kane County, Illinois.

At the trial of the case, the circuit court permitted King to prove that McNamara was a wealthy individual who had no children and only a small family, but that he, King, was a poor individual with a large family to support. McNamara objected to the admission of this evidence.

The jury returned a verdict in favor of King for the amount of $650.00, which was more than the annual wage that an average man earned in those days. The circuit court entered a judgment upon the verdict. McNamara appealed from the judgment to the Illinois Supreme Court.

Lincoln and another attorney named J. B. Thomas represented McNamara in prosecuting the appeal.

On the appeal Lincoln argued, first, that the damages which had been awarded to King were grossly excessive. He argued, second, that it was improper for the circuit court to have allowed King to present evidence of his own poverty and large family, in contrast to McNamara's wealth and small family.

As to the appropriateness of the $650.00 award of damages, the Illinois Supreme Court stated, "The amount of recovery and actions for personal injuries rests so much in the discretion of juries, that courts will not disturb their verdicts on the ground that the damages are excessive, unless it is manifest that they have been governed by passion, partiality or corruption; and to draw such a conclusion, is not enough that the damages, in the opinion of the court are too high, or that a less amount would have been a sufficient satisfaction for the injury. It must be apparent at first blush that the damages are glaringly excessive." This essentially remains the law in the State of Illinois.

As to the propriety of the circuit court's having allowed King to present evidence of his poverty and large family, in contrast to McNamara's wealth and small family, the Illinois Supreme Court held that both parties' "pecuniary circumstances may be inquired into." The law is quite to the contrary today. It is appropriate now to present evidence of a defendant's net worth if a plaintiff is seeking punitive damages against him, but in no case would it be appropriate to present evidence either of the smallness of the defendant's family, or of the plaintiff's own poverty, or of the largeness of the plaintiff's family.

In any event, the Illinois Supreme Court rejected both of Lincoln's arguments, and affirmed the judgment in favor of George King and against Charles McNamara. Lincoln had thus lost his appeal for his client.

60

Usury is the charging of an excessive and illegal rate of interest. The question of whether a mortgage holder was guilty of usury, for having charged an excessive rate of interest on a mortgage loan, arose in the case of *Ellis vs. Locke,* 7 Ill. 459 (1845).

On February 6, 1841, Ezra Ellis executed a promissory note payable to John Locke, for the amount of $247.50, one year after the date of the note, with interest thereon at the rate of 12 percent per year. He also executed a mortgage on land which he owned, in order to secure his payment of the note.

In April, 1845, Locke brought an action in the Circuit Court of Cook County in order to foreclose the mortgage. Ellis thus apparently had failed to pay what he owed on the promissory note.

The only defense which Ellis asserted, to Locke's action for a foreclosure of the mortgage, was that the 12 percent rate of interest which he had been required to pay on the promissory note was usurious, and that Locke himself was guilty of usury.

The circuit court tried the case without a jury, and examined Locke, Ellis, and another witness named E. H. Haddock. The court found the issues in favor of Locke, and assessed his damages at $361.63. Ellis filed a motion for a new trial. The circuit court denied that motion, and entered a judgment of foreclosure in favor of Locke.

Ellis appealed from that judgment to the Illinois Supreme Court. Lincoln and another lawyer named J. B. Thomas represented Ellis in prosecuting the appeal.

Lincoln pressed the same argument that Ellis had made in the circuit court: namely, that the 12 percent interest rate was usurious, and that Locke had been guilty of usury.

The Illinois Supreme Court concluded that the circumstances, to which Locke had testified, negated the allegation of usury. It also concluded that Locke's testimony had been corroborated by the witness, Haddock, who knew of all the transactions between the parties concerning the promissory note and mortgage. The Illinois Supreme Court stated, "The scale of evidence, therefore, strongly inclined to the plaintiff's side, and the court was not only authorized, but required, to find the issues against the defendant."

The Illinois Supreme Court thus affirmed the judgment of foreclosure which the Circuit Court of Cook County had entered against Lincoln's client, Ezra Ellis.

61

The case of *Bryan vs. Wash,* 7 Ill. 557 (1845), involved a family dispute, the resolution of which turned upon the question whether a particular deed had been effectively "delivered" to the grantee named therein.

George Bryan was the father of Nicholas Bryan, and, so, the grandfather of Nicholas Bryan's own daughter, Mary Jane Bryan. George Bryan owned land in Sangamon County, Illinois.

On September 28, 1837 -- while Mary Jane Bryan was apparently still a minor -- George Bryan signed and dated a deed which purported to convey his land to his granddaughter, Mary Jane Bryan. He deposited the deed with his son, Nicholas Bryan, with instructions to him to give the deed to Mary Jane Bryan, when he, Nicholas Bryan, saw fit to do so.

Mary Jane Bryan married Milton Wash in July, 1840. The young woman, Mary Jane, and her new husband, Milton Wash, apparently knew that the deed to the land -- from George Bryan to his granddaughter, Mary Jane -- had not yet been recorded in the Recorder's Office of Sangamon County.

The young woman, Mary Jane Wash, had a sister named Eliza C. Taylor, whose husband was named James Taylor. The mother of Mary Jane Wash and Eliza T. Taylor -- and the wife of Nicholas Bryan -- was Mary D. Bryan.

In the fall of 1840, Mary D. Bryan handed the deed in question to James Taylor, to be recorded in the Recorder's Office of Sangamon County. Her daughter, Eliza C. Taylor, was present at that transaction, but her husband, Nicholas Bryan, apparently was not present. After James Taylor obtained the deed, he recorded it on November 5, 1840.

Mary Jane Wash and her husband, Milton Wash, thereafter mortgaged the land on November 10, 1841, to Tinsley and Company in order obtain a loan for the amount of $1,200.00. Nicholas Bryan and Mary D. Bryan, the parents of Mary Jane Wash, then still lived on that land.

Nicholas Bryan -- the father of Mary Jane Wash -- perhaps disapproved of having the land, on which he still lived, mortgaged for an amount which was large in that day. The grandfather, George Bryan, was then apparently incompetent. Nicholas Bryan brought an action against his daughter, Mary Jane Wash, and his son-in-law, Milton Wash, as the "next friend" (that is, the representative) of the incompetent George Bryan. Nicholas Bryan sought, in that action, to obtain a decree that the deed in question had never taken effect because it supposedly had never been delivered to Mary Jane Wash. Nicholas Bryan contended that possession of the deed had been obtained from his own wife, Mary D. Bryan, by deceit on the part of James Taylor, who was Mary Jane Wash's brother-in-law.

The case thus turned on the question whether an effective delivery of the deed had been made to Mary Jane Wash. The Circuit Court of Sangamon County concluded that a delivery had been made, and entered a judgment in favor of Mary Jane Wash and her husband, Milton Wash.

George Bryan -- by his son and next friend, Nicholas Bryan -- appealed from that judgment to the Illinois Supreme Court.

Both Lincoln and his former partner, Stephen Logan, are listed as having represented the "defendants in error" on appeal. It is likely that one of them represented one set of defendants in error -- Mary Jane Wash and her husband, Milton Wash -- and that the other of them represented the other set of defendants in error -- the bankers who had made the $1,200.00 loan and had obtained the mortgage on the land. It is impossible to know for certain which lawyer represented which set of defendants in error, but -- because Stephen Logan was the more established lawyer -- he most likely represented the bankers. Lincoln probably represented the young couple, Mary Jane Wash and Milton Wash.

The Illinois Supreme Court observed that, "A delivery is essential to the validity of every deed. In order to constitute a complete delivery, it is requisite that there should be an acceptance by or on behalf of the grantee." The Court also remarked that -- in the case of a gift of land, especially when the

153

recipient of the gift was an infant -- a presumption arose in favor of finding that delivery of the deed had occurred. The Court concluded that the necessary delivery had occurred in this case when the grandfather, George Bryan, had initially deposited the deed with his own son, Nicholas Bryan, in behalf of his granddaughter, Mary Jane. The Court concluded that the discretion which the grandfather gave to his son, as to when the son should turn the deed itself over to the granddaughter, concerned only the physical evidence of the title to the land, but did not concern the question whether the grandfather had intended to accomplish a delivery in favor of his granddaughter at the moment that he deposited the deed with his own son, Nicholas Bryan.

The Illinois Supreme Court affirmed the judgment of the Circuit Court of Sangamon County in favor of the granddaughter, Mary Jane Wash, and her husband, Milton Wash. Lincoln had thus successfully defended against the appeal in behalf of his clients.

62

The case of *Wright vs. Bennett,* 7 Ill. 587 (1845), demonstrates that even Lincoln could sometimes -- as a result of taking the cases that came his way -- be found making an argument which was legally correct but intrinsically unfair. The case involved the duty -- of a father of an illegitimate child -- to support that child.

Under the traditional common law, as it was developed in England, the father of an illegitimate child was not entitled to take custody of that child away from the child's mother. The father of an illegitimate child also apparently did not have any legal duty to support an illegitimate child.

The Illinois legislature enacted a statute on January 23, 1827, concerning a father's duty to support an illegitimate child. The statute provided that a man -- who had been convicted in a paternity case of being the father of an illegitimate child -- should give a bond and security in the amount of $500.00, in order to guarantee his payment of support for that illegitimate child for a period not to exceed seven years. The statute authorized a circuit court to require the father of an illegitimate child to pay child support in an amount not exceeding $50.00 per year, during that seven-year period.

The statute also contained a provision that -- if the illegitimate father should begin to pay the child support ordered by a circuit court, for the support of his illegitimate child -- he was entitled "to take charge and have the control of said child": that is, the father was absolutely entitled to take the child away from the mother. The statute provided also that -- if the mother refused to surrender the child to the father -- then the father would be released from any further duty to pay support for the child.

Richard Bennett had an illegitimate child by Jane Davidson. On June 4, 1844, Richard Bennett was convicted in the Circuit Court of Menard County, Illinois, of being the father of Jane Davidson's illegitimate child. The circuit court ordered Richard Bennett to pay child support in the amount of $40.00 per year during the seven-year period which began on November 6,

1843, for the support, maintenance, and education of his illegitimate child.

Richard Bennett promptly posted his bond and security for the amount of $500.00 but then, on June 8, 1844, demanded that Jane Davidson, the mother of the child, surrender the child to him. The mother, Jane Davidson, apparently refused to surrender her child to Richard Bennett.

Richard Bennett asserted that -- as a result of Jane Davidson's refusal to surrender the child to him -- he was released from any further obligation to support the child.

Jane Davidson brought an action in the Circuit Court of Menard County, Illinois, for the use and benefit of her child, in an effort to collect from Richard Bennett, and from the surety on his child support bond, the amount of child support which Richard Bennett should have paid for the child. Richard Bennett tendered to her the amount of $3.55 before the trial of the case, and asserted that that was all the child support that had accrued before her refusal -- to turn over the child to him -- terminated his obligation to pay child support. Jane Davidson replied to Richard Bennett's argument, about the supposed termination of his obligation to pay child support, by asserting that the statute in question contemplated the father's executing two bonds so that -- if the father demanded custody of the child and the mother refused to turn the child over to the father, thereby terminating the father's obligation under the first bond -- the second bond would remain, and would provide for the father's continuing support of the child. The circuit court agreed with Richard Bennett, however, and entered a judgment in his favor.

In behalf of her child, Jane Davidson appealed from that judgment to the Illinois Supreme Court. Lincoln represented Richard Bennett in defending him against the appeal.

Lincoln filed a brief, for Richard Bennett, which stated as follows: "Only one bond is necessary under the statute. The rule of the common law, it is admitted, did not permit it, but we are to be governed by the statute in this case."

Judge Purple of the Illinois Supreme Court wrote, in the Court's decision, "I regret that, upon a careful and attentive consideration of the law, I can find nothing in its various provisions to warrant this construction [that is, the construction of the statute advanced by Jane Davidson's attorney], and am reluctantly compelled to admit that, if the reputed father of an illegitimate child, under the law as it existed at the time of the commencement of this suit, will have the inhumanity, in its helpless and dependent infancy, to demand its surrender by the mother, the law, upon her refusal, imposes upon him no further obligation to aid in its maintenance and support, at least so long as she persists in her refusal. . . . the law is plain, and admits of but one interpretation. But one bond is required. If this be given, and the child unnaturally and unfeelingly demanded, it must be surrendered, or the unfortunate mother must struggle with her own adversity as best she may." The Illinois Supreme Court affirmed the judgment in favor of Lincoln's client, Richard Bennett.

63

The case of *Kincaid vs. Turner*, 7 Ill. 618 (1845), involved the intentional setting of a prairie fire, which grew out of the control of the person who had set it and which destroyed another man's property.

John Kincaid had set the prairie fire in Menard County, Illinois. Starling Turner was the man whose property the prairie fire had destroyed.

Starling Turner sued John Kincaid in the Circuit Court of Menard County. He brought an action for "trespass on the case," in which he alleged that Kincaid had set the fire on the prairie, and had so negligently watched it as to permit it to grow out of control and to destroy his (Turner's) property.

Before the case went to trial, Turner and Kincaid decided to submit their dispute to three arbitrators, who were to decide the case, if possible, by rendering a unanimous decision. The three arbitrators were unable to reach a unanimous decision. They approached Turner and Kincaid and gave them three options: to withdraw the case from arbitration; or to choose three other men to act as arbitrators in a new arbitration proceeding; or to allow a majority of the three arbitrators to decide the case. Both of the parties stood silent in the face of these suggestions. A bystander then remarked that he supposed that the parties thought that they could not do better than for a majority of the arbitrators to make a decision. A majority of the arbitrators then wrote and signed an award in favor of Kincaid.

Starling Turner rejected this award and returned to the Circuit Court of Menard County to litigate the matter. The circuit court submitted the case to a jury, which returned a verdict in favor of Turner for the amount of $150.00. The circuit court entered a judgment upon that verdict in favor of Turner, and Kincaid appealed from the judgment to the Illinois Supreme Court.

Lincoln and another lawyer named T.L. Harris represented Turner in defending against the appeal.

Kincaid's lawyer argued that the parties' silence, when the arbitrators made the three suggestions to them, amounted to their consent that a majority -- rather than a unanimity -- of the arbitrators should decide the case. Kincaid's lawyer submitted a brief to the Illinois Supreme Court which asserted this point quaintly:

> "Silence gives consent, for instance, the marriage ceremony. If a man bawled out 'aye!' when his assent was asked by the minister, he would be considered as caring nothing about it. It is the silence that gives the consent."

Lincoln and Harris submitted a brief in which they argued simply, "When questions of fact are submitted to the jury, they are the sole judges."

The Illinois Supreme Court concluded that it fell within the jury's discretion to decide what the parties' silence meant in the face of the three suggestions made by the arbitrators. The Court stated that -- although the jury, if it had wished, could have concluded that the parties had agreed, by their silence, to allow a majority of the arbitrators to make the award -- the jury was completely free to decide that the parties had not so agreed, and to return a verdict in favor of Starling Turner. The Illinois Supreme Court thus refused to disturb the jury's verdict, and affirmed the circuit court's judgment in favor of Lincoln's client, Starling Turner.

64

The case of *Cunningham vs. Fithian,* 7 Ill. 650 (1845), was related to the earlier case of *McDonald vs. Fithian,* 6 Ill. 269 (1844). The Illinois Supreme Court's decision in the second case, *Cunningham vs. Fithian,* states that Stephen Logan, Abraham Lincoln, and E.D. Baker had all been attorneys for the appellees in both cases, but that their names had been accidently omitted from the reported decision in the earlier case of *McDonald vs. Fithian.*

The two cases involved a land speculation in Milwaukee, Wisconsin Territory, in which several citizens of Vermillion County, Illinois, engaged in 1836. Isaac Moores (as the agent for Alexander McDonald), James Murphy (as the agent for John Murphy), Hezekiah Cunningham, and William Fithian went to Milwaukee in March, 1836, for the purpose of purchasing lots in that city. After they arrived in Milwaukee, Fithian proposed to act in behalf of their group, as the agent to contract with Solomon Juneau for the purpose of purchasing four acres of land from him. Fithian told the others that he had had dealings with Juneau, and that he would succeed better in the negotiations with Juneau than they would.

The others agreed that Fithian should act as the agent for the group in negotiating with Juneau. The individuals' agreement was that -- after Fithian's purchase of the four acres of land from Juneau -- each of the four individuals in the group was to own one acre of land.

After the four individuals in the group of prospective purchasers entered in this agreement, Fithian negotiated with Juneau for the purchase of four acres of land. Juneau demanded the enormous sum of $3,000.00 per acre. Fithian persuaded his associates that they -- and he, as a member of their group -- should agree to pay a total of $12,000.00 for the four acres.

Fithian, however, had supposedly entered into a secret agreement with Juneau. The terms of that secret agreement were that Juneau was actually willing to sell the land to the group of four investors for the total amount of $9,000.00; but that, in return for Fithian's getting that $9,000.00 out of his three associates, for Juneau, Fithian should receive his one acre from Juneau free of charge.

In making the purchase of the four acres, McDonald, Murphy, and Cunningham gave Fithian their promissory notes for their share of the exorbitant purchase price, and Fithian paid his own money over to Juneau. Fithian later sued McDonald and Cunningham on their promissory notes and obtained judgments against them. McDonald and Cunningham then sought injunctions against Fithian, in order to prevent him from collecting the judgments which he had obtained against them on their promissory notes.

The Circuit Court of Vermillion County refused to grant the injunctions which McDonald and Cunningham had requested, and dismissed their respective pleadings. McDonald and Cunningham appealed to the Illinois Supreme Court from the dismissal of their pleadings. Lincoln, Logan, and Baker represented Fithian in defending him against the appeals taken by McDonald and Cunningham.

McDonald and Cunningham argued, before the Illinois Supreme Court, that Fithian had been guilty of fraud, and that, in consequence, their promissory notes to him should be rescinded. The Illinois Supreme Court stated, in the *Cunningham* case, that Cunningham had not filed his "bill" to rescind the sale until June 12, 1841, more than five years after he had discovered Fithian's alleged fraud. In the meantime, the value of the four acres in Milwaukee declined greatly. The Illinois Supreme Court stated, "It is a well settled rule in equity, that where a party seeks to rescind a contract for fraud, he must ask the aid of the court in a reasonable time, and be in a situation to restore to the opposite party whatever he may have received from him. He has no right to lie by for a long time, however, for the purpose of first ascertaining whether he may not be able to realize a profit out of the contract . . . ." The Court held -- in the *Cunningham* case -- that Cunningham had waited too long to sue Fithian, and that he had thereby lost his right to rescind the contract on the basis of Fithian's alleged fraud. In the earlier *McDonald* case, the Court had held, after considering the evidence in minute detail, that there was insufficient evidence of fraud on Fithian's part. In both cases, therefore, the Illinois

Supreme Court affirmed the circuit court's judgment in favor of Lincoln's client, William Fithian.

One gets the impression, from reading the decisions of the Illinois Supreme Court in the first half of the 1800s, that cases frequently dragged on for years, and even decades. The case of *Wilson vs. Van Winkle,* 7 Ill. 684 (1845), provides an example of such delay.

On March 11, 1816, George Eller had made a promissory note to Thomas Wilson for the amount of $450.00, which he was to pay on October 15, 1818. Thomas Wilson assigned the promissory note to Hiram Van Winkle on October 29, 1818.

In February, 1819, (when Abraham Lincoln would have been a boy 10 years of age in Indiana) Hiram Van Winkle commenced an action against George Eller, and recovered a judgment against him for the principal amount of the promissory note, plus interest. In the same year, 1819, George Eller filed an action for an injunction against both Hiram Van Winkle and Thomas Wilson, and alleged that he had given the promissory note to Thomas Wilson in payment for a tract of land which he had purchased from Thomas Wilson. He alleged further that Thomas Wilson had had no title to the land, and that, in consequence, the sale contract between George Eller and Thomas Wilson should be rescinded and an injunction should be issued against Thomas Wilson and his assignee of the promissory note, Hiram Van Winkle, prohibiting them from collecting the judgment which Hiram Van Winkle had obtained on the promissory note. George Eller initially obtained an injunction staying (that is, delaying indefinitely) proceedings by Hiram Van Winkle or Thomas Wilson to collect the judgment entered against George Eller on the promissory note. In his answer to the complaint for an injunction, Van Winkle alleged that he had paid a valuable consideration to Thomas Wilson in order to acquire the promissory note, and denied that Thomas Wilson had practiced any fraud upon George Eller. Wilson, in his answer to the complaint for an injunction, essentially denied that he had committed any fraud.

The injunction action -- among George Eller, Thomas Wilson, and Hiram Van Winkle -- then was continued until

April, 1835: that is, for a period of 16 years. The circuit court entered a final decree in April, 1835, in which it determined that Thomas Wilson had defrauded George Eller, rescinded the contract between George Eller and Thomas Wilson, and entered a perpetual injunction against Hiram Van Winkle which prohibited him from collecting the judgment which he had obtained in 1819 against George Eller on the promissory note. As a result of the entry of this decree, Hiram Van Winkle was then out the money that he had paid to Thomas Wilson on October 29, 1818, for the promissory note.

In 1841, Thomas Wilson died. Greenup Wilson was appointed the executor of the will of Thomas Wilson.

In June, 1842, Hiram Van Winkle -- 24 years after he had paid Thomas Wilson for the assignment of George Eller's promissory note -- commenced an action before the probate justice of the peace of Edgar County, Illinois, against the Estate of Thomas Wilson, Deceased, to recover the consideration which he had paid to Thomas Wilson for the assignment of the promissory note. The case was tried before a jury, which returned a verdict in favor of Van Winkle for the amount of $873.45. The probate justice of the peace entered a judgment upon that verdict. The executor of Thomas Wilson's estate appealed to the Circuit Court of Edgar County, where a trial *de novo* was held before the judge alone, without a jury. The trial judge entered a judgment in favor of Van Winkle for the amount of $1,015.15, which included accrued interest, on December 21, 1844. Thomas Wilson's executor appealed from that judgment to the Illinois Supreme Court.

In 1845, the case arrived before the Illinois Supreme Court. Lincoln (who was then 36 years of age) and two other attorneys represented an aging Hiram Van Winkle in defending against the appeal.

Thomas Wilson's executor made several arguments on appeal, which he had not thought to make, in the first instance, to the trial court. One such argument was that Hiram Van Winkle had allowed the statute of limitations, applicable to his claim against Thomas Wilson, to expire before having commenced his lawsuit against Thomas Wilson's estate in 1842. The Illinois Supreme Court remarked that the executor could not raise this defense for the first time on appeal, and that -- if he had wanted to rely upon it -- he should have raised the defense before the trial court.

The Illinois Supreme Court affirmed the judgment in favor of Hiram Van Winkle, and against the Estate of Thomas Wilson, Deceased, for the amount of $1,015.15, and Lincoln had successfully represented his client, Hiram Van Winkle, on appeal.

66

The law concerning defamation (that is, slander and libel) has always been quite different from the law concerning other torts. The common law of England did not regard it as necessarily defamatory of another person to say that that other person had been unchaste, or that he had committed adultery or fornication. The Illinois legislature adopted a statute -- which remains in effect today -- which declares that it is defamatory *per se* (that is, on its face) to say of another that he has been guilty of adultery or fornication. One of the earliest decisions which concerned that statute -- *Patterson vs. Edwards,* 7 Ill. 720 (1845) -- arose from a case in which Lincoln represented the plaintiffs.

A woman identified only as Mrs. Patterson had said of another woman, identified only as Mrs. Edwards, that "Mrs. Edwards has raised a family of children by a negro, and I can prove it." Because Mrs. Edwards' husband, Ambrose Edwards, was not black, both she and he took this as an accusation that she had been guilty of the crime of fornication or the crime of adultery with one not her husband.

In those days, a woman could not simply bring an action -- nor have an action brought against her -- in her own name. Rather, her husband had to join in bringing the action with her. Consequently, Mrs. Edwards and her husband, Ambrose Edwards, brought an action against Mrs. Patterson and her husband, William Patterson, for slander in the Circuit Court of Mason County, Illinois.

Mr. and Mrs. Edwards proved at the trial of the case that Mrs. Patterson had made the statement in question. Mr. and Mrs. Patterson made the dubious defense that, on another occasion, Mrs. Patterson had made a similar statement about "Mrs. Edwards," meaning Ambrose Edwards' mother. The Pattersons apparently contended that the statement in question had been made about Ambrose Edwards' mother, rather than his wife, and that, in consequence, Ambrose Edwards and his wife could not recover damages for defamation.

A jury returned a verdict in favor of Mr. and Mrs. Edwards for the amount of $220.00, which was a substantial amount in that day. The circuit court entered a judgment in favor of Mr. and Mrs. Edwards on the verdict, and denied Mr. and Mrs. Patterson's motion for a new trial.

The Pattersons appealed from that judgment to the Illinois Supreme Court. Lincoln and another attorney named M. McConnell represented Mr. and Mrs. Edwards in defending against the appeal.

The Illinois Supreme Court found that Mr. and Mrs. Edwards' complaint was defective because it did not set forth enough facts to show that Mrs. Patterson's accusation was one of fornication or adultery. The Court apparently believed that Mr. and Mrs. Edwards should also have alleged, in their complaint, that Mr. Edwards was not black, and that the accusation necessarily implied that Mrs. Edwards had engaged in a relationship with a man who was not her husband.

The Illinois Supreme Court reversed the judgment in favor of Mr. and Mrs. Edwards, and remanded the case to the circuit court to permit Mr. and Mrs. Edwards to amend their complaint. Lincoln had lost his defense against the appeal.

67

The case of *Griggs vs. Gear,* 8 Ill. 2 (1845), involved a larger amount of damages -- $36,208.02 -- than any other case in which Lincoln had previously participated. The case concerned a partnership formed for the purpose of conducting lead mining at Galena, Illinois.

In 1835, David Griggs and his company, Griggs & Weld, entered into a partnership agreement with Hezekiah Gear for the purpose of engaging in the lead business at Galena, Illinois. Pursuant to the terms of that partnership agreement, Griggs & Weld were to supply Gear with all the money that he should require for the business, and Gear was to superintend the business at Galena, and to ship the lead to Boston, where it was to be sold by Griggs & Weld.

Griggs & Weld had a falling out with Gear. The firm had furnished goods to Gear worth more than $13,000.00, and had demanded payment from Gear. Gear had refused to pay. On his part, Gear claimed that Griggs & Weld had refused to furnish the capital that he had required to engage in the lead busines successfully and that, in consequence, he had suffered damage in excess of $100,000.00.

Griggs & Weld retained attorneys in Jo Daviess County, Illinois, to bring an action at law against Gear for the $13,000.00 in goods which the firm had supplied to him.

In response, Gear filed a bill in equity, by which he sought to enjoin Griggs & Weld from maintaining its action at law against Gear. Gear apparently was successful in obtaining the injunction which he desired, and Griggs & Weld were enjoined from proceeding with its action at law against Gear.

In 1839, without having obtained any authority from Griggs & Weld to do so, the attorneys which represented Griggs & Weld in the action at law filed a motion, in behalf of Griggs & Weld, in the equity case, for the purpose of seeking to have the injunction against Griggs & Weld dissolved. The Circuit Court of Jo Daviess County denied that motion in 1841, and, in 1842, the circuit court further ordered that an official known as a "special master" take evidence concerning Gear's allegations that Griggs & Weld's failure to supply capital to him had caused him to suffer a great loss in the lead mining business. The special master reported to the circuit court, in 1844, that the failure of Griggs & Weld to fulfill its obligations under the partnership agreement had caused Gear to suffer a loss of $50,000.00. From that amount, the special master had deducted the value of the goods furnished by Griggs & Weld to Gear -- that is $13,791.98 -- leaving a balance of $36,208.02 owed by Griggs & Weld to Gear. The circuit court approved the report and entered a decree requiring Griggs & Weld to pay Gear damages in the amount of $36,208.02.

The first that the firm of Griggs & Weld learned of its involvement in the separate equity action, in which the circuit court had ordered to pay the huge amount of $36,208.02, was apparently when Gear sought to collect that amount from the firm of Griggs & Weld.

Griggs & Weld, realizing that it had not been served well by its initial attorneys, obtained different attorneys, who filed a "bill of review" in the Circuit Court of Jo Daviess County, Illinois, in which they asserted that Griggs & Weld had never authorized its initial attorneys to enter an appearance for it in the equity action and that the circuit court had had no jurisdiction over it for the purpose of ordering it to pay Gear anything. Gear filed a demurrer -- that is, a motion to dismiss -- Griggs & Weld's bill of review. The circuit court sustained the demurrer, and dismissed Griggs & Weld's bill of review.

Griggs & Weld appealed from the dismissal, of its bill of review, to the Illinois Supreme Court. An attorney named J.W. Chickering filed a brief for Griggs & Weld. Three other lawyers participated in filing two briefs in behalf of Hezekiah Gear. Lincoln, representing Griggs & Weld, then "replied at length to the arguments of the counsel" for Hezekiah Gear.

The Illinois Supreme Court remarked, in its opinion, that Griggs & Weld had not retained its initial attorneys to appear in the equity case at all and that, rather, Griggs & Weld had not even known of the existence of the equity case until after the final decree, requiring it to pay $36,000.00 to Gear, had been entered. The Court proceeded to say, of Griggs & Weld's initial attorneys, "It further appears, that those attorneys are irresponsible. Can it be tolerated for a moment, that parties are to be bound by a decree to pay more than $36,000.00 which is entered up behind their backs, and without even an implied knowledge of the existence of the suit, and without their having any adequate remedy over against anyone? . . . . We cannot consent to attach such a sanctity to the character and conduct of a solicitor, that he may bind strangers, without their privity or consent in proceedings which may be utterly ruinous to them, and without their being able to respond for the damages which they may occasion, no matter how honest may be their motives. If the fortunes of all our citizens are held by so frail a tenure as this, -- if they may be utterly ruined without redress, either by the carelessness, the ignorance or the dishonesty of everyone who may get a license to practice law in a country where there are so many facilities for obtaining a license as in this, it is quite time that everyone should know it."

Having thus reproached Griggs & Weld's intial attorneys, the Illinois Supreme Court concluded that Griggs & Weld had never truly entered its appearance in the equity case, that the circuit court had never had personal jurisdiction over the equity case, and that, therefore, the circuit court's decree -- requiring Griggs & Weld to pay more than $36,000.00 to Gear -- could not stand.

The Illinois Supreme Court reversed the decree of the circuit court which had dismissed Griggs & Weld's bill of review. The Court remanded the case to the Circuit Court of Jo Daviess County for further proceedings on Griggs & Weld's bill of review. Lincoln and his co-counsel, J.W. Chickering, had saved Griggs & Weld from financial ruin.

The case of *Edgar County vs. Mayo,* 8 Ill. 82 (1846), involved the question whether the clerk of a circuit court of a county was entitled to recover, from the county, his fee for having issued two legal writs at the request of the county's state's attorney.

Two individuals in Edgar County, Illinois -- Andrew J. Hanks and Enos Rawley -- apparently had been charged with the commission of crimes by that county's state's attorney. Both Andrew J. Hanks and Enos Rawley had been freed on a "recognizance." A recognizance, in a criminal case, is the mere promise by an accused person to comply with the conditions set forth in the recognizance, or, upon his failure to do so, to pay the penalty specified in the recognizance.

Andrew J. Hanks and Enos Rawley apparently violated the terms of their recognizances, perhaps by failing to show up at their respective criminal trials. The state's attorney sought the issuance of a legal writ, known as a *"scire facias,"* from the Clerk of the Circuit Court of Edgar County, Illinois, as part of his effort to collect from Andrew J. Hanks and Enos Rawley the penalties specified in their recognizances.

Jonathan Mayo was the Clerk of the Circuit Court of Edgar County, Illinois. As requested by the state's attorney, he issued two writs of *scire facias,* one of which was directed against Andrew J. Hanks, and the other of which was directed against Enos Rawley.

In those days, the office of clerk of the circuit court of a county was apparently operated as a "fee office": that is, the circuit clerk collected his pay by charging a fee for each official act which he performed. In this case, Jonathan Mayo, the circuit clerk, charged Edgar County the amount of $5.87 for having issued the writ of *scire facias* directed against Andrew J. Hanks, and the additional amount of $2.06 for having issued the writ of *scire facias* directed against Enos Rawley.

The state's attorney was unable to collect anything, in behalf of the State of Illinois, under either writ, from Andrew J.

Hanks or Enos Rawley. The circuit clerk, Jonathan Mayo, submitted his bill, for the amount of $7.93, to the Commissioners of Edgar County.

The Commissioners of Edgar County refused to pay the circuit clerk's bill for $7.93.

The circuit clerk, Jonathan Mayo, then filed an action against Edgar County -- in the Circuit Court of Edgar County -- in order to collect the amount of $7.93 for his having issued the two writs of *scire facias*. The circuit court rendered a judgment in favor of the Circuit Clerk, Jonathan Mayor.

Edgar County appealed from that judgment to the Illinois Supreme Court. Lincoln represented the Circuit Clerk, Jonathan Mayo, in defending against the appeal.

Lincoln filed a brief which read, in part,

"By the common law, the defendant in error is entitled to remuneration for his services. The county called upon him to perform those services, and he has performed them. There is no law of the state, which contravenes the common law.
Cases have been cited by counsel to show that the United States never pay costs. This is not strictly true. No judgment can be rendered against the government, and to this point, only do the decisions go."

Lincoln concluded his brief with a reference to cases decided in two other states, and a reference to one case previously decided by the Illinois Supreme Court.

The Illinois Supreme Court concluded that the state's attorney "as the people's representative, prosecutes forfeited recognizances according to his own discretion or sense of duty, and acknowledges no controlling power on the part of the county officers; he cannot, therefore, by his acts, bind persons or corporations who are not his principals, but strangers to the proceeding." The Court thus concluded that -- although the states attorney's decision, to attempt to collect from Andrew J. Hanks and Enos Rawley on their forfeited recognizances, had created work for the circuit clerk, Jonathan Mayo -- the circuit clerk was not entitled to be paid by the county for his work.

The Illinois Supreme Court reversed the judgment of the Circuit Court of Edgar County, Illinois, and Lincoln had lost his defense against the appeal.

A short opinion in a case can sometimes reveal a depth of human woe. This is true of the decision in *Roney vs. Monaghan,* 8 Ill. 85 (1846).

Owen Monaghan brought an action of trespass for criminal conversation against John Roney: that is, Monaghan sought money damages from Roney on the ground that Roney allegedly had had sexual relations with Monaghan's wife. Monaghan filed his action in the Circuit Court of Lake County, Illinois.

The case was tried before a jury, which returned a verdict in favor of Monaghan, and against Roney, for the amount of $225.00. The circuit court entered a judgment, in favor of Monaghan and against Roney, on that verdict.

Roney filed a motion for a new trial, in which he asserted that the verdict was contrary to the law and the evidence. The circuit court denied the motion for a new trial, and Roney appealed to the Illinois Supreme Court.

Lincoln and two other lawyers -- G. Spring and G. Goodrich -- represented Owen Monaghan in defending against the appeal.

The Illinois Supreme Court held that the case was properly tried, and that Roney's motion for a new trial was properly denied. The Court stated, "We deem it unnecessary to review the evidence taken altogether, it is of a character to warrant the inference which the jury has drawn; that a criminal intercourse existed between Roney and the wife of Monaghan. In such cases, a court will never disturb the verdict of a jury."

Lincoln had successfully represented the agrieved husband, Owen Monaghan, in defending against the appeal.

A "voluntary nonsuit" was formerly the term used to describe a party's voluntarily dismissing, upon his own motion, his case.

A "bill of exceptions" was a list of the rulings of the trial court, upon points of evidence, to which a party took exception. For a party to rely upon a bill of exceptions as a basis for taking an appeal to the Illinois Supreme Court, it was apparently necessary that the trial judge, who had made the evidentiary rulings, sign the bill of exceptions, thereby verifying that it correctly reported both his rulings and the party's exceptions thereto.

A "writ of mandamus" is a writ issued by a court to some official, requiring that official to perform an official duty.

In the case of *People ex rel. Harris vs. Browne,* 8 Ill. 87 (1846), an individual named Daniel S. Harris had filed a law suit in the Circuit Court of Jo Daviess County, Illinois, in October, 1842. The case was tried before a jury. In the course of the jury trial, however, the trial judge -- Thomas C. Browne -- made various rulings that Harris thought to be wrong. Harris asked that his exceptions to those rulings be noted in the record of the case.

Rather than allow the case to proceed to a verdict of the jury, however, Harris then decided to take a voluntary nonsuit: that is, he voluntarily dismissed his case.

After having voluntarily dismissed his case, Harris sought to take an appeal from the adverse rulings by the trial judge, on the points of evidence, to the Illinois Supreme Court. In preparing to take his appeal, he sought to have the trial judge, Thomas C. Browne, sign the bill of exceptions which Harris had prepared.

The trial judge, Thomas C. Browne, refused to sign the bill of exceptions on the ground that -- in view of Harris' having voluntarily dismissed his case -- there was nothing to which he could thereafter take exception.

In the face of Browne's refusal to sign the bill of exceptions, Harris applied to the Illinois Supreme Court for a writ of mandamus, which he sought to have directed against Browne, and which would have required Browne to sign the bill of exceptions. Harris applied to the Illinois Supreme Court for the writ of mandamus in December, 1842, but his attorney did not press the matter until August 28, 1846.

The trial judge, Thomas C. Browne, persisted in his refusal to sign the bill of exceptions. Lincoln represented Browne in defending against the writ of mandamus.

The Illinois Supreme Court concluded that Harris "took a voluntarily nonsuit in the circuit court, and having voluntarily gone out of court, he cannot call upon this court to reverse a judgment, which was entered at his own solicitation, whether the court committed errors in the proceedings of the course previous to the nonsuit or not." The Illinois Supreme Court denied Harris' motion for a writ of mandamus.

Lincoln had successfully defended the trial judge, Thomas C. Browne, against the motion for a writ of mandamus.

71

In the parlance of Lincoln's era in Illinois, a "grocery" was an establishment which made retail sales of alcoholic liquor: that is, in other words, a bar. During the first of the Lincoln-Douglas debates -- on August 21, 1858, in Ottawa, Illinois -- Douglas accused Lincoln of having been a "flourishing grocery-keeper in the town of Salem" (meaning the village of New Salem) as a young man. Lincoln answered this charge in a humorous fashion, in his reply to Douglas, in the following words: "Now I pass on to consider one or two more of these little follies. The Judge [that is, Douglas] is woefully at fault about his early friend Lincoln being a 'grocery-keeper.' I don't know as it would be a great sin, if I had been; but he is mistaken, Lincoln never kept a grocery anywhere in the world. It is true that Lincoln did work the latter part of one winter in a little still-house, up at the head of a hollow."

For any contract to be binding upon the parties thereto, each party must have given to the other a "consideration." If the consideration given by one party is illegal, and against the public policy of the State, however, the contract itself is illegal and is not enforceable by either party to the contract.

The case of *Munsell vs. Temple,* 8 Ill. 93 (1846), involved the purported transfer of a liquor license, and the validity of the transferee's promise to pay the treasurer of McLean County, Illinois, the amount of $21.38 for that transfer.

Even in the 1840s, the State of Illinois restricted the operation of groceries (that is, bars) by requiring that a grocery be operated only pursuant to a liquor license issued by the county commissioners. The relevant statute -- known as the License Act -- provided as follows: "County commissioners may grant licenses to keep groceries upon the following conditions, to wit: First, the applicant shall pay into the county treasury, for the privilege granted, a sum not exceeding $300.00, nor less than $25.00, in the discretion of the court . . . ."

The County Commissioners of McLean County, Illinois, had initially issued a license to James E. Parke in March, 1843, to operate a grocery in the Bloomington Hotel in Bloomington, Illinois. Parke gave the treasurer of McLean County, Illinois, a promissory note for $25.00 for that license. In June, 1843, Roswell Munsell applied to McLean County to have Parke's license transferred to him. The county approved that transfer, and Munsell gave his promissory note to William H. Temple, the treasurer of McLean County, for the sum of $21.38, for the transferred license. The amount of Munsell's promissory note had apparently been calculated to correspond to the portion of the term of the liquor license which remained unexpired.

Munsell did not pay the $21.38 to William H. Temple, the Treasurer of McLean County. The treasurer sued Munsell in the Circuit Court of McLean County in order to collect the amount of that promissory note.

The Circuit Court of McLean County entered a judgment against Roswell Munsell on his promissory note for the amount of $24.68. The judgment apparently included interest on the face amount of the promissory note.

Roswell Munsell appealed from that judgment to the Illinois Supreme Court. Lincoln represented him in prosecuting the appeal.

Lincoln filed the following brief in behalf of his client, Munsell:

> "The note of Parke was void because the license was not valid; the money was not paid for it, as required by law. Besides, it was not a license to the plaintiff, but to Parke, and it was not legally transferrable. Rev. Stat. 342, Sec. 9.

The note given by Munsell to the treasurer was also void. He could not, in his official capacity, take a note. *Berry v. Hanby,* 1 Scam. 468."

The Illinois Supreme Court ruled in favor of Lincoln's client, although not precisely for the reasons advanced by Lincoln.

The Illinois Supreme Court noted that, under the License Act, no license for a grocery could be legally granted for a sum of money less than $25.00. The Court held that McLean County could not take it upon itself to prorate the cost of a license over the term of the license, and that McLean County should have required Munsell to pay at least $25.00 for a liquor license, rather than only the amount of $21.38.

The Illinois Supreme Court also ruled that liquor licenses were not transferable from one person to another, and that McLean County should not have approved the transfer of James E. Parke's liquor license to Roswell Munsell. (This continues to be the law in Illinois: namely, that liquor licenses are not transferable from one person to another, but must be issued anew to the purchaser of a tavern or liquor store.)

The Court concluded, finally, that it was a violation of the statute for McLean County to permit a transfer of a liquor license to Roswell Munsell on credit, rather than for an immediate payment of cash.

The Court thus concluded that Roswell Munsell's promise to pay the amount of $21.38, to the Treasurer of McLean County, Illinois, was founded upon a contract which violated both the law and the public policy of the State of Illinois and which was, in consequence, illegal and void. The Court reversed the judgment of the Circuit Court of McLean County.

Lincoln had thus won the appeal for his client, Roswell Munsell.

72

The case of *Fell vs. Price,* 8 Ill. 186 (1846), involved an effort, by two different judgment creditors of a single judgment debtor, to seize and sell the same tract of land twice in order to collect the respective judgment debts owed to them.

The facts of the case are so convoluted as to make it helpful to identify the various parties involved in it.

Jesse W. Fell of McLean County, Illinois, owned three tracts of land near Bloomington, Illinois: namely, (1) Lot Number 2 in the NE 1/2 of Section 16, Township 23 North, Range 2 East of the Third Principal Meridian; (2) a separate five-acre tract of land near Bloomington; and (3) a piece of timberland described as Lot Number 16 in Section 16, Township 23 North, Range 2 East of the Third Principal Meridian.

Jesse W. Fell's father, who also played a part in this case, was Jesse Fell, Sr.

Nathan Low was the father of John N. Low.

About May, 1838, Nathan Low obtained a judgment against Jesse Fell for the amount of $220.81, plus costs, and an "execution" (that is, a writ authorizing the sheriff's seizure and sale of a judgment debtor's property) was issued on March 10, 1839, which was levied upon the first two tracts of land owned by Jesse W. Fell. The two tracts of land were sold, pursuant to that execution, on June 16, 1839. John N. Low -- the son of Nathan Low -- appeared at the sale and acted as the agent for his father. John N. Low purchased the two tracts of land by bidding in the amount of the judgment obtained by Nathan Low against Jesse W. Fell. The sheriff delivered a certificate of purchase to John N. Low in his own name, since Nathan Low had not appeared personally at the execution sale. The certificate of purchase indicated that John N. Low would be entitled to receive a deed for the two tracts of land after the expiration of twelve months after the date of sale -- that is, after June 16, 1840 -- if the judgment debtor, Jesse W. Fell, did not redeem the tracts of land from the execution sale by paying the judgment debt which he owed to Nathan Low.

On May 11, 1840, when Jesse W. Fell had only about a month left in which to redeem his tracts of land, he entered into an agreement with his judgment creditor, Nathan Low, in order to extend his redemption time. Under that agreement, Jesse W. Fell delivered to Nathan Low a deed to his first two tracts of land and, as additional security to Nathan Low, a deed to the third tract of land. Nathan Low executed an agreement by which he promised to reconvey these three tracts to Jesse W. Fell upon Jesse W. Fell's having paid the amount of the judgment debt to him within a certain time.

Jesse W. Fell was not able to pay the amount which he owed to Nathan Low, however, and, with Jesse W. Fell's consent, Nathan Low sold the first two tracts of land to an individual named C. H. Perry on November 20, 1840. C. H. Perry paid the fair market value of the land at that time, which was apparently $100.00.

C. H. Perry thereafter sold the land to Jesse W. Fell's father -- Jesse Fell, Sr. -- on November 20, 1842. After his purchase of the land, Jesse Fell, Sr., made improvements worth about $1,000.00 on the land.

Between the date of the execution sale to John N. Low (June 16, 1839) and the date of Jesse W. Fell's deed to Nathan Low (May 11, 1840) another of Fell's creditors -- Robert Price -- had obtained a judgment against Fell for $513.97 in October, 1839. Robert Price caused the Sheriff of McLean County to levy a second execution against Jesse W. Fell's first two tracts of land.

When Robert Price was on the verge of having the two tracts of land sold, the individuals who had purchased those two tracts of land, in succession, from Nathan Low -- namely, C. H. Perry and Jesse Fell, Sr. -- filed a bill for an injunction in the Circuit Court of McLean County, Illinois, in an effort to prohibit Robert Price from selling the tracts of land again pursuant to the execution which he obtained. Robert Price's theory was apparently that the deed of May 11, 1840, from Jesse W. Fell to Nathan Low, vi\iated the effect of the first execution sale held on June 16, 1839, and thereby permitted Robert Price to enforce the execution lien which he obtained on the tracts of land in October, 1839.

The circuit court agreed with Robert Price's view of the case. The circuit court entered an injunction against Robert Price, as sought by C. H. Perry and Jesse Fell, Sr., but conditioned the effectiveness of the injunction upon the payment, by those individuals, of the amount of $100.00 to Robert Price. That amount -- $100.00 -- was the fair market value of the land as of the time that Robert Price's execution lien attached to the land, and before Jesse Fell, Sr., made $1,000.00 in improvements on the land.

C. H. Perry and Jesse Fell, Sr., appealed to the Illinois Supreme Court from that decree entered by the Circuit Court of McLean County. Lincoln represented C. H. Perry and Jesse Fell, Sr., in prosecuting the appeal.

The Illinois Supreme Court agreed with Lincoln's arguments, and concluded that the deed -- from Jesse W. Fell to Nathan Low on May 11, 1840 -- did not vitiate the first execution sale. The Court concluded, therefore, that Robert Price acquired no rights in the land by reason of his subsequent judgment. The Court stated, "The injunction ought to have been made perpetual without a condition, and at the cost of the defendants."

The Court reversed the decree of the Circuit Court of McLean County, Illinois, and ordered that the injunction should be made perpetual, against Robert Price, and without any condition requiring C. H. Perry and Jesse Fell, Sr., to pay Robert Price anything. Lincoln had thus won the appeal for his clients, C. H. Perry and Jesse Fell, Sr.

73

The case of *Wright vs. Taylor*, 8 Ill. 193 (1846), involved a promissory note that had been assigned to the State Bank of Illinois, which bank had become bankrupt and had been put in liquidation by a statute passed on January 24, 1843.

John Wright had executed three promissory notes, for the amount of $672.08 each, payable to John Taylor. The promissory notes were to become due one year, two years, and three years, respectively, after John Wright executed them on March 6, 1841. To secure his payments of the promissory notes, John Wright delivered a mortgage, of land that he owned, to John Taylor.

Wright paid the amount of the first promissory note on time. He defaulted, however, in paying the second promissory note.

Taylor filed, in the Circuit Court of Menard County, Illinois, a bill to foreclose his mortgage on Wright's land.

Wright filed an answer to the bill, in which he admitted that he had executed the second promissory note and that he had not paid the promissory note. He raised as a defense, however, the fact that Taylor had assigned that second promissory note, for the amount of $672.08, to the State Bank of Illinois, in payment of a debt which he, Taylor, owed to that bank. Taylor's assignment of the promissory note to the State Bank of Illinois was relevant to the issues in this case because an Illinois statute, passed on December 22, 1842, provided "That all debts or demands due by note or otherwise, unto the President, Directors and Company of the Bank of Illinois, or to the State Bank of Illinois, or that may hereafter become due unto either of said banks, may, after or before suit brought thereon, be discharged and paid in notes and bills of said Banks respectively to which said debt or demand may be due, whether the same be in possession of said Bank or Banks, or assigned or transferred to any corporation, person or persons."

In that day, notes issued by local banks were apparently used as currency, just as the official currency issued by the United States Treasurer is used today. Because the State Bank of Illinois was bankrupt, the value of the notes that it had issued had sunk in value to only 26 cents on the dollar.

John Taylor had assigned that second promissory note to the State Bank of Illinois in payment of $672.08 worth of debt which he himself owed to the State Bank of Illinois. John Taylor bought it back from the bank, with bank paper, for only 26 cents on the dollar; that is, for the amount of $174.74. Yet John Taylor insisted that Wright pay him the full $672.08, in order to prevent his mortgaged land from being sold.

Wright's argument was that he should likewise be allowed to pay the promissory note for $672.08 -- which Taylor then held for the second time -- in notes that had been issued by the State Bank of Illinois. If he did so, he would be able to discharge his debt, on the promissory note, by paying only 26 cents on the dollar: that is, by paying Taylor only $174.74.

The Circuit Court of Menard County agreed with Taylor, however, and entered a decree of foreclosure which would have required Wright to pay the full $672.08 to Taylor, in order to redeem his land from the decree of foreclosure.

Wright appealed from that decree to the Illinois Supreme Court. Lincoln represented John Taylor in defending against the appeal.

The Illinois Supreme Court concluded that -- after the State Bank of Illinois had become the holder and legal owner of the promissory note in question -- "The maker had an unquestionable right in law to pay it in the paper of the bank." The Court stated further, "In no event could he be compelled to pay in any funds except the paper of the bank. . . . Having been once the absolute property of the bank, and over due, the maker's right to discharge the bank's indebtedness accompanied it into whose hands soever it might afterwards fall, as fully as to all intents and purposes, as it would have done if it had been so stipulated upon the note itself." In other words, once the note had passed through the hands of the State Bank of Illinois, Wright was authorized by the statute to discharge his indebtedness on the note by paying the holder thereof (Taylor, for a second time) bank paper, or the equivalent thereof: namely, 26 cents on the dollar.

The Illinois Supreme Court reversed the decree of the Circuit Court of Menard County in part, so as to require Wright to pay Taylor only the amount of $174.74, with interest thereon at the rate of six percent per year, from March 7, 1843, (the day after its maturity) in order to redeem his land from the decree of foreclosure. Lincoln thus had lost his defense against the appeal for the holder of the note and mortgage, John Taylor.

74

The case of *Welch vs. Sykes,* 8 Ill. 197 (1846), involved an effort by a resident of Maryland to enforce -- in an Illinois circuit court -- against a resident of Illinois, a judgment of a Maryland trial court. The effort, by the Maryland resident to enforce the Maryland trial court's judgment in an Illinois trial court, invoked the Full Faith and Credit Clause of the United States Constitution, which states,

> "Full Faith and Credit shall be given in each State to the public Acts, Records, and judicial Proceedings of every other State." *See* U.S. Const. art. IV, section 1.

James Sykes was a resident of Maryland. He had sued a man named Watson in the County Court of Ann Arundel County, Maryland. He obtained a judgment against Watson, in the Maryland court, for "$340.00 debt, and $10.84 damages" on October 26, 1835.

James Sykes apparently thereafter located Watson in Clark County, Illinois. James Sykes brought an action against Watson, in the Circuit Court of Clark County, Illinois, based upon the judgment rendered by the Maryland trial court. Sykes sought to have the Illinois circuit court give full faith and credit to the judgment of the Maryland trial court, and to render an Illinois judgment against Watson on the basis of the Maryland judgment. The rendition of an Illinois judgment, in Sykes' favor, would have permitted Sykes to take action to collect the amount of the judgment from Watson in Illinois: that is, by having the Sheriff of Clark County, Illinois, seize and sell whatever property Watson owned within Clark County, Illinois, for the purpose of collecting enough money to pay Sykes' judgment against Watson.

The defendant, Watson, filed a demurrer (that is, a motion to dismiss) with respect to Sykes' complaint. In his demurrer, Watson raised as his third and fourth pleas the allegations that -- from the commencement of the lawsuit in Maryland until the rendition of the judgment therein -- he had resided in Ohio, outside the jurisdiction of the Maryland trial court. Watson thus argued that the Maryland trial court lacked jurisdiction over his person, and, so, could not enter a valid judgment against him. Watson asserted, in the fourth plea in his demurrer, that he had not appeared in the suit voluntarily by means of having an attorney represent him in the suit.

The Circuit Court of Clark County, Illinois, sustained Watson's demurrer with respect to the third and fourth pleas. James Sykes appealed from the ruling by the circuit court to the Illinois Supreme Court.

Lincoln represented James Sykes in prosecuting the appeal.

The Illinois Supreme Court remarked that a record of the proceedings in the suit in Maryland had not been made a part of the record in this case: that is, the record of the proceedings had not been submitted to the Circuit Court of Clark County, Illinois, and, so, was not properly a part of the record on appeal. The Illinois Supreme Court stated, however, that "a copy of the record of proceedings of the suit in Maryland, has been submitted to the inspection of the court." Lincoln had thus apparently obtained the record of the proceedings in the lawsuit in Maryland, and had submitted that record directly to the Illinois Supreme Court. It would be impossible today to submit such a document -- which had not been first submitted to the trial court below -- directly to the Illinois Supreme Court for its consideration. Nonetheless, the Illinois Supreme Court both received the document from Lincoln, and considered it.

The record of the proceedings in the lawsuit in Maryland stated that an attorney had appeared therein for the defendant Watson. The Illinois Supreme Court indicated that this statement, in the record of the proceedings in the suit in Maryland, must be taken as "conclusive proof that the attorney appeared for him, but only *prima facie* evidence of the authority of the attorney to appear, and which latter fact the defendant is at full liberty to disprove." The Illinois Supreme Court concluded that, on the basis of the record of the proceedings in the lawsuit in Maryland, James Sykes should be considered, in the first instance, to have proved that the defendant Watson had voluntarily submitted to the jurisdiction of the Maryland trial court by engaging an attorney to appear for him in that lawsuit. The Court indicated, however, that the defendant Watson was

187

free to attempt to prove that the attorney which appeared in that proceeding had not been authorized by him, Watson, so to appear.

The Illinois Supreme Court reversed the circuit court's sustaining the third and fourth pleas contained in the defendant Watson's demurrer, and remanded the case for further proceedings. Lincoln had won the appeal for his client, James Sykes.

75

The case of *Hawks vs. Lands,* 8 Ill. 227 (1846), involved an unhappy end to a partnership of two men.

Samuel Lands and Matthew Hawks had been partners in trade, apparently in McLean County, Illinois. They had dissolved their partnership, and had caused the partnership's property to be transferred to Hawks. Hawks had agreed to pay all of the partnership's debts. Hawks had failed to pay a $500 debt owed by the partnership to Thomas C. Rockhill & Co., which company had then collected the $500 from Lands.

Lands brought an action of *assumpsit* (that is, an action based upon a contract) against Hawks in the Circuit Court of McLean County, Illinois. Lands alleged in his declaration (that is, his complaint) that he had paid a $500 debt owed by the partnership, which Hawks should have paid, and that, in consequence, he was entitled to recover $500 from Hawks. Before trial, Lands obtained the circuit court's permission to amend his declaration slightly, for the purpose of stating that the creditor -- to which he had paid the partnership's debt of $500 -- was Thomas C. Rockhill & Co. Hawks used this amendment of the declaration as an occasion for asking the circuit court to continue the trial of the case. The circuit court refused to continue the case, to which refusal Hawks excepted.

Hawks filed an answer in the case which consisted of three defenses. He asserted, first, *non assumpsit:* that is, that he had made no such contract with Lands. He contended, second, that -- in 1838 -- he had paid Lands $1,200 for the conveyance of land located in "the town of Washington"; that Lands had made the conveyance with a "covenant of seizin" (that is, with a representation that he owned a good title to the land); and that Lands had not owned a good title to the land, as a result of which Hawks had lost the value of the $1,200 which he had paid to Lands. Hawks alleged that his own $1,200 loss -- from dealing with Lands -- should be set off against the $500 that Lands claimed from him, thereby reducing Lands' claim to nothing. Hawks asserted, as his third defense, that he had already paid to Lands the amount which he sought.

Lands filed a demurrer to (that is, he moved to strike) the second plea concerning the alleged set-off against his own claim. The circuit court sustained his demurrer, and dismissed Hawks' plea of a set-off.

The circuit court rendered a judgment in favor of Lands, and against Hawks, for the amount of $419.43. Hawks appealed from the judgment to the Illinois Supreme Court.

Lincoln represented Hawks in prosecuting the appeal. He filed a brief in which he argued that Hawks' motion for a continuance should have been allowed, and that Hawks' plea of a set-off should have been permitted. His brief read as follows:

"As to the sufficiency of the plea of set-off, that it shows a cause of action in Covenant, see 2 Cond. R. 157, 160; 1 Ohio 171-2; 2 Mass. 455; and that being such a cause of action, it may by our statute be set-off. Edwards v. Todd, 1 Scam. 464; Nichols v. Ruckels, 3 do. 298.

As to the question of continuance, see Covell v. Marks, 1 Scam. 525; Ewing v. French, 1 Blackf. 170; Kelly v. Duignan, 2 do. 420; and as to matter of substance, see 1 Eng. Com. Law R. 136; Cooper 286, 288, head paging; 9 Johns.291; 3 J.J. Marsh. 332."

The Illinois Supreme Court indicated that -- if Lands' amendment to his pleading, by which he had simply named the creditor to which he had paid the partnership's $500 debt -- had caused a *material* change in his action, Hawks might have been entitled to a continuance on the basis of the amendment. The amendment in question, however, changed nothing of significance in Lands' pleading, and, so, Hawks was not entitled to a continuance of the trial on the basis of the amendment.

The Illinois Supreme Court also concluded, that under an Illinois statute concerning the pleading of set-offs, Hawks could not properly allege -- as a set-off to Lands' claim against him -- his loss from his earlier real estate transaction with Lands. The Court stated, in reaching this conclusion, "Unliquidated damages arising out of covenants, contracts, or torts totally disconnected with the subject matter of the plaintiff's claim, are not such 'claims or demands' as constitute the subject matter of set-off under our act of assembly. To give this construction to the statute would invest justices of the peace with full jurisdiction over questions involving the title to and covenants concerning real estate, compel parties to litigate all their rights, of whatever nature or kind, in one action, and result in irremediable injustice and endless confusion." (This reasoning has not been justified by developments in the law since the Illinois Supreme Court decided this case in 1846. For several decades at least, it has been possible in Illinois for a defendant in a case to file as a counterclaim against the plaintiff any claim that he has against the plaintiff, regardless of the nature or kind of that counterclaim, and regardless of its not being related to the plaintiff's original action against the defendant. Yet no one today asserts that such a procedure "result[s] in irremediable injustice and endless confusion.")

The Illinois Supreme Court affirmed the judgment of the Circuit Court of McLean County. Lincoln had lost the appeal for his client, Matthew Hawks.

76

The case of *Garrett vs. Stevenson,* 8 Ill 261 (1846), is perhaps more interesting for the glimpse -- of the building trade in Illinois in the 1840s -- that it gives us than for the law involved in the decision of the case.

Augustus O. Garrett and his wife, Mary G. Garrett, owned land in Peoria described as "Lots No. four and five, in block No. eight, in the town and county of Peoria." They decided to build a house on their land. Augustus O. Garrett signed a contract with builders known as Stevenson & Wardell, for the construction of a house on the land, on March 3, 1840. One of the partners and workmen in the building firm was Andrew O. Stevenson.

The contract provided that the landowner, Garrett, was to pay the builders, Stevenson & Wardell, for their labor and materials on July 1, 1840.

Stevenson & Wardell apparently commenced work on the house as soon as the weather permitted them to do so after the signing of the contract on March 3, 1840. The house and the outbuildings were of brick construction, and -- according to the Illinois Supreme Court's decision in the case -- the builders laid the following numbers of bricks in the various structures:

"Laid in the house,	575,000
" " privy,	45,000
" " ice house,	13,500
" " cistern,	3,000
" " front wall,	7,000
In all amounting to	643,500"

Stevenson & Wardell agreed to lay the brick at a charge of $4 per thousand for the first 600,000 bricks, and thereafter at a charge of $5 per thousand.

Stevenson & Wardell also applied 4,400 yards of plaster in the house, which amount included 400 yards of plaster for a rough coating for the house's ballroom. The firm's charge for applying the plaster was 21 cents per yard.

The landowner, Garrett, did not pay the builders, Stevenson & Wardell, all that they claimed from him on July 1, 1840. Garrett was apparently unhappy with the quality of their work, and asserted that it was not "workmanlike": that is, not up to the standard generally expected of workmen in their particular trade.

On October 27, 1841, Stevenson & Wardell filed a petition for a mechanic's lien -- on Garrett's land -- in the Circuit Court of Peoria County. The case was later taken, by a change of venue, into the Circuit Court of Tazewell County, where it lingered for five years before being tried.

A mechanic's lien is a lien on land which exists in favor of a "mechanic" (that is, a workman) who does work on, or supplies material to, an improvement located upon the land. If the mechanic follows the necessary procedures, he can have the land sold in order to compel the payment of his bill out of the proceeds of the sale. Even if the landowner is without funds, or has hidden away his cash assets, the mechanic is thereby enabled to use the value of the land itself in obtaining payment of his bill.

Mechanics' liens -- which are still much in use today -- were apparently first recognized in Illinois by "An Act for the benefit of mechanics," passed on February 22, 1833. That first mechanic's lien statute, however, required the mechanic claiming the lien to file his petition, to enforce the lien, in the circuit court within three months after his money became due to him.

The jury that tried this case returned a verdict in favor of the builders, Stevenson & Wardell, for the amount of $2,595.20. The circuit court entered a decree which allowed the enforcement of the mechanic's lien on the land, by requiring the sale of the land, in order to pay Stevenson & Wardell's bill.

The landowner, Garrett, appealed from the decree to the Illinois Supreme Court. Lincoln and another lawyer named H.O. Merriman represented Garrett in prosecuting the appeal.

Lincoln relied primarily on the three-month filing deadline established by the 1833 Illinois mechanic's lien statute. He asserted that -- because Stevenson & Wardell had waited until October 27, 1841, to file their petition, which date was almost 16 months after their bill had become due -- they should be barred from enforcing a mechanic's lien against the land.

The Illinois Supreme Court pointed out, in rejecting this argument by Lincoln, that a second mechanic's lien statute had become effective in the State of Illinois on December 10, 1839, and that it did not set forth any deadline for the filing of a petition to enforce a mechanic's lien. Lincoln had been aware of this argument, but had asserted -- on the basis of the Illinois Supreme Court's earlier decision in *Turney vs. Saunders,* 5 Ill. 527 (1841) -- that the first mechanic's lien statute, with its three-month filing deadline -- should apply to this case. The Court "distingushed" (that is, explained away) its earlier decision in *Turney vs. Saunders,* and ruled against Lincoln on this point.

The Illinois Supreme Court did not leave Lincoln entirely comfortless, however. In an opinion so lengthy as to seem to have one word for each of the more than 600,000 bricks in the house, the Court concluded that Garrett owed Stevenson & Wardell only $1,284.06, rather than the $2,595.20 awarded by the jury and the circuit court. The Court reformed the circuit court's decree, to permit the sale of the house in order to compel the payment of the amount of $1,284.06 to Stevenson & Wardell.

77

A "chose in action" is a somewhat old-fashioned name for one individual's cause of action against another individual: that is, one individual's right to commence a lawsuit against another individual in an effort to recover damages from that other individual. Some choses in action -- such as a claim for damages because of a personal injury inflicted by another's tortious conduct -- are not assignable. Other choses in action -- such as a claim arising under a promissory note or other contract -- are assignable.

The case of *Henderson vs. Welch,* 8 Ill. 340 (1846), involved the assignment of a chose in action (which had apparently arisen under a contract) from David Welch to Eli Henderson.

David Welch apparently had entered into a contract with Samuel Shaw and Daniel Shaw. On the basis of that contract, David Welch believed that he had a claim for damages against Samuel Shaw and Daniel Shaw.

David Welch assigned his chose in action (that is, his claim for damages arising under the contract) to Eli Henderson. Eli Henderson then commenced a lawsuit, against Samuel Shaw and Daniel Shaw, in the Circuit Court of DuPage County, Illinois. Because Henderson was asserting Welch's right against Samuel Shaw and Daniel Shaw, the case in the Circuit Court of DuPage County was entitled, on the plaintiff's side, as "Welch for the use of Henderson."

Only one defendant, Samuel Shaw, was served with process (that is, a summons) in that case, and so, the other defendant, Daniel Shaw, never became a party to that case.

The Circuit Court of DuPage County dismissed Henderson's lawsuit. Because Samuel Shaw had incurred court costs in that suit, however, he obtained a judgment from the circuit court that both Welch and Henderson should pay his court costs. In addition, Henderson had incurred fees (charged by the Clerk of the Circuit Court of DuPage County) as the plaintiff in that case, which he apparently did not pay. A fee bill was issued by the clerk of the circuit court against David Welch, for court costs incurred by Eli Henderson, in the amount $14.87 1/2 cents.

An execution was issued against David Welch for the court costs due to both Samuel Shaw and Daniel Shaw.

David Welch paid the court costs adjudged to be due to Samuel Shaw and Daniel Shaw, and also paid the fee bill owed by Eli Henderson for his own court costs to the Clerk of the Circuit of DuPage County. David Welch then sued Eli Henderson -- in the Circuit Court of McHenry County, Illinois -- to recover the amount that he had been required to pay as a result of Eli Henderson's having prosecuted the lawsuit in the Circuit Court of DuPage County.

David Welch obtained a judgment, against Eli Henderson, for the amount of $95.24. Eli Henderson made a motion for a new trial, but the circuit court denied the motion. Eli Henderson appealed from the judgment of the Circuit Court of McHenry County to the Illinois Supreme Court.

Lincoln represented Eli Henderson in prosecuting the appeal.

The Illinois Supreme Court stated, "The equitable assignee of a chose in action may sue upon it in the name of the party having the legal title, but he is bound to indemnify such party against the payment of costs." The Court concluded that Eli Henderson was required to indemnify (that is, to reimburse) David Welch for the court costs which David Welch was forced to pay as a result of Eli Henderson's unsuccessful lawsuit in the Circuit Court of DuPage County.

Lincoln had apparently argued, in behalf of Eli Henderson, that the record developed in the circuit court did not clearly indicate whether David Welch had, in fact, paid the amount of the judgment owed to Samuel Shaw and Daniel Shaw. Lincoln also pointed out that the judgment was in error to the extent that it purported to require anyone to pay anything to Daniel Shaw, because Daniel Shaw had never been served with process and, so, had never been made a party to the lawsuit.

The Illinois Supreme Court stated that there was no reasonable doubt that David Welch had paid the judgment for the court costs owed to Samuel Shaw. The Court also concluded that the fact that the judgment was in favor of both Samuel Shaw and Daniel Shaw -- despite Daniel Shaw's absence from the lawsuit -- was a variance that was "not material for this case."

The Illinois Supreme Court affirmed the judgment of the Circuit Court of McHenry County, against Eli Henderson, for the amount of $95.24. Lincoln thus lost the appeal that he had made for his client, Eli Henderson.

78

The case of *Cowls vs. Cowls*, 8 Ill. 435 (1846), involved a question of child custody that arose out of a divorce.

Ann Cowls had been the wife of Thomas Cowls. They had two children: a daughter, Mary Jane, and a son, Thomas.

Ann Cowls had brought an action for divorce against her husband, Thomas Cowls, in the Circuit Court of Edwards County, Illinois. She obtained a decree of divorce. At the time of the entry of the divorce decree, their daughter, Mary Jane, was six years of age, and their son, Thomas, was four years of age. The divorce decree made no provision concerning the children, and did not specify which parent was to have custody of the children.

In the absence of such a provision in the divorce decree, the father apparently was entitled to have custody of the children. This was in keeping with an astonishing doctrine of the English common law, which apparently had been imported into the Illinois common law: namely, that the children of a marriage belonged to the father.

After having obtained a divorce from Thomas Cowls, Ann Cowls later returned to the Circuit Court of Edwards County and filed a "bill" (that is, a complaint) by which she sought to have custody of the two children removed from Thomas Cowls and granted to her. Ann Cowls alleged in her bill that -- after the divorce -- Thomas Cowls had lived with a prostitute until a few weeks before Ann Cowls had filed her bill, at which time Thomas Cowls finally married the woman in question. Ann Cowls further alleged that Thomas Cowls was "addicted to excessive and frequent intoxication"; that he neglected his children and left them entirely in the care of the woman that he had married; that that woman was entirely unqualified to attend to the care and education of the children; that Thomas Cowls was in the habit of quarreling with that woman, in the presence of the children, and of driving her from the house; and that Thomas Cowls habitually used profane, indecent, immoral, and vulgar language before the children.

The circuit court found these allegations to be true, and it decreed that the children should be taken from their father, Thomas Cowls, and placed in the custody of their mother, Ann Cowls. The circuit court also required the father, Thomas Cowls, to pay to the mother, Ann Cowls -- for the support of the two children -- the amount of $30.00 per year per child, for the period of five years.

Thomas Cowls appealed from that decree, to the Illinois Supreme Court. Lincoln represented Thomas Cowls in presenting his appeal.

From the comments made by Justice Caton of the Illinois Supreme Court, in his written opinion, one may deduce that Lincoln argued that Ann Cowls was unfit to have custody of the two children herself, and that her unfitness was revealed by her having failed to seek, in the original divorce action, to obtain custody of the children. Lincoln also apparently argued that Ann Cowls was "more anxious to obtain the money that may be awarded for their maintenance, than to secure the welfare of the children." Lincoln also asserted that the child support awarded by the circuit court -- $30.00 per year per child -- was too high.

The Illinois Supreme Court rejected all of Lincoln's arguments. In writing the Court's opinion, Justice Caton composed a passage which remains true 145 years later, and which merits repetition:

> "The power of the court of chancery to interfere with and control, not only the estates but the persons and custody of all minors within the limits of its jurisdiction, is of very ancient origin, and can not now be questioned. This is a power which must necessarily exist somewhere, in every well-regulated society, and more especially in a republican government, where each man should be reared and educated under such influences that he may be qualified to exercise the rights of a freeman and take part in the government of the country. It is a duty, then, which the country owes as well to itself, as to the infant, to see that he is not abused, defrauded or neglected, and the infant has a right to this protection."

Lincoln thus lost his appeal for Thomas Cowls.

Our impression of Lincoln is that eloquence and justice were ranged on his side of every contest in which he engaged. Although we cannot know the details of the child custody dispute involved in this case, as Lincoln perceived them, it is possible that eloquence and justice were *against* Lincoln in this instance.

79

A "verdict" is the decision rendered by a jury before which a case has been tried. A judge never renders a "verdict." Rather, a judge may enter his judgment upon a jury's verdict, but he himself never renders a "verdict."

In a jury trial, both the jury's verdict and the judge's judgment upon that verdict are necessary to bring the case to a conclusion. A party can not appeal from an adverse verdict, but can only appeal from the judgment entered upon that adverse verdict.

The case of *Wilcoxon vs. Roby,* 8 Ill. 475 (1846), involved an error in a jury's verdict.

Levi Wilcoxon and William Roby both had made claims to a tract of "government land" in the State of Illinois: that is, to land which had never been privately owned by any person, but had remained in the ownership of the United States since Illinois had come within its jurisdiction.

Wilcoxon and Roby signed a contract between themselves, by which they agreed to "desist from all interference with a certain tract of government land, to which both had previously set up a claim, until the merits of the respective claims could be settled and adjusted between them." They both apparently had been petitioning a government officer to recognize their respective claims, and they wanted an opportunity to settle their claims between themselves, without worrying about what the other was attempting to accomplish with the government officer. Despite the existence of this contract, Levi Wilcoxon apparently continued his efforts to have a government officer recognize the superiority of his claim to the tract of land in question. William Roby then sued him in the Circuit Court of Stephenson County, Illinois, for the $400.00 penalty specified in the contract, for a breach of the contract. Such a penalty provision in a contract would probably not be enforced today.

The case was tried before a jury, and the jury returned a verdict in favor of William Roby for the amount of the $400.00 penalty.

The jury's verdict, however, apparently failed to find, first, that Wilcoxon was legally indebted to Roby under the contract. The jury's verdict jumped over this question, and apparently assessed Roby's damages, against Wilcoxon, at $400.00.

After having returned this verdict, the jury was discharged: that is, dismissed from further service. After the discharge of the jury, the judge of the circuit court entered his judgment upon the verdict, for the amount of $400.00 in favor of Roby and against Wilcoxon.

Levi Wilcoxon appealed from that judgment to the Illinois Supreme Court. Lincoln and two other lawyers -- T. Campbell and M. Y. Johnson -- represented Wilcoxon in prosecuting the appeal.

The attorney for William Roby conceded that an error had occurred in the circuit court's rendition of the judgment.

The Illinois Supreme Court stated, "The finding of the jury and the judgment of the Court are not responsive to the issues made. There can be no assessment of damages unless the debt be first found. This defect in the verdict could not have been corrected in the circuit court after the jury had delivered their verdict and been discharged. The circuit court could enter no proper judgment upon such a verdict."

The Illinois Supreme Court reversed the judgment, and remanded the case to the Circuit Court of Stephenson County for a new trial. Lincoln had won his appeal for Levi Wilcoxon.

80

The case of *Trumbull vs. Campbell,* 8 Ill. 502 (1846), involved an action by the then Secretary of State for the State of Illinois against his predecessor in office for money damages.

A Belleville lawyer named Lyman Trumbull was appointed Secretary of State for the State of Illinois on February 27, 1841. He held that office for slightly more than two years, until March 4, 1843, when an individual named Thompson Campbell was appointed to succeed him.

On March 3, 1843 -- the day before Lyman Trumbull was unceremoniously booted out of office -- the Illinois legislature made an appropriation to the Secretary of State "for making index to the journals of the senate and house of representatives and laws, for copying laws, and making marginal notes and index to laws, the sum of six hundred dollars."

Lyman Trumbull, being aware of the $600.00 appropriation which the Illinois legislature had made, presented to the State Auditor, on the morning of March 4, 1843, an order for two-thirds of the amount appropriated: that is, for the amount of $400.00. In response to Trumbull's order, the State Auditor issued a warrant to Lyman Trumbull requiring the State Treasurer to pay Lyman Trumbull $400.00. Lyman Trumbull asserted that he had already completed two-thirds of the work for which the appropriation had been made, and that, in consequence, he should be paid two-thirds of the amount of the appropriation.

After Thompson Campbell assumed the office of Secretary of State, Trumbull presented his warrant to the State Treasurer for $400.00, and he received payment.

Thompson Campbell labored to complete the work of indexing the journals of the senate and house of representatives, indexing the laws of the State of Illinois, making marginal notes to the laws, and making copies of the laws. Thompson Campbell finished the work, convinced that he had done more than one-third of the entire job, and that Lyman Trumbull had been paid too much out of the $600.00 appropriation.

Thompson Campbell brought an action of *assumpsit,* for money had and received, against Lyman Trumbull in the Circuit Court of Sangamon County, Illinois. The parties agreed as to the relevant facts (though obviously not as to the conclusions to be drawn from those facts) and submitted an "agreed case" to the trial judge for his decision. The trial judge decided that Lyman Trumbull had not performed more than one-third of the entire work involved; that Lyman Trumbull thus should not have been paid more than $200.00, representing one-third of the $600.00 appropriation; that Lyman Trumbull had been overpaid by the State Treasurer to the extent of $200.00; and that, finally, Lyman Trumbull should pay the excess, $200.00, to the present Secretary of State, Thompson Campbell. The trial judge entered his judgment to this effect.

Lyman Trumbull appealed from the judgment to the Illinois Supreme Court. Lincoln represented Trumbull in prosecuting the appeal. Lincoln's former partner, Stephen Logan, and another lawyer named A. T. Bledsoe, represented Thompson Campbell in defending against the appeal.

Lincoln filed a brief, the following portion of which appears in the report of the case:

"No action at law will lie in the case,

1. Because Trumbull being in office when the appropriation was made, the legal right to the whole was instantly vested in him. Jones v. Shore, 3 Peters' Cond. R. 624; Buel v. Van Ness, 5 do. 445.

2. Because it involves an apportionment of the appropriation, which a court of law is incompetent to make. 1 Story's Eq. Jur. §§ 471-2; Robson v. Andrede, 2 Eng. Com. Law R. 432; Waddell v. Morris, 14 Wend. 76.

No action at law will lie in the case by Campbell against Trumbull, because there is no privity between them. 2 Comyn on Cont. 7; 6 Saunders' Pl. & Ev. 675; Chitty on Cont. 184; Tiernan v. Jackson, 5 Peters, 580."

The Illinois Supreme Court stated that "The only point in the case is, whether the action as between these parties can be maintained." It indicated that the attorneys on both sides of the case had discussed the question "with much ability," as one would expect Lincoln and Logan to do.

The Court concluded that an action of *assumpsit,* for money had and received, was based upon one person's wrongfully receiving and retaining the money of another. In this case, the Court held, the $200.00 which Lyman Trumbull had wrongfully received and retained belonged not to Thompson Campbell, but to the State of Illinois itself. Consequently, Thompson Campbell could not bring an action, in his own name, directly against Lyman Trumbull for the recovery of the $200.00. Instead, Thompson Campbell would have to bring an action against Lyman Trumbull in the name of the State of Illinois.

The Court concluded further that, in an appropriate action, the State of Illinois could force Lyman Trumbull to repay $200.00, and that the then Secretary of State, Thompson Campbell, had a right to be paid $400.00 by the State Treasurer, for his performance of two-thirds of the work involved in the project, regardless of whether the State Treasurer had erred by paying Lyman Trumbull $200.00 too much.

The Illinois Supreme Court reversed the judgment for $200.00 against Lyman Trumbull. Lincoln thus had won the appeal for his client, Lyman Trumbull.

This was the same Lyman Trumbull, who, in 1855, beat out Lincoln for the position of United States Senator, as a result of Lincoln's having to break an impasse in the State Senate (which then chose the Illinois Senators) by throwing his own support to Trumbull. Trumbull also went on to write, at the end of the Civil War, the Thirteenth Amendment to the United States Constitution, which abolished slavery.

In this case, therefore, the eventual author of the Emancipation Proclamation represented the eventual author of the Thirteenth Amendment to the United States Constitution.

A "mortgagor" is one who conveys a mortgage on his land to another person, usually a lender, for the sake of giving security to back up his promise to repay the loan as agreed. A "mortgagee" is the person, usually a lender, to whom a mortgage on land has been conveyed.

When a mortgagor conveys a mortgage on his land to the mortgagee, he retains an "equity of redemption," in the land. That equity of redemption -- under the law which prevailed in Illinois in Lincoln's day -- permitted the mortgagor to redeem his land from a mortgage foreclosure sale by paying the successful bidder at that sale, within a specified time, the amount of his bid plus interest thereon at the rate of 10 percent per year.

A "mistake of fact" is a mistake which a party, to a transaction, has made concerning an essential fact pertinent to the transaction. A party may sometimes have a transaction rescinded -- that is, undone -- if he entered into the transaction with a mistake of fact in mind.

A "mistake in law" is a mistake, not as to an essential *fact* relating to the transaction, but, rather, as to the consequences of applying the law to those facts. If a party has made a mistake of law, with respect to a transaction, he ordinarily has no hope of having the transaction rescinded.

In the case of *Cooper vs. Crosby,* 8 Ill. 506 (1846), the plaintiff, Hugh Cooper, made a mistake of law -- as to the significance of a mortgagor's equity of redemption -- and thereby threw away more than half the amount of the mortgage debt which the mortgagor owed to him.

Israel Crosby owned several lots in the City of Springfield, Illinois. On July 8, 1843, Israel Crosby conveyed a mortgage on his lots to Hugh Cooper, in order to secure his payment of his debt to Hugh Cooper. Israel Crosby thereafter conveyed his equity of redemption in those lots to a third party named Robbins.

Israel Crosby apparently failed to pay his debt to Hugh Cooper on schedule. On March 24, 1846, Hugh Cooper, in an action which he had filed in the Circuit Court of Sangamon County, Illinois, foreclosed his mortgage on Israel Crosby's lots. The circuit court entered a decree which adjudged that Israel Crosby then owed Hugh Cooper the amount of $608.00, and that the lots in question were to be sold to raise the proceeds necessary to pay that amount to Hugh Cooper.

The report of this decision suggests that the lots were indeed worth at least $608.00, and that a fair bid for the lots would have yielded enough to pay Hugh Cooper his $608.00.

The mortgage foreclosure sale was scheduled to occur on October 24, 1846: that is, seven months after the entry of the decree of foreclosure.

Hugh Cooper's attorney -- who was probably Lincoln himself -- met with Hugh Cooper before the mortgage foreclosure sale. Cooper's attorney made out a list of the price that Cooper was to bid on each of the lots that was being sold, in order to ascribe to each lot a proportionate part of the $608.00 indebtedness plus the costs which Cooper had incurred. Cooper's attorney's advice to Cooper, therefore, was that Cooper should bid in the entire amount of his indebtedness, $608.00, plus the costs that he had incurred.

It was crucial, for Cooper's own protection, that he do this. A ridiculously low bid by Cooper, for the lots, would permit Robbins, as the owner of the equity of redemption, to take the lots back from Cooper simply by paying Cooper the amount of his bid.

Greed may have gotten the better of Cooper at the mortgage foreclosure sale, because Cooper did not follow his attorney's advice. Instead, Cooper bid only $269.50 for the lots, rather than the $608.00 due on the mortgage, plus costs.

When Cooper took the news of this purchase back to his attorney, his attorney probably pointed out to him immediately that he would lose the lots to Robbins, if Robbins stepped forward and exercised his equity of redemption by paying over to Cooper the amount of $269.50. If Robbins were to do so, Cooper would then be forced to try to obtain the $338.50 difference -- between $608.00 and $269.50 -- from Israel Crosby. Israel Crosby was bankrupt, however, and Cooper would never be able to recover anything further from Israel Crosby. Cooper's only chance to collect the amount owed to him, in full, was to have bid that full amount, plus costs, in at the mortgage foreclosure sale.

Cooper's attorney, probably Lincoln, prepared and filed a motion in the circuit court, in which Cooper and the attorney, in attached affidavits, indicated that Cooper had become confused at the mortgage foreclosure sale, and had thought that his role, at the mortgage foreclosure sale, was to make certain that no other person was permitted to purchase any lot for less than the value which Cooper's attorney had ascribed to it. Cooper thus alleged that he had essentially regarded the value ascribed to each lot, by his attorney, as the maximum value, up to which he would bid on that particular lot. In reality, however, the value ascribed to each lot by Cooper's attorney was the mimimum amount that the attorney desired Cooper to bid on each lot, in order to ensure that Cooper would be able to collect the entire amount of the mortgage indebtedness owed to him plus costs.

Cooper undoubtedly gave such an explanation to his attorney for his failure to follow his attorney's advice. Cooper may simply have thought, however, that he knew better than his attorney did, how to extract the greatest possible benefit for himself from a mortgage foreclosure sale.

Cooper's motion in the Circuit Court of Sangamon County requested that the circuit court set aside the mortgage foreclosure sale, and schedule another mortgage foreclosure sale of the lots. The circuit court denied the motion, though, and approved the report of the official, known as a "master," who had made the sale.

Cooper then appealed from the denial of his motion to the Illinois Supreme Court. Lincoln represented Cooper in prosecuting the appeal.

Lincoln was opposed by his former partner, Stephen Logan, who apparently represented Robbins, the owner of the equity of redemption. The Illinois Supreme Court stated,

"In this case there is no pretence [sic] that there had been misrepresentation or fraud, and it is only alleged that Cooper was mistaken in reference to the advice or instructions of counsel, as to the proper course to be pursued by him. It is difficult to perceive how this misapprehension of his can be considered more or less, than an error in relation to the law bearing upon the case, against which it is plain a court of equity could not relieve him. . . ."

The Illinois Supreme Court concluded that granting Cooper the relief which he sought would, in effect, invite every mortgagor to make an unreasonably low bid for the land at a mortgage foreclosure sale in the expectation that -- should the owner of the equity of redemption attempt to redeem the land for that low price -- the mortgagor would then be able to file a motion in the circuit court, alleging mistake or confusion on his part, and seeking to have the mortgage foreclosure sale set aside, and a new mortgage foreclosure sale scheduled.

The Illinois Supreme Court affirmed the circuit court's denial of Cooper's motion to set aside the mortgage foreclosure sale. Lincoln thus lost the appeal for his client, Hugh Cooper.

After this disposition of the appeal, Robbins certainly must have redeemed the land from Hugh Cooper for the amount of $269.50, and Cooper was simply out the other $338.50 of the mortgage indebtedness owed to him, plus his costs. Cooper could have avoided all of this, simply by bidding what the lots were worth at the mortgage foreclosure sale.

82

The term "common law" refers to that body, of principles of law, developed by judges over a period of centuries, in England and America, as they decided the cases pending before them. It thus represents tradition, built up from the accretion of precedents over a long period of time. It is quite possible to find reports of decisions -- and the precedents contained therein -- rendered by English courts in the 1500s. Illinois long ago, in fact, adopted a Reception Statute by which it absorbed, as its own, the common law of England which predated the fourth year of King James the First (that is, the common law of England which predated March 24, 1606).

Law set forth in a statute should be distinguished from common law. A statute and the law it contains are made by legislators in an instant, as it were, whereas common law is made by judges slowly, case by case. Although, under the common law, married women had few property rights, they were not entirely bereft of property rights. The common law recognized a right of "dower" in a married woman. A married woman's right of dower gave her a life interest in (that is, a right, during her life, to possess, use, and gain the benefit of) one-third of her husband's lands. If her husband were to die, her right of dower in one-third of his lands, would give her something with which to support herself.

As distinguished from the common law right of dower, a mechanic's lien exists -- in favor of a workman who has built an improvement upon land, or in favor of a supplier who has delivered materials for the building of that improvement on land -- only by virtue of a statute adopted by the Illinois legislature.

Both a widow's right of dower in, and workman's mechanic's lien on, land were involved in the case of *Shaeffer vs. Weed,* 8 Ill. 511 (1846).

William Weed had resided in White County, Illinois. He had a wife, Harriet, and a son, William.

William Weed had contracted with William Shaeffer for the construction of a house on William Weed's land. William

Shaeffer began the work on the house, and apparently made considerable progress on it, but then stopped his work when William Weed died.

An individual named John Gillison was appointed administrator of the Estate of William Weed, Deceased.

About seven months after William Weed's death, the workman, William Shaeffer, filed a petition in the Circuit Court of White County, Illinois, under the Illinois mechanic's lien statute. He sought, by means of that petition, to assert a mechanic's lien on the house and land owned by the Estate of William Weed, Deceased. Shaeffer joined, as defendants to his mechanic's lien proceeding, the administrator of William Weed's estate, John Gillison; William Weed's widow, Harriet; and William Weed's son, William.

The administrator, Gillison, filed a "replication" (that is, an answer) to Shaeffer's petition for a mechanic's lien. In his replication, the administrator, Gillison, asserted that the widow, Harriet Weed, was entitled to dower in the land despite the claim for a mechanic's lien, and that, in addition, Shaeffer was not entitled to claim a mechanic's lien because he had not filed his petition within six months after payment had become due to him for his work.

Shaeffer demurred (that is, objected) to these defenses and sought to have them stricken. The circuit court upheld these defenses, however. In the face of this decision by the circuit court, Shaeffer had no further allegations or arguments to offer, and the circuit court entered a judgment in favor of the administrator, John Gillison, for his court costs.

William Shaeffer appealed from that judgment to the Illinois Supreme Court. Lincoln represented Shaeffer in prosecuting the appeal.

The Illinois Supreme Court decided one issue against, and a second issue in favor of, Lincoln's client, William Shaeffer.

The Illinois Supreme Court concluded, first, "That the widow's dower cannot be affected by the lien created by the

212

statute." The Court thus concluded that the widow's rights in the land must be satisfied before the workman, Shaeffer, received anything for his work.

The second principal issue in the case concerned the six-month limitation, for the filing of a petition to enforce a mechanic's lien, set forth in the Illinois mechanic's lien statute. The administrator, John Gillison, argued that -- if a workman failed to file his petition within six months after payment was due to him -- his claim, even against the party with whom he had contracted, was extinguished. After analyzing the Illinois mechanic's lien statute at length, the Illinois Supreme Court concluded, however, that the six-month deadline for filing a petition, established by the statute, only concerned the question of the *priority* of the workman's claim with respect to claims presented by other creditors. Because the workman, William Shaeffer, had not filed his petition to enforce his mechanic's lien within six months after payment became due to him, he had lost whatever priority he otherwise might have had, and other creditors of the decedent, William Weed, would be able to satisfy their claims, out of the value of the land, before the workman, William Shaeffer, would be able to satisfy his claim out of the value of the land. This did not mean, though, that the claim of the workman, William Shaeffer, against the land owned by the Estate of William Weed, Deceased, was extinguished. Rather, the workman, William Shaeffer, was still able to prosecute his petition to enforce his mechanic's lien against that land.

The Illinois Supreme Court reversed the judgment of the Circuit Court of White County, Illinois, and remanded the case to that circuit court for further proceedings consistent with its opinion in the case. Lincoln had achieved a partial victory for his client, the workman, William Shaeffer.

The case of *Anderson vs. Ryan,* 8 Ill. 583 (1846), involved an action by a father, against the seducer of his daughter, for damages for the seduction.

Michael Ryan resided in Coles County, Illinois. He had a daughter, whose name was not revealed in the report of the decision in this case.

Elias Anderson seduced Michael Ryan's daughter, and made her pregnant. The daughter apparently still lived in the household of her father, Michael Ryan.

When the daughter was four months advanced in pregnancy, the father, Michael Ryan, brought an action for damages against Elias Anderson, in the Circuit Court of Coles County, Illinois, for the seduction of Michael Ryan's daughter.

The common law, of England and America, had long permitted a father to bring such an action for damages against the seducer of his daughter. To bring the action, however, the father had to allege that -- by reason of his daughter's pregnancy -- he had lost the service of his daughter in his household. The father could not simply base his case on the fact that he was outraged by what had happened to his daughter.

This particular case was tried before a jury, which necessitated the trial judge's instructing the jury as to the applicable law. The trial judge instructed the jury "that the law required the plaintiff to prove some loss of service and of the comfort and society of his daughter, but that proof of the slightest loss was sufficient, and if the jury should believe that the daughter of the plaintiff lived with the father and had been pregnant by the defendant for the term of four months before the commencement of the action they might infer and ought to infer the loss of service." The defendant objected to the last clause of this instruction, which told the jury that it ought to infer the father's loss of his daughter's service because of the daughter's pregnancy.

The jury returned a verdict in favor of the father, Michael Ryan, and assessed his damages at $656.00, a large sum for that day. The trial judge entered a judgment upon that verdict, in favor of the plaintiff father and against the defendant.

The defendant, ~~Michael Ryan~~ *Elias Anderson*, moved for a new trial, but the trial judge denied that motion.

~~Michael Ryan~~ *Elias Anderson* then appealed from the judgment to the Illinois Supreme Court. Lincoln represented ~~Ryan~~ *Anderson* in prosecuting the appeal.

Lincoln filed a brief which set forth the following two points:

"1. The court below by instructing the jury that they ought to infer a loss of service, withdrew the consideration of the question of the loss of service from the jury, which was contrary to the law. Trotter v. Saunders, 7 J.J. Marsh. 321; Sullivan v. Enders, 3 Dana 66; Tufts v. Seabury, 11 Pick. 140; 3 U.S. Dig. 571, sections 563 - 565; United States v. Tillotson, 12 Wheat. 180; Allen v. Kopman, 2 Dana 221.

2. Although there may be evidence apparently sufficient to sustain the verdict, yet, as the court could not see whether the jury based their verdict as to loss of service on the evidence, or on the misdirection of the court, a new trial should have been granted. Gaines v. Buford, 1 Dana 481, 502; Gillespie v. Gillespie, 2 Bibb 89, 93; Wardell v. Hughes, 3 Wend. 418."

The Illinois Supreme Court disagreed with Lincoln. The Court stated, "It has long been considered as a standing reproach to the common law, that it furnished no means to punish the seducer of female innocence and virtue, except through the fiction of supposing the daughter was a servant of her parent, and that in consequence of her seduction, the parent had lost some of her services as a menial. It is high time this reproach should be wiped out. . . . This action ought, then, no longer to be considered as a means of recovering damages for the loss of menial services, but as an instrument to punish the perpetrator of

215

a flagitious outrage upon the peace and happiness of the family circle."

The Illinois Supreme Court affirmed the large judgment against Lincoln's client, Elias Anderson. Lincoln had lost the appeal.

A RETROSPECTION
ON THE FIRST HALF OF LINCOLN'S CAREER
BEFORE THE ILLINOIS SUPREME COURT

Lincoln was elected to the United States House of Representatives on August 3, 1846. In accordance with the law that prevailed in his era, he did not take his seat in Congress until December 6, 1847.

He remained in Congress until March 4, 1849, and did not return to the practice of law in the State of Illinois until the summer or fall of 1849. A two-year gap thus exists in Lincoln's participation in cases before the Illinois Supreme Court, which corresponds to his attendance at Congress.

This two-year gap divides Lincoln's career, before the Illinois Supreme Court, in half. Before he left for Congress, Lincoln was involved in 83 cases before the Illinois Supreme Court. After Lincoln returned from Congress, he was involved in an additional 83 cases before the Illinois Supreme Court.

It is interesting to note that -- although Lincoln had taken on William Herndon as his junior partner in 1844 -- Herndon's name never appeared with Lincoln's, in the report of a decision of the Illinois Supreme Court, until after Lincoln's return from Congress in 1849. Then, in the first case which Lincoln handled before the Illinois Supreme Court after his return -- *Wright vs. M'Neely,* 11 Ill. 241 (1849) -- the firm's name, "Lincoln & Herndon," appeared.

A retrospection upon the first half of Lincoln's career before the Illinois Supreme Court reveals the determined work of an able man. Whenever any of Lincoln's writing appears in the reports of the Illinois Supreme Court's decisions, from the first half of his career, regardless of how small that bit of writing may be, it invariably is concise and illuminating.

This quality, which suffuses all of Lincoln's legal writing, discloses that Lincoln, in his own way, was a proud man. It is a deep-seated pride in himself, and in the goodness of what he loves and believes, that drives a man to strive to be truly eloquent in all of his utterances. Lincoln undoubtedly had that pride, and it helped him to do all that he had to do -- and to bear all that he had to bear -- in his life.

An examination of Lincoln's appellate cases, from the first half of his legal career, also reveals that he dealt with ordinary people in a great variety of situations. In other words, he enjoyed the opportunity -- that a small-town Illinois law practice has always given a man -- to learn much about people and about life as he performed his daily work.

NOTES ON INDICES

Five indices, concerning the content of Lincoln's cases before the Illinois Supreme Court during the first half of his career, are here set forth. Index A lists the names of all people and organizations mentioned in the Illinois Supreme Court's opinions in the cases. Index B lists all place names -- including Illinois counties and cities -- mentioned in the Illinois Supreme Court's opinions. Index C is a case-by-case listing of all legal topics covered in the cases. Index D is an alphabetical listing of the legal topics covered in the cases. Index E sets forth all of the legal authorities cited in the briefs which Lincoln submitted to the Illinois Supreme Court in support of his arguments in the cases.

In each index, the first number listed to the right of an entry appears in boldface type. This number, in boldface type, corresponds to the number of the case as set forth in the Table of Contents near the beginning of this book. The subsequent number, or numbers, on a given line appear in regular typeface, and represent the page number in this book at which the particular item may be found.

In Indices A, B, and E, some items have only the case number in boldface type, listed for them, without any listing of a page in this book. This means, for such an item, that the item is mentioned by the Illinois Supreme Court in its opinion in the case in question, but that the item is not mentioned in this book's study of that particular case. For example, in Index A, the second reference to "Baker, E. D." (a close friend of Lincoln) is to case 11; that is, to the case of *Averill vs. Field,* 4 Ill. 390 (1842). An examination of the Illinois Supreme Court's opinion, reported in that volume and at that page, will reveal that E. D. Baker was one of two attorneys for the appellee in that case. This book's discussion of the case of *Averill vs. Field* in chapter 11, however, does not refer to E. D. Baker by name.

219

In Index A, the appearance of an asterisk after an individual's name indicates that that individual was one of Lincoln's clients, whom Lincoln represented in either prosecuting, or defending against, an appeal before the Illinois Supreme Court.

Index C, the case-by-case listing of legal topics, and Index D, the alphabetical listing of legal topics, set forth only the numbers of the cases in which various legal topics appear. They do not state the page, or pages, in this book at which the discussion of a particular subject occurs.

INDEX A

Index of People and
Organizations
(Lincoln's clients on
appeal marked with *)

Case and Page Numbers
(Case number bolded
and listed first, page
number regular typeface)

Abrams, William G. *	**8**, 19
Alexander, David C.	**12**, 28
Alexander, M. K.	**17**, 39
Allen, E. Z.	**36**, 90
Allen, Joseph	**12**, 28
Anderson and Flanders	**40**, 100
Anderson, Elias *	**83**, 214
Arnold, I. N.	**77**
Averill, Riley*	**11**, 25
Bailey & Marsh	**33**
Bailey, Daniel M.	**47**
Bailey, David *	**4**, 11
Baker, E. D.	**9**, 22
	11
	16
	21, 47
	26
	28
	31
	40
	42, 106
	64, 160
Ballance, Charles	**49**
Ballentine, Harvey	**5**, 13
Ballentine, Robert	**5**
Baltimore & Western Land Association	**32**, 70
Beall, Joshua *	**5**, 13
Beaumont, G. A. O.	**44**, 114

Benedict, Kirby	7, 17
Bennett	56
Bennett, John *	62
Bennett, Richard E.	62, 155
Berrien County Bank *	44, 113
Betts, Josias T.	43, 110
Bigelow, Lewis	49, 124
Bledsoe, A. T.	9
	11
	16
	21
	22
	26
	28
	73
	77
	78
	80, 204
	82
	83
Blucher, Daniel	56
Bobo, Letitia	46
Bobo, Nancy	46
Bobo, Sarah	46
Bogardus, John L.	49, 124
Bradford, V. L.	44
Brayman, M.	15
	25
	28
	58
Breese, Sidney, Justice	2
	3, 10
	6
	18
	19
Bridges, Milton	29
Briggs, Benjamin	9, 21
Broadwell, David	42, 106

Broadwell, John B. *	42, 106
Broadwell, Moses	42, 106
Broadwell, Sarah	42, 106
Broadwell, William	42, 106
Brown, J. J.	64
	69
Browne, Thomas C., Justice	25
	57
	67
	79
Browne, Thomas C., Justice *	70, 175
Browning, O. H	32
Bruce, Green W.	25, 54
Bryan, George	61, 152
Bryan, Mary D.	61, 152
Bryan, N.	61
Bryan, Nicholas	61, 152
Bryan, Robert	61
Bryan, W. F.	53
	56
Buckmaster, N., Sheriff of Madison County	18
Bunn, Lewis	31
Bunn, Marjory	31
Burnett, Isaac	53, 134
Bushnell, N.	32
Butterfield, J.	38
	49
	67
Byrd, Adam *	57, 144
Cabiness, John M.	61
Camp, William	8, 19
Campbell, James *	24, 52
Campbell, T.	57
	70
	79, 202
Campbell, Thomas	80, 203
Cannon, Manly F.*	2, 7

Carson, William — 42
Cassell, Jacob * — 37, 92
Caton, John D., Justice — 13
35
36
38
42
48
49
52
53
56
59
63
67
78, 199
82
Cave, Sidney — 82
Chase, Bishop — 56, 141
Chase, Henry J. — 56, 141
Cheney, Owen — 47, 120
Cheny, Thomas — 47
Chesseldine, Henry * — 22, 48
Chestnut — 15
Chickering, J. W. — 18
67, 169
City of Springfield * — 51, 129
Clark, Henry — 26, 56
Cline, Cornelius * — 1, 5
Collins & Hannay — 23, 50
Colton, W. — 31
Colton, Wells — 27
Conklin, J. C. — 10
20
Conklin, James C. — 51, 129
Constable, C. H. — 40, 102
74
Constant, John — 16, 37

Cook, Amasa *   38, 94
Cook, B. C.   36
Cook, Edward C. *   40, 101
Cooper, Hugh K. *   81, 206
Correll, Andrew   5, 13
Cowgil, Wm.   61
Cowles, A.   18
                                       33
Cowls, Ann   78, 198
Cowls, Mary Jane   78, 198
Cowls, Thomas *   78, 198
Cowls, Thomas, Jr.   78, 198
Craig & Warner   33, 85
Craig & Warner *   19, 43
Crane, William B. *   20, 45
Cromwell, Nathan (deceased)   4, 11
Cromwell, William   4, 11
Crosby, Israel W.   81, 206
Crothers, Samuel W.   55
Cunningham, Hezekiah   64, 160
Dabney   24, 52
Daniel, Justice   13
Darnell, William D.   68
Davidson, Jane   62, 155
Davis, David   31, 66
Davis, E.   29
Davis, Levi   14
Debolt, George *   56, 141
Dibrell   65
Dickey, Hugh T., Justice   60
                                       69
Dickey, John *   43, 110
Dickey, T. L.   35, 89
                                       36, 90
                                       38, 95
Dillehunt, Benjamin *   7, 17
Dillion, Daniel   47
Dorman, William M., and wife   30

Douglas, Stephen A., Justice   11, 27
                                20, 46
                                22
Dryden, Joshua *   32, 70
Duncan, Joseph   18
Eddy, H.   41, 105
Edgar County   68, 171
Edwards, Ambrose P. *   66, 166
Edwards, B. F.   33, 85
Edwards, B. S.   19
                                26
                                33
                                47
Edwards, Benjamin F.   19, 43
Edwards, Mrs.   66, 166
Edwards, Old Mrs.   66, 166
Edwards, Richard   72
Eldridge, Barnabas, E.   48, 122
Elkin, Garret *   6, 15
Eller, George   65, 163
Ellers, O.   25, 54
Ellis, Ezra *   60, 150
Emerson, C.   7
England, George *   26, 56
Favor, Kimball *   35, 88
Fay, Thomas S.   18, 41
Fell, Jesse *   72, 180
Ferguson   16
Ferguson & Lukins   26, 56
Ferguson, W. I.   51, 130
Ficklin, O. B.   13
                                14
                                17
Field, Alexander P.   41, 104
Field, Spencer   11, 25
Fisher   13
Fitch, George W.   18, 41
Fithian, William *   64, 160

Foster, George	**29**, 62
Foster, Peyton *	**29**, 62
Francis, Simeon *	**23**, 50
Frazier, Samuel *	**17**, 39
Frisby, Ellen *	**49**
Frye, Smith	**46**, 118
Garrett, Augustus O. *	**44**, 113
	76, 192
Garrett, Mary G.	**76**, 192
Gatton, Benjamin H.	**50**, 127
Gear, Hezekiale H.	**67**, 168
Gibbs	**47**
Gillison, John	**82**, 211
Goodrich, G.	**69**, 174
Gosnell, Samuel	**32**, 70
Grable, William G.	**10**, 23
Grant, Franklin M.	**35**, 88
Gray	**33**
Greathouse, John S.	**15**, 35
Greely, Benjamin	**9**, 21
Griffin, Young *	**39**, 97
Griggs & Weld	**67**, 168
Griggs, David R. *	**67**, 168
Griswald, Eliha	**48**
Grubb, Samuel	**20**, 45
Gunn & Fox	**39**, 97
Haddock, E. H.	**60**, 150
Hailey, Elizabeth	**55**
Hains, Benjamin C.	**31**
Hains, Thomas H.	**31**, 66
Hall, Bryant	**40**, 102
Hall, Henry H.	**50**, 127
Hall, J.	**32**
Hall, Junius	**18**
	19
Hall, Samuel	**28**, 60
Hallock, Serjeant	**83**
Hamilton, Artois	**58**, 146

Hamlin, Orin	**49**
Hancock, John	**9**, 21
Hanks, Andrew J.	**68**, 171
Harbock	**67**
Hardin, J. J.	**18**
	22
	65
	67
Harkness, Elisha *	**31**, 66
Harkness, Esther	**31**
Harkness, Samuel (deceased)	**31**, 66
Harlan, Justin, Justice	**17**
	45
Harris, Daniel S.	**70**, 175
Harris, Jame	**2**, 7
Harris, John	**2**, 7
Harris, Robert	**2**, 7
Harris, T. L.	**62**
	63, 158
Harvey, E. E.	**77**
Hatchett, William	**55**
Hawks, Matthew H. *	**75**, 189
Helm, Hohn B.	**33**, 85
Helm, John B.	**19**, 43
Henderson, Eli *	**77**, 195
Hickox & Brothers	**51**, 129
Hickox, Horace	**51**
Hickox, V.	**51**, 129
Hill, Leroy L.	**55**, 138
Hill, Paulena S.	**55**, 138
Hill, Silas P.	**55**
Hinde	**45**, 115
Hodgson, Daniel	**9**, 21
Hoes, J. V. A.	**38**
Hogue, James M.	**40**, 100
Houtt, Elisha	**68**
Irwin, David M. *	**50**
Jefferds, John	**4**, 100

Johnson	49
Johnson, Andrew	27, 58
Johnson, M. Y.	79, 202
Jones	52
Jones, John A.	3
Jordan, J. P.	39
Jubilee College	56, 141
Juneau, Solomon	64, 160
Kelly, Royal *	44, 113
Kimball, Lovell	38, 94
Kincaid, John K.	63, 158
King, George	59, 148
Kinney, Matthew P.	2, 7
Kinzie, James	44, 113
Klein	8, 19
Knowlton, L. B.	76
Koerner, J.	50
	52
	66
	68
	71
	72
	83
Krieder, Issac	12, 28
Krum, J. M.	32, 69
	33, 85
Lake	48, 122
Lamborn, J.	7
	8
Lands, Samuel	75, 189
Lane, John	30, 64
Law, John N.	72, 180
Law, Nathan	72, 180
Lazell, George A. B.	23, 50
Lazell, John A.	23, 50
Leonard, W. H	28
Lesher, Jacob *	45, 115
Linder, U. F.	72

	83
Littledale, Justice	83
Locke, John	60, 150
Lockridge, E.	29
Lockridge, John	29, 62
Lockwood, Samuel D. Justice	3
	15
	39
	64
	83
Logan, S. T.	2
	4
	6
	8, 19
	9, 21
	11, 25
	20, 46
	22, 48
	23, 50
	24
	25, 54
	29
	31, 66
	43, 110
	44, 114
	45, 116
	54
	55, 139
	60
	61, 153
	64, 160
	80, 204
	81, 208
Loop, J. L.	1, 5
Lowell, Alfred	11, 25
Magahee, John H. *	21, 47
Margrave, Thomas *	10, 23
Marlett, Isaac	35, 88

Marsh, Hankinson & Co.	**18**, 41
Martin, John T.	**32**, 71
Martin, W.	**33**
Martin, William	**18**
	19
Mason, George	**14**, 33
Maus, Jacob S.	**3**, 10
Maus, W. S.	**3**, 10
Maxey, James	**16**, 37
Mayo, Jonathan *	**68**, 171
McCall, Henry	**45**
McCall, James B.	**45**
McCall, Julia, (deceased)	**45**, 115
McCall, Mary S.	**45**
McCall, William	**45**
McClure, Harkness, Hannah	**31**
McClure, John	**31**, 66
McConnel, M.	**15**
	66
McCormick, Andrew, Mayor	**51**, 129
McDonald, Alexander	**64**, 160
McDougall, J. A.	**39**
	41
	51
	65
McIntire, Fleming F.	**6**, 15
McIntosh, William	**45**
McNamara	**59**, 148
Menard, Peter	**9**, 21
Merriman, H. O.	**46**
	56, 141
	76
Miller,	**38**, 95
Miller, Abram	**29**
Miller, William	**33**
Milnor, Daniel	**9**, 21
Minshall, W. A.	**50**
	66

Monaghan, Owen *	**69**, 174
Moore, Joshua J. *	**58**, 146
Moores, Isaac	**64**, 160
Morgan, Thomas	**39**, 97
Morris, B. S.	**69**
Moss, William S.	**46**, 118
Mullanphy, Mr.	**33**
Munsell, Roswell	**71**, 178
Murphy, James	**64**, 160
Murphy, James *	**54**, 136
Murphy, John	**64**, 160
Nance	**4**, 11, 12
Neely, Alexander, Justice of the Peace	**1**
Negus, Isaac	**18**
Nelson, Chief Justice	**83**
Nesbit, Matthew	**52**, 132
Nye	**47**, 120
Nye, Sheriff	**22**
Olmstead, William	**52**, 132
Park, Benjamin F. *	**14**, 33
Parke, James E.	**71**, 177
Parker, James M.	**36**, 90
Parsons, Henry	**48**
Patterson, Maria	**66**, 166
Patterson, William	**66**, 166
Patterson, Zera	**47**, 120
Payne, Morgan L.	**17**, 39
Payne, Thomas (deceased)	**50**, 126
Pearson, J.	**69**
Pentecost, Hugh L.	**21**, 47
Perkins, Elisha M.	**28**, 60
Perkins, H. H.	**9**
Perkins, M. A.	**9**
Perry, Carlton H.	**72**, 180
Peters, O.	**35**
	38, 95
	48
	52

Peters, O.	**76**
Petit	**48**
Pettus, Mrs.	**61**
Pettus, Thomas	**61**
Petty, M.	**55**
Pickering	**21**, 47
Pierce, S. C.	**18**
Pinckard, William G. *	**18**, 41
Powell, E. N.	**46**, 119
	49, 125
	53
	56
Price, Robert	**72**, 181
Purple, Norman H., Justice	**51**
	55
	58
	62, 156
	69
	73
	75
	79
	81
	82
Ranlett, Seth A.	**53**, 134
Rawley, Enos	**68**, 171
Rawlings, Moses M.	**41**, 104
Redman, George	**68**
Ridges, James	**29**
Risinger, Daniel S. *	**47**, 120
Risley, Joshua *	**13**, 31
Robbins, S. W.	**23**
	24
	29
	42
	55
	61
	63
	81, 207

Robbins, George	**18**
Robinson, Christopher	**30**, 64
Robinson, Greenleaf, C.	**22**, 48
Roby, William	**79**, 201
Rogers	**13**
Rogers, Edward K.	**43**, 110
Roney, John	**69**, 174
Ross, Joseph	**52**, 132
Rountree, John H.	**70**
Rowe, Nelson *	**48**, 122
Ryan, Michael	**83**, ~~213~~ 214 *errata w*
Scammon, Jonathan Y.	**1**, 5
	43
Scates, Walter B., Justice	**10**
	18
	19
	22
	26
	27
	30
	33
	36
	37
	41
	44
	46
	49
	50
	54
Schlencker, Gideon	**13**, 31
Schooly, Palemon	**40**, 100
Semple, James, Justice	**16**
	32
Shaeffer, William *	**82**, 210
Shaw, Aaron	**14**
Shaw, Daniel	**77**, 195
Shaw, Samuel	**77**, 195
Sherman, E. L.	**44**

Shields, James, Justice	10
	20 ,46
	28, 60
	30
	33, 86
	41
Shumate, W.	29
Simpson, Joshua B. *	53, 134
Skinner	38
Skinner, M.	44, 114
Slentz, Jacob	40, 100
Sloan, John S.	54, 136
Smedes, A. K.	24
	42
Smith, D. A.	18
	22
	39, 98
	65
	67
Smith, David A. *	15, 35
Smith, George F.	57, 144
Smith, Joseph H.	57, 144
Smith, Norman *	36, 90
Spear, David	24, 52
Spear, Issac P.	24, 52
Spear, J. P.	24
Spring, G.	1
	69, 174
State Bank of Illinois	73, 183
Stevenson & Wardell	76, 192
Stevenson, Andrew	76, 192
Stickney, John C.	37, 92
Stickney, W. H.	37
Stone, Dan, Justice	1
Story, Justice	78
Strong, N. D.	18
	19
	32

Strong, N.D.	33
Strong, S.	6
	24
Stuart, J. T.	33
	47
Summerville, Alexander	54, 136
Sweat, Mary Jane	42, 106
Sweezy, David	40, 100
Sykes, James *	74, 186
Talbot, Benjamin	61
Taylor, E. D.	61
Taylor, Eliza C.	61, 152
Taylor, G. W.	29
Taylor, Hays (deceased)	5, 13
Taylor, James	61, 152
Taylor, John *	73, 183
Temple, William H.	71, 178
Thomas C. Rockhill & Co.	75, 189
Thomas, Jesse B., Justice	9
	12
	23
	36
	46
	59, 149
	60, 150
	64
	71
	75
	76
	79
Thomas, William	31
	50, 127
Thomas, William, Justice	4, 11
Thompson, Michael	42, 107
Thompson, Mary Jane	42, 108
Thompson, William H.	47
Tinsley & Co.	61, 152
Tinsley, S. M.	61

Trailor, Joel   55, 138
Treat, Samuel H., Justice   2
                                                     5
                                                     7
                                                     8
                                                     9
                                                    10
                                                    11
                                                    12
                                                    14
                                                    15
                                                    16
                                                    17
                                                    20
                                                    21
                                                    23
                                                    24
                                                    26
                                                    27
                                                    28
                                                    29
                                                    31
                                                    39
                                                    40
                                                    42
                                                    43
                                                    45
                                                    47
                                                    50
                                                    51
                                                    54
                                                    55
                                                    57
                                                    58
                                                    59
                                                    60
                                                    61
                                                    62

Treat, Samuel H., Justice	63
	65
	66
	68
	71
	72
	73
	74
	75
	76
	77
	80
	81
Truett, Miers F.	25, 54
Trumbull, L.	7, 17
	30, 65
	41
Trumbull, Lyman *	80, 203
Turner, Starling *	63, 158
Underhill, Isaac	49, 124
Urquhart, J. D.	26
Van Winkle, Abraham	65
Van Winkle, Hiram *	65, 163
Van Winkle, Micajah	65
Vanderbergh, Eliza	45
Vanderbergh, Ferdinand (deceased)	45, 115
Vanderbergh, Francis	45
Vanderbergh, Henry	45, 115
Vanderbergh, Joseph C.	45
Vandever, N. M.	55
Vanscoyac	47
Wallace	13, 31
Ware, N. A.	19, 43
Ware, Nathaniel A.	33, 85
Warfield, Charles A.	32, 70
Warner, Alfred *	33, 85
Warren, D.	36, 90
Wash, Bryan, Mary Jane	61, 152

Wash, Milton H. * **61**, 152
Washburne, E. B. **25**
  70
Waterman, Hiram, Justice of the Peace **1**
Watkins, Thomas * **16**, 37
Watson **74**, 186
Webb, E. B. **5**
Weed, Harriet **82**, 210
Weed, William (deceased) **82**, 210
Weed, William **82**, 210
Weedman, John * **27**, 58
Welch, David **77**, 195
Welch, Upton D. **74**
White, John **16**, 37
Wilcoxon, Levi * **79**, 201
Wilder, R. **35**
Williams **13**, 31
Williams, A. **49**
Wilson, Greenup **65**, 164
Wilson, I. G. **77**
Wilson, James * **12**, 28
Wilson, Joseph L., (deceased) **5**, 13
Wilson, L. G. **59**
Wilson, Samuel **12**, 28
Wilson, Thomas (deceased) **65**, 163
Wilson, William, Justice **1**
  6
  13
  14
  17
  21
  25
  26
  37
  40
  64
  65
  74

Wilson, William, Justice   78

    82

    83

Wise, Mary   13, 32

Wood, Nicholas   32, 70

Worthing, Amos H. *   3, 10

Wren, Aquilla   46, 118

Wren, Clarissa *   46, 118

Wren, Thomas   46

Wright, Asa, D.   62

Wright, John   73, 183

Young, Richard M., Justice   43

    44

    46

    47

    48

    50

    53

    77

INDEX B

Index of Places	Case and Page Numbers (Case number bolded and listed first, page number regular typeface)
Alton, City of	**18**, 41
	19, 43
	33, 86
Ann Arundel County, Maryland	**74**, 186
Aurora, Illinois	**35**
Baltimore, Maryland	**32**, 70
Berrien County	**44**, 113
Bloomington, Illinois	**47**, 120
	71, 177
Bloomington, Hotel	**71**, 177
Boone County	**1**, 5
Boston	**67**, 168
Brown County	**22**, 48
Carlisle, Ohio	**31**, 66
Cass County	**50**, 126
Christian County	**55**, 138
Clark County	**74**, 186
Clay County	**40**, 100
Coles County	**83**, 213
Cook County	**43**, 110
	44, 113
	60, 150
DeKalb County	**52**, 132
Delaware	**25**, 54
DeWitt County	**27**, 58
DuPage County	**77**, 195
Edgar County	**54**, 136
	65, 164
	68, 171
Edwards County	**21**, 47

Edwards County	**78**, 198
Edwardsville, Illinois	**33**
England	**12**
Galena, Illinois	**67**, 168
Gallatin County	**10**, 23
	30, 64
	37, 92
	41, 104
Grand Rapids, Michigan	**45**
Hancock County	**58**, 146
Jo Daviess County	**1**, 5
	25, 54
	57, 144
	67, 168
	70, 175
Kane County	**35**, 88
	59, 148
Kendall County	**38**, 94
	48, 122
Kentucky	**32**
	43, 111
	61
Lake County	**69**, 174
LaSalle County	**36**, 90
	38, 94
Lead Mines	**2**, 7
Macon County	**7**, 17
Macoupin County	**15**, 35
	33
Madison County	**18**, 41
	19, 43
	33, 85
	32, 69
Marseilles, Town of	**38**, 94
Mason County	**66**, 166
Massachusetts	**32**
McHenry County	**77**, 196
McLean County	**31**, 66

McLean County   **47**, 120

71, 177

75, 189

Menard County   **26**, 56

62, 155

63, 160

73, 183

Montogomery County   **55**, 138

New York   **43**, 111

Niles, Illinois   **44**, 113

Pekin, Illinois   **11**, 24

47, 120

Peoria County   **46**, 118

49, 124

56, 141

58, 146

76, 192

Putnum County   **53**, 134

Richland County   **14**, 33

40

Sangamon County   **2**, 7

6, 15

8, 19

16, 37

20, 45

23, 50

24, 52

29, 62

42, 106

43, 110

50, 127

51, 131

55, 138

61, 152

80, 204

81, 206

Scott County   **39**, 97

Springfield, Illinois   **16**, 37

	81, 206
St. Louis, Missouri	**4**, 11
	33
	53, 134
Stephenson County	**79**, 201
Tazewell County	**3**, 10
	4, 11
	9, 21
	11, 25
	12, 28
	28, 60
	47, 120
	76, 193
Texas	**4**, 11
Vermillion County	**17**, 39
	64, 160
Wabash County	**5**, 13
	13, 31
	45, 114
White County	**82**, 211
Xenia, Ohio	**31**, 66
Yager's Addition, Washington	**75**

INDEX C

LEGAL TOPICS
Listed Case by Case

Topics	Case Numbers
Appeal, dismissal of	1
Appeal bond, timeliness of filing	1
Appellate jurisdiction of circuit court	1
Circuit clerk, creation of office in new county	1
County, creation of	1
Justice of the peace	1
Timeliness of filing, appeal bond	1
Bailee	2
Bailment	2
Constructive possession of personal property	2
Damages for trespass to personal property	2
Horse	2
Lien, on horse	2
Possession of personal property, as sufficient to permit bringing of action for trespass to personal property	2
Theft, of horse	2
Trespass to personal property, action of	2
Trover, action of	2
Agent, authority of; to bind principal by deed	3
Appeal bond, surety on	3
Power of attorney	3
Seal, necessity of; to make power of attorney valid	3
Surety on appeal bond	3
Consideration, failure of	4

Consideration, Illegal	4
Illegality of sale of free person	4
Presumption, evidentiary (that every person in Illinois is free rather than slave)	4
Promissory note	4
Servitude, indentured	4
Slavery	4
Execution	5
Execution, return of *nulla bona*	5
Fraudulent conveyance, setting aside	5
Steamboat	5
Bond, of sheriff	6
Execution sale of land	6
Redemption money, paid to redeem land from execution sale	6
Sheriff's bond	6
Surety on bond	6
Surety, liability of; on sheriff's bond	6
Suretyship	6
Appeal bond	7
Judgment, sufficiency of	7
Justice of the peace	7
Trial *de novo*	7
Gambling debt, as illegal consideration for promissory note	8
Illegality of consideration	8
Injunction by equity against enforcement of judgment obtained at law	8
Privilege against self-incrimination	8
Promissory note	8
Res judicata	8
Consideration, alleged lack of	9
Mortgage	9

Mortgage foreclosure proceeding 9
Promissory note 9
Usury 9

Damages, punitive; in action for seduction 10
Financial circumstances of defendant, 10
    as admissible evidence in action for
    seduction
Financial circumstances of plaintiff, 10
    as admissible evidence in action for
    seduction
Punitive damages in action for seduction 10
Seduction, action for damages for 10
    defendant's seduction of plaintiff's
    daughter

Burden of proof, maker of promissory note's 11
    burden of proving non-occurrence
    of condition precedent to his duty
    under promissory note
Pleading, maker of promissory note's 11
    burden of pleading
    non-occurrence of condition
    precedent to his duty under
    promissory note
Promissory note 11
Subdividing of land 11
Subdivision lots 11

Administrator 12
Bona fide purchaser 12
Forgery 12
Note, promissory forgery of 12
Note, promissory; party bound by his 12
    acceptance of an instrument bearing
    a forgery of a signature
Note, promissory; warranty 12
    concerning genuine

247

Arrest   13
Damages, for false arrest   13
Duress, not a defense against action for   13
    false arrest
False arrest   13
Justice of Peace   13
New trial, motion for; on basis on   13
    newly discovered evidence
Newly discovered evidence   13
Posse, citizen's obligation to join   13
Warrant, for arrest   13

Admissions, of defendant; as insufficient   14
    to prove plaintiff's title of the land
Best evidence rule   14
Damages, timber; recovery of damages for   14
    unauthorized cutting of timber
Documentary originals rule   14
Evidence, proof of ownership of land   14
Land, proof of ownership   14
Timber   14

Debt, action of   15
Execution sale, statute restricting   15
    execution sale of land
Judgment, enforcement of   15
Judgment, execution upon   15
Land, sale of; in execution on judgment   15
Res judicata   15

Delay in enforcing rights,   16
    whether it should cause loss of rights
Horse, theft of   16
Limitations, statute of   16
Ratification of wrongful sale of horse   16
Replevin, action of   16
Statute of limitations   16

Assignment of judgment   17
Delay in enforcing rights,   17
    as causing a loss of those rights
Discharge of obligor; by his payment   17
    to assignor before having received
    notice, from assignee, of the assignment
Injunction against a party's   17
    payment of judgment to another
Judgment, assignment of   17
Just compensation,   17
    for land taken for public use
Public works, state board of   17
Railroad   17

Deed, sheriff's   18
Deed, tax   18
Ejectment, action of   18
Execution sale of land   18
Land, sale of; for payment of real estate taxes   18
Levy, certificate of levy on land   18
    defective because of vague description
    of land
Sheriff's deed   18
Tax deed   18
Tax deed void because of uncertainty   18
    as to owner's payment of real estate
    tax on portion of land sold
Title to land   18

Apportionment of value of land   19
    among competing creditors
Execution sale   19
Foreclosure, strict   19
Mortgage foreclosure   19
Note, promissory   19
Promissory note   19
Redemption, equity of   19
Strict foreclosure   19

Surety   19

Commissioner's report of sale of land   20
Commissioner's report of sale of land,   20
    motion to set aside
Decree *pro confesso*   20
Execution sale of land   20
Execution, writ of   20
Note, promissory   20
Promissory note   20

Injunction, dissolution of; as being an   21
    interlocutory, unappealable order
Injunction issued by court of equity   21
    against a party's enforcement of
    judgment entered by a court of law
Interlocutory order, as insufficient   21
    to permit the taking of an appeal therefrom
Judgments, finality of   21
Judgments, final; necessity of,   21
    as prerequisite to party's
    taking an appeal

Execution sale of land,   22
    alleged irregularities in procedure
    followed by sheriff
Execution, writ of   22
Injunction, in equity; against a party's   22
    enforcement of judgment entered at law
Note, promissory   22
Promissory note   22

Affirmative defense of payment of   23
    promissory note
Discharge of indebtedness   23
Note, promissory   23
Parol evidence rule   23

Payment of promissory note,   23
    as affirmative defense
Promissory note   23

Fraudulent conveyance   24
Indispensable party   24
Indispensable party, absence of; as a defect   24
    the objection to which cannot be waived
    by a party
Indispensable party, absence of; as requiring 24
    reversal of a judgment
Necessary party   24
Parties, joinder of necessary parties   24
Parties, joinder of indispensable parties   24

Appeal, record on   25
Bill of exceptions   25
New trial, motion for; on basis of newly   25
    discovered evidence
Newly discovered evidence, as basis for a   25
    motion for a new trial
Record on appeal   25
Record on appeal, ambiguities worked by   25
    omissions from record on appeal
    resolved against the appellant

Caveat emptor   26
Consideration, failure of;   26
    as not constituting a ground for
    recovering money paid at an execution sale
Execution sales   26
Horses   26
Judgments, enforcement of   26
Replevin, action of   26

Agistment   27
Bailment   27
Conversion   27

Damages, nominal	27
Damages for wrongful use of horse	27
Horse, damages for wrongful use of	27
Horse, conversion of	27
Nominal damages	27
Bond for deed	28
Condition precedent, party's failure	28
to perform; as barring his right	
to recover damages on a contract	
Deed, warranty	28
Note, promissory	28
Promissory note	28
Title bond	28
Administrator of decedent's estate	29
Delay in enforcing rights, as a waiver	29
of those rights	
Delay in rescinding contract for fraud	29
as a confirmation of contract and	
waiver of the right to rescind	
Election to rescind contract	29
on basis of seller's fraud,	
time within which election must be made	
Fraud	29
Injunction, to restrain holder of	29
promissory note from collecting thereon	
Note, promissory	29
Promissory note	29
Rescission of contract on basis	29
of seller's fraud	
Title to land, defective	29
Administrator, appointment of creditor	30
of decedent as administrator	
Delay in enforcing rights, as a waiver	30
of those rights	

Heir's rights in decedent's land   **30**

Laches   **30**
Limitations, period of; applicable to   **30**
   administrator's petition to sell
   decedent's land to pay debts
Mesne profits   **30**

Action by ward to compel guardian   **31**
   to reimburse him for misappropriation
   of ward's estate
Administrator   **31**
Dissipation of estate, guardian's   **31**
   dissipation of ward's estate
Fraud, stepfather's defrauding of his   **31**
   stepchildren out of their inheritance
Guardian's dissipation of ward's estate   **31**
Guardian of minors   **31**
Guardian of minors, duty to use interest
   only to maintain and educate children,
   and to leave principal untouched   **31**
Guardian of minors; guardian's invention of
   artificial wants for their wards, court's
   disapproval of   **31**
Minors   **31**

Admissions in one party's answer;   **32**
   whether binding on another party
Agency   **32**
Appearance by party in action,   **32**
   effect on attachment of party's land
Attachment lien   **32**
Attachment   **32**
Bail, special   **32**
Bona fide purchaser   **32**
Cestui que trust   **32**
Champerty   **32**
Constructive notice, given by recording   **32**

of deed

Creditor, judgment   32

Deed, recording of; as being necessary   32
   to give the grantee priority over
   attachment of land by grantor's creditor

Injunction against attachment action   32

Judgment creditor   32

Lien, obtained by attachment   32

Lis pendens   32

Necessary parties   32

Parties, necessary   32

Partnership   32

Pendente lite, purchase of land   32

Pendente lite, nihil innovetur   32

Principal, undisclosed   32

Priority of competing interest   32
   of creditors in a debtor's land

Purchaser, bona fide   32

Purchaser *pendente lite,* as being bound   32
   by the decree although not a party
   to the suit

Recording Act   32

Relation back of attachment lien   32
   (which leads to a judgment) to the
   date of the levy

Representation of parties not joined   32
   to action, by parties who have been
   joined to action

Special bail   32

Trust   32

Execution sale of land   33

Foreclosure, strict   33

Mortgage   33

Mortgage foreclosure   33

Note, promissory   33

Promissory note   33

Public sale of land in mortgage   33
   foreclosure action
Recording of mortgage, as giving   33
   constructive notice thereof
   to mortgagor's other creditors
Strict foreclosure   33
Title to land, defective   33
Title search, failure to make   33

Distraint of personal property   35
Distress for rent   35
Witness, incompetence to testify   35
   because of financial interest
   in the matter being tried

Execution, void for lack of notice   36
   of proceeding to defendant
Execution, writ of   36
Judgment, void for lack of notice   36
   of proceeding to defendant
Levy of writ of execution   36
Steers   36

Bill of exceptions   37
Breach of contract   37
Carpenter   37
Construction contract   37
Contract for construction of building 37
Discretion, exercise of that discretion 37
   granted to a party by a contract
   as not constituting a breach of that contract

Deposition testimony, use of in evidence 38
Deposition testimony, waiver of certain   38
   objections to; if not asserted before trial
Lien, mechanic's   38
Mechanic's lien   38

Mechanic's lien proceeding as an action   38
    at equity
Mill, flour; contract for construction of   38
Millwright work   38
Substantial performance of construction   38
    contract
Witness, competence of party to testify   38
    in his own case at equity
Witness, incompetence of party to testify   38
    in his own case at law

Affidavit, by sheriff, uncontradicted;   39
    to be taken as true
Consent of party to procedure,   39
    as waiver of his right to object
    to procedure
Execution   39
Execution sale   39
Judgment creditor   39
Settlement of litigation   39
    as removing all matters left for trial
Trial of right of personal property   39
    seized upon levy of execution

Deed, priority of; with respect
    to competing judgment lien   40
Deed, sheriff's   40
Ejectment, action of   40
Execution sale   40
Judgment creditor   40
Judgment lien   40
Recorder, County   40
Recorder, State   40
Recorder's misplacing of deed   40
    delivered for recording,
    effect on rights of grantor
    named in deed
Recording Act   40

Sheriff's deed   **40**

Bond, given by state official   **41**
Condition precedent to sureties'   **41**
   liability on officials' bond
Debt, action of   **41**
Fee office   **41**
Fund commissioner   **41**
   in connection with issuance
   if state bonds
Legislative action, action by both   **41**
   house of the legislature as
   necessary for
Secretary of State   **41**
State bonds   **41**
Sureties on official's bond   **41**

Conveyance of land, conditional upon   **42**
   support of minors
Deed to land, conditional upon   **42**
   support of minors
Minors, grandfather's effort   **42**
   to provide for his grandchildren
   after his death
Mistake of law, as defeating an   **42**
   action for specific performance
Parol evidence   **42**
Specific performance   **42**

Distraint   **43**
Distress for rent   **43**
Execution sale   **43**
Execution, writ of; priority between   **43**
   a competing writ of execution and
   a distress for rent
Priority, as between competing writ of   **43**
   execution and a distress for rent
Rent, amount owed for   **43**

Endorser's liability on promissory note **44**
 to holder
Instructions to jury **44**
Jury instructions **44**
Note, promissory; assignment of **44**
Presumption, evidentiary; drawn from **44**
 date on bearer notes, as to time
 that holder had obtained possession
 of notes
Promissory note, assignment of **44**
Set-off **44**

Appeal bond, alleged defect in **45**
Necessary party **45**
Party, necessary **45**
Process, service of; upon necessary **45**
 parties, as a prerequisite to
 circuit court's entry of judgment
Suggestion of death **45**

Abatement of divorce action **46**
 by reason of the death of one
 of the parties
Alimony **46**
Divorce **46**
Dower **46**
Writ of error, motion for a rule **46**
 requiring necessary parties
 to join in the proceeding in error
 before the Illinois Supreme Court

Consideration, failure of **47**
Impossibility of performance; **47**
 one contracting party's preventing
 the other's performance,
 as excusing the other's non-performance
Mill, steam **47**
Note, promissory **47**

Promissory note 47

Condition precedent to party's right 48
 to recover on contract
Contract for farm labor 48
Labor, contract for labor of farmhand 48
Quantum meruit 48
Wages, sought by farmhand 48

After-acquired title 49
Deed, quitclaim; sufficiency 49
 to pass grantor's after-acquired
 title to grantee
Ejectment, action of 49
Quitclaim deed, sufficiency of; 49
 to pass grantor's after-acquired
 title to grantee

Administrator with the will annexed 50
Ejectment, action of 50
Land, sale of; by administrator with 50
 the will annexed; petition for court's
 approval of sale a prerequisite
Minors, father's effort to provide 50
 for his children after his death
Power of sale, conferred by will 50
 on executor; as not authorizing
 administrator with the will annexed
 to sell land without court approval

Business license issued by municipality 51
City orders 51
Counterclaim 51
General funds of municipality 51
License, business; issued by municipality 51
Municipalities 51
Real estate taxes 51
Set-off 51

Tax anticipation warrants   51
Trial *de novo*   51

Arbitration, agreement for   52
Jurisdiction of circuit court   52
     to hear matter, in face of parties'
     agreement to arbitrate
Trespass *quare clausum fregit*   52

Endorsement of promissory note   53
Note, promissory   53
Pleading, sufficiency of declaration's   53
     allegation of endorsement of
     promissory note over to plaintiff
Promissory note   53

Bail bond   54
Condemnation money   54
Pleading, common law   54
Pleading; insufficiency of declaration   54
     to recover on bail bond for having
     failed to allege, with certainty,
     the entry of a judgment against
     the principal on the bail bond
Surety on bail bond   54

Bond for deed contract for sale of land   55
Misdescription of land   55
Note, promissory   55
Promissory note   55
Quarter-quarter section   55
School Commissioners   55
Section 16, in township,   55
     as owned by School Commissioners
Specific performance   55
Specific performance, action for;   55
     defeated by lack of clarity in the evidence

Agent's liability on contract negotiated   **56**
   by him, if he has failed to disclose
   his principal   **56**
Jubilee College   **56**
Principal, undisclosed   **56**
Labor of workman, contract for   **56**
Trial *de novo*   **56**

Arbitration   **57**
Jurisdiction, personal, over party;   **57**
   necessary to validity of judgment
   or award against party
Necessary party, personal jurisdiction   **57**
   over; as prerequisite to validity
   of any part of judgment entered in case

Attachment, as being available only   **58**
   to enforce a right growing out of
   contract, rather than to recover
   damages for a tort
Jurisdiction, personal; over defendant,   **58**
   as necessary to support a judgment
   against a defendant in a tort action
Publication of notice as insufficient notice   **58**
   to defendant in tort action

Assault and battery   **59**
Damages, excessiveness of;   **59**
   in a personal injury case
Evidence of sizes of plaintiff's and   **59**
   defendant's families, respectively,
   as admissible evidence in personal
   injury action
Financial circumstances of defendant,   **59**
   as evidence admissible in a personal
   injury action

Financial circumstances of plaintiff,   59
    as evidence admissible in a personal
    injury action
Jury's discretion, as to amount of damages   59
    which should be awarded
Trespass, action of   59

Mortgage   60
Mortgage foreclosure proceeding   60
Note, promissory   60
Promissory note   60
Usury   60

Acceptance of deed by grantee,   61
    as necessary to complete delivery of deed
Deed, on delivery of; to an escrow holder   61
    for benefit of minor
Deed, delivery of; what constitutes   61
Delivery of deed   61
Minor   61
Next friend for incompetent adult   61
Presumption in favor of delivery of deed,   61
    in the case of gift of land to an infant

Child custody, of illegitimate child   62
Child support bond   62
Child support obligation, of father with   62
    respect to illegitimate child
Custody of illegitimate child   62
Father of illegitimate child, his right   62
    to take custody of child; if child's
    mother accepts child support payments
    from him
Illegitimate child, father's duty to support   62
Paternity proceeding   62
Termination of child support obligation,   62
    of father of illegitimate child

Arbitration   63
Jury, as sole judges of questions of fact   63
Negligence, in allowing set fire   63
    to grow out of control on the prairie
Prairie fire, setting   63
Silence of parties, not taken as consent   63
    to decision by a majority, rather than
    by a unanimity; of arbitrators
Trespass on the case   63

Agent, self-dealing by   64
Delay in enforcing rights, as causing   64
    a loss of those rights
Evidence, insufficiently of, to prove fraud   64
Fraud, rescission of contract for   64
Injunctions against enforcement   64
    of judgments at law obtained on
    promissory notes
Land speculation   64
Note, promissory   64
Promissory note   64
Rescission of contract for one party's fraud,   64
    necessity of defrauded party's electing
    to rescind within a reasonable time
    after having learned of fraud
Self-dealing by agent   64
Status quo ante, restoration of parties to;   64
    in event of rescission of contract for fraud

Continuance of trial   65
Fraud   65
Injunction against collection of judgment   65
    obtained at law on a promissory note
Limitations, statute of   65
Note, promissory   65
Promissory note   65
Statute of limitations   65
Trial *de novo*   65

Waiver on appeal of defenses not raised   **65**
   in the trial court

Adultery, accusation of; as being slanderous   **66**
Defamation   **66**
Fornication, accusation of;   **66**
   as being slanderous
"Of and concerning" element of tort   **66**
   of defamation
Pleading, declaration in slander action   **66**
   defective because of lack of specificity
Slander and Libel Act   **66**

Appearance, party's entry of   **67**
Attorneys' entering client's appearance   **67**
   in case without client's consent
Entry of appearance by party in case,   **67**
   what constitutes
Injunction against proceeding with   **67**
   action at law
Jurisdiction, personal, over defendant;   **67**
   as necessary to support decree entered
   by equity court against defendant
Lead mining   **67**
Master in chancery   **67**
Partnership   **67**

Clerk of circuit court, action to recover   **68**
   fees allegedly owed to him (for work done
   at state's attorney's request) from county
Fee office   **68**
Recognizance   **68**
Scire facias   **68**

Criminal conversation   **69**
Evidence, sufficiency of; to support verdict   **69**
   and judgment for plaintiff in action for
   criminal conversation

Trespass for criminal conversation, action for   **69**

Bill of exceptions, necessity of trial judge's   **70**
    signature thereon
Mandamus, writ of; application   **70**
    to Illinois Supreme Court for issuance of,
    against trial judge
Nonsuit, voluntary   **70**
Voluntary dismissal, as rendering   **70**
    alleged previous errors in proceeding
    unappealable by party who obtained it
Voluntary nonsuit   **70**

Consideration   **71**
Grocery   **71**
Illegality of consideration,   **71**
    as rendering promissory note void
License Act   **71**
License, liquor   **71**
Liquor license, nontransferability of   **71**
Note, promissory   **71**
Promissory note   **71**

Execution   **72**
Execution sale, vitiation of   **72**
Executions, successive; on same tracts of land   **72**
Injunction against enforcement of   **72**
    execution lien
Redemption form execution sale   **72**
Redemption time   **72**

Depreciation of value of bank paper   **73**
Discharge of indebtedness held or endorsed   **73**
    by the State Bank of Illinois, by payment
    in depreciated bank paper
Mortgage   **73**
Mortgage foreclosure proceeding   **73**
Note, promissory   **73**

Promissory note   73
State Bank of Illinois, bankruptcy of   73

Appearance by attorney, with party's   74
    authorization, as a submission to the
    court's personal jurisdiction
Foreign judgments, enforcement of;   74
    in Illinois circuit court
Full Faith and Credit Clause   74
    of the United States Constitution
Judgments, foreign; enforcement of   74
Jurisdiction, personal, over defendant;   74
    necessity of, in order to make court's
    judgment against defendant valid
Record on appeal   74

Amendment of pleading causing a material   75
    change in the action, as providing
    a basis of a continuance
Assumpsit, action of   75
Continuance, motion for   75
Land, defective title to   75
Partnership   75
Set-off, defendant's inability to assert,   75
    as set-off, unliquidated damages arising
    out of claims not connected to subject
    matter of plaintiff's claim
Title to land, defective   75

Building, construction of   76
Construction contract   76
Damages awarded in mechanic's lien   76
    foreclosure proceeding
Limitation, on time for filing petition   76
    to enforce mechanic's lien
Mechanic's lien proceeding   76
Workmanlike performance   76
    of construction work

Assignment of chose in action   77
Chose in action   77
Court costs   77
Execution   77
Fee bill from circuit clerk   77
Indemnification for court costs   77
Liability of assignee of chose in action,   77
     to his assignor, for court costs
     assessed against both in action brought
     by the assignee

Child support, alleged excessiveness of   78
Child custody, modification of   78
Custody of children, father's right to have   78
Divorce   78
Minors   78

Breach of contract   79
Contract, breach of   79
Discharge of jury, as ending circuit court's   79
     ability to correct errors
     in the jury's verdict
Government land, competing claims to   79
Judgment, entered upon defective   79
     jury defective; as being itself defective
Land, government; competing claims to   79
Liability, jury's finding of; as   79
     prerequisite to jury's assessment
     of damages

Appropriation by legislature   80
Assumpsit, action of   80
Journals of house and senate,   80
     indexing of
Laws, making copies of   80
Secretary of State   80
Standing or party to bring suit   80
State Auditor   80

Stipulated facts   **80**
Warrant for payment of funds   **80**
    by State Treasurer

Equity of redemption   **81**
Mistake of law   **81**
Mortgage   **81**
Mortgage foreclosure proceeding   **81**
Mortgage foreclosure sale,   **81**
    purchaser's motion to set aside
Redemption, equity of   **81**

Administrator   **82**
Dower   **82**
Limitations, on time for filing   **82**
    petition for enforcement
    of mechanic's lien
Mechanic's lien   **82**
Mechanic's lien foreclosure proceeding   **82**
Priority, of mechanic's lien   **82**
    with respect to claims of other
    creditors

Damages recovered by father,   **83**
    against another, for that other's
    seduction of the father's daughter
Instructions to jury   **83**
Jury instructions   **83**
Loss of daughter's services,   **83**
    as no longer being an element
    of father's action for damages for
    another's seduction of his daughter
Seduction of daughter,   **83**
    action for damages for
Trespass *vi et arms*   **83**

INDEX D

INDEX OF LEGAL TOPICS
in Alphabetical Order

Topics	Case Numbers

Abatement of divorce action
  by reason of the death of one
  of the parties
	46

Acceptance of deed by grantee as necessary to complete delivery of deed	**61**

Action by ward to compel guardian
  to reimburse him for misappropriation
  of ward's estate
	31

Administrator	**12**
Administrator	**31**
Administrator	**82**
Administrator, appointment of creditor of decedent as administrator	**30**
Administrator of decedent's estate	**29**
Administrator with the will annexed	**50**
Admissions in one party's answer, whether binding on another party	**32**
Admissions, of defendant, as insufficient to prove plaintiff's title to the land	**14**
Adultery, accusation of, as being slanderous	**66**
Affidavit, by sheriff, uncontradicted; to be taken as true	**39**
Affirmative defense of payment of promissory note	**23**
After-acquired title	**49**
Agency	**32**
Agent, authority of, to bind principal by deed	**3**

Agent's liability on contract negotiated
  by him, if he has failed to disclose
  his principal
	56

Agent, self-dealing by	**64**

269

Agistment	27
Alimony	**46**
Amendment of pleading causing a material change in the action, as providing a basis of a continuance	75
Appeal bond	7
Appeal bond, alleged defect in	45
Appeal bond, surety on	3
Appeal bond, timeliness of filing	1
Appeal, dismissal of	1
Appeal, record on	25
Appearance by attorney, with party's authorization, as a submission to the court's personal jurisdiction	74
Appearance by party in action, effect on attachment of party's land	32
Appearance, party's entry of	67
Appellate jurisdiction of circuit court	1
Apportionment of value of land among competing creditors	19
Appropriation by legislature	80
Arbitration	57
Arbitration	63
Arbitration, agreement for	52
Arrest	13
Assault and battery	59
Assignment of chose in action	77
Assignment of judgment	17
Assumpsit, action of	75
Assumpsit, action of	80
Attachment	32
Attachment, as being available only to enforce a right growing out of contract, rather than to recover damages for a tort	58
Attachment lien	32
Attorneys' entering client's appearance in case without client's consent	67

Bail bond	54
Bail, special	32
Bailee	2
Bailment	2
Bailment	27
Best evidence rule	14
Bill of exceptions	25
Bill of exceptions	37
Bill of exceptions, necessity of trial judge's signature thereon	70
Bona fide purchaser	12
Bona fide purchaser	32
Bond for deed	28
Bond for deed contract for sale of land	55
Bond, given by state official	41
Bond, of sheriff	6
Breach of contract	37
Breach of contract	79
Building, construction of	76
Burden of proof, maker of promissory note's burden of proving non-occurrence of condition precedent to his duty under promissory note	11
Business license issued by municipality	51
Carpenter	37
Caveat emptor	26
Cestui que trust	32
Champerty	32
Child custody, modification of	78
Child support, alleged excessiveness of	78
Child support bond	62
Child support obligation, of father with respect to illegitimate child	62
Child custody, of illegitimate child	62
Chose in action	77
Circuit clerk, creation of office in new county	1
City orders	51

Clerk of circuit court, action to recover 68
    fees allegedly owed to him (for work done
    at state's attorney's request) from county
Commissioner's report of sale of land 20
Commissioner's report of sale of land, 20
    motion to set aside
Condemnation money 54
Condition precedent to party's right 48
    to recover on contract
Condition precedent, party's failure 28
    to perform, as barring his right
    to recover damages on a contract
Condition precedent to sureties' 41
    liability on officials' bond
Consent of party to procedure, 39
    as waiver of his right to object
    to procedure
Consideration 71
Consideration, alleged lack of 9
Consideration, failure of 4
Consideration, failure of 47
Consideration, failure of, 26
    as not constituting a ground for
    recovering money paid at an execution sale
Consideration, illegal 4
Construction contract 37
Construction contract 76
Constructive notice, given by recording 32
    of deed
Constructive possession of personal property 2
Continuance of trial 65
Continuance, motion for 75
Contract, breach of 79
Contract for construction of building 37
Contract for farm labor 48
Conversion 27
Conveyance of land, conditional upon 42
    support of minors

Counterclaim	51
County, creation of	1
Court costs	77
Creditor, judgment	32
Criminal conversation	69
Custody of children, father's right to have	78
Custody of illegitimate child	62
Damages awarded in mechanic's lien foreclosure proceeding	76
Damages, excessiveness of, in a personal injury case	59
Damages, for false arrest	13
Damages for trespass to personal property	2
Damages for wrongful use of horse	27
Damages, nominal	27
Damages, punitive, in action for seduction	10
Damages recovered by father, against another, for that other's seduction of the father's daughter	83
Damages, timber; recovery of damages for unauthorized cutting of timber	14
Debt, action of	15
Debt, action of	41
Decree *pro confesso*	20
Deed, delivery of; to an escrow holder for benefit of minor	61
Deed, delivery of; what constitutes	61
Deed, priority of; with respect to competing judgment lien	40
Deed, quitclaim; sufficiency to pass grantor's after-acquired title to grantee	49
Deed; recording of; as being necessary to give the grantee priority over attachment of land by grantor's creditor	32
Deed, sheriff's	18
Deed, sheriff's	40
Deed, tax	18

Deed to land, conditional upon   42
  support of minors
Deed, warranty   28
Defamation   66
Delay in enforcing rights,   16
  whether it should cause loss of rights
Delay in enforcing rights,   17
  as causing a loss of those rights
Delay in enforcing rights, as a waiver   29
  of those rights
Delay in enforcing rights, as a waiver   30
  of those rights
Delay in enforcing rights, as causing   64
  a loss of those rights
Delay in rescinding contract for fraud   29
  as a confirmation of contract and
  waiver of the right to rescind
Delivery of deed   61
Deposition testimony, use of in evidence   38
Deposition testimony, waiver of certain   38
  objections to, if not asserted before trial
Depreciation of value of bank paper   73
Discharge of indebtedness   23
Discharge of indebtedness held or endorsed   73
  by the State Bank of Illinois, by payment
  in depreciated bank paper
Discharge of jury, as ending circuit court's   79
  ability to correct errors
  in the jury's verdict
Discharge of obligor, by his payment   17
  to assignor before having received
  notice, from the assignee, of the assignment
Discretion, exercise of that discretion   37
  granted to a party by contract
  as not constituting a breach of that contract
Dissipation of estate, guardian's   31
  dissipation of ward's estate
Distraint   43

Distraint of personal property	35
Distress for rent	35
Distress for rent	43
Divorce	46
Divorce	78
Documentary originals rule	14
Dower	46
Dower	82
Duress, not a defense against action for false arrest	13
Ejectment, action of	18
Ejectment, action of	40
Ejectment, action of	49
Ejectment, action of	50
Election to rescind contract on basis of seller's fraud, time within election must be made	29
Endorsement of promissory note	53
Endorser's liability on promissory note to holder	44
Entry of appearance by party in case, what constitutes	67
Equity of redemption	81
Evidence, insufficiency of, to prove fraud	64
Evidence of sizes of plaintiff's and defendant's families, respectively; as a admissible evidence in personal injury action	59
Evidence, proof of ownership of land	14
Evidence, sufficiency of; to support verdict and judgment for plaintiff in action for criminal conversation	69
Execution	5
Execution	39
Execution	72
Execution	77
Execution, return of *nulla bona*	5
Execution sale	19

Execution sale   39
Execution sale   40
Execution sale   43
Execution sales   26
Execution sale of land   6
Execution sale of land   18
Execution sale of land   20
Execution sale of land   33
Execution sale of land,   22
   alleged irregularities in procedure
   followed by sheriff
Execution sale, vitiation of   72
Execution, writ of; priority between   43
   a competing writ of execution and
   a distress for rent
Execution sale, statute restricting   15
   execution sale of land
Executions, successive, on same tracts of land   72
Execution, void for lack of notice   36
   of proceeding to defendant
Execution, writ of   20
Execution, writ of   22
Execution, writ of   36
False arrest   13
Father of illegitimate child; his right   62
   to take custody of child, if child's
   mother accepts child support payments
   from his
Fee bill from circuit clerk   77
Fee office   41
Fee office   68
Financial circumstances of defendant,   10
   as admissible evidence in action for
   seduction
Financial circumstances of defendant,   59
   as evidence admissible in a personal
   injury action

Financial circumstances of plaintiff,   **10**
as admissible evidence in action for
seduction

Financial circumstances of plaintiff,   **59**
as evidence admissible in a personal
injury action

Foreclosure, strict   **19**

Foreclosure, strict   **33**

Foreign judgments, enforcement of,   **74**
in Illinois circuit court

Forgery   **12**

Fornication, accusation of,   **66**
as being slanderous

Fraud   **29**

Fraud   **65**

Fraud, rescission of contract for   **64**

Fraud, stepfather's defrauding of his   **31**
stepchildren out of their inheritance

Fraudulent conveyance   **24**

Fraudulent conveyance, setting aside   **5**

Full Faith and Credit Clause   **74**
of the United States Constitution

Fund commissioner   **41**
in connection with issuance
if state bonds

Gambling debt, as illegal consideration   **8**
for promissory note

General funds of municipality   **51**

Government land, competing claims to   **79**

Grocery   **71**

Guardian of minors   **31**

Guardian of minors; duty to use interest   **31**
only to maintain and educate children,
and to leave principal untouched

Guardian of minors; guardian's invention of   **31**
artificial wants for their wards, court's
disapproval of

Guardian's dissipation of ward's estate   **31**

Heir's rights in decedent's land	**30**
Horse	**2**
Horses	**26**
Horse, conversion of	**27**
Horse, damages for wrongful use of	**27**
Horse, theft of	**16**
Illegality of consideration	**8**
Illegality of consideration, as rendering promissory note void	**71**
Illegality of sale of free person	**4**
Illegitimate child, father's duty to support	**62**
Impossibility of performance; one contracting party's preventing the other's performance, as excusing the other's non-performance	**47**
Indemnification for court costs	**77**
Indispensable party	**24**
Indispensable party, absence of, as a defect the objection to which cannot be waived by a party	**24**
Indispensable party, absence of, as requiring reversal of judgment	**24**
Injunction against a party's payment of judgment to another	**17**
Injunction against attachment action	**32**
Injunction against collection of judgment obtained at law on a promissory note	**65**
Injunction against enforcement of execution lien	**72**
Injunctions against enforcement of judgments at law obtained on promissory notes	**64**
Injunction against proceeding with action at law	**67**
Injunction by equity against enforcement of judgment obtained at law	**8**
Injunction, dissolution of, as being an interlocutory, unappealable order	**21**

Injunction, in equity, against a party's enforcement of judgment entered at law	22
Injunction issued by court of equity against a party's enforcement of judgment entered by a court of law	21
Injunction, to restrain holder of promissory note from collecting thereon	29
Instructions to jury	44
Instructions to jury	83
Interlocutory order, as insufficient to permit the taking of an appeal therefrom	21
Journals of house and senate, indexing of	80
Jubilee College	56
Judgment, assignment of	17
Judgment creditor	32
Judgment creditor	39
Judgment creditor	40
Judgment lien	40
Judgment, enforcement of	15
Judgments, enforcement of	26
Judgment, entered upon defective jury verdict, as being itself defective	79
Judgment, execution upon	15
Judgments, final; necessity of, as prerequisite to party's taking an appeal	21
Judgments, finality of	21
Judgments, foreign; enforcement of	74
Judgment, sufficiency of	7
Judgment, void for lack of notice of proceeding to defendant	36
Jurisdiction of circuit court to hear matter, in face of parties' agreement to arbitrate	52
Jurisdiction, personal, over defendant; as necessary to support a judgment against a defendant in a tort action	58

Jurisdiction, personal, over defendant;   67
    as necessary to support decree entered
    by equity court against defendant
Jurisdiction, personal, over defendant;   74
    necessity of, in order to make court's
    judgment against defendant valid
Jurisdiction, personal, over party;   57
    necessary to validity of judgment
    or award against party
Jury, as sole judges of questions of fact   63
Jury instructions   44
Jury instructions   83
Jury's discretion, as to amount of damages   59
    which should be awarded
Just compensation,   17
    for land taken for public use
Justice of the Peace   1
Justice of the Peace   7
Justice of the Peace   13
Labor, contract for labor of farmhand   48
Labor of workman, contract for   56
Laches   30
Land, defective title to   75
Land, government; competing claims to   79
Land, proof of ownership   14
Land, sale of, by administrator with   50
    the will annexed; petition for court's
    approval of sale a prerequisite
Land, sale of, for payment of real estate taxes   18
Land, sale of, in execution on judgment   15
Land speculation   64
Laws, making copies of   80
Lead mining   67
Legislative action, action by both   41
    house of the legislature as
    necessary for

Levy, certificate of levy on land   **18**
   defective because of vague description
   of land
Levy of writ of execution   **36**
Liability, jury's finding of; as   **79**
   prerequisite to jury's assessment
   of damages
Liability of assignee of chose in action,   **77**
   to his assignor; for court costs
   assessed against both in action brought
   by the assignee
License Act   **71**
License, business, issued by municipality   **51**
License, liquor   **71**
Lien, mechanic's   **38**
Lien, obtained by attachment   **32**
Lien, on horse   **2**
Limitation, on time for filing petition   **76**
   to enforce mechanic's lien
Limitations, on time for filing   **82**
   petition for enforcement
   of mechanic's lien
Limitations, period of, applicable to   **30**
   administrator's petition to sell
   decedent's land to pay debts
Limitations, statute of   **16**
Limitations, statute of   **65**
Liquor license, nontransferability of   **71**
Lis pendens   **32**
Loss of daughter's services,   **83**
   as no longer being an element
   of father's action for damages for
   another's seduction of his daughter
Mandamus, writ of; application   **70**
   to Illinois Supreme Court for issuance of,
   against trial judge
Master in chancery   **67**
Mechanic's lien   **38**

Mechanic's lien	82
Mechanic's lien foreclosure proceeding	82
Mechanic's lien proceeding	76
Mechanic's lien proceeding as an action at equity	38
Mesne profits	30
Mill, flour; contract for construction of	38
Mill, steam	47
Millwright work	38
Minor	61
Minors	31
Minors	78
Minors, father's effort to provide for his children after his death	50
Minors, grandfather's effort to provide for his grandchildren after his death	42
Misdescription of land	55
Mistake of law	81
Mistake of law, as defeating an action for specific performance	42
Mortgage	9
Mortgage	33
Mortgage	60
Mortgage	73
Mortgage	81
Mortgage foreclosure	19
Mortgage foreclosure	33
Mortgage foreclosure proceeding	9
Mortgage foreclosure proceeding	60
Mortgage foreclosure proceeding	73
Mortgage foreclosure proceeding	81
Mortgage foreclosure sale, purchaser's motion to set aside	81
Municipalities	51
Necessary parties	32
Necessary party	24
Necessary party	45

Necessary party, personal jurisdiction   57
   over; as prerequisite to validity
   of any part of judgment entered in case
Negligence, in allowing set fire   63
   to grow out of control on the prairie
New trial, motion for; on basis of   13
   newly discovered evidence
New trial, motion for; on basis of newly   25
   discovered evidence
Newly discovered evidence   13
Newly discovered evidence, as basis for a   25
   new trial
Next friend for incompetent adult   61
Nominal damages   27
Nonsuit, voluntary   70
Note, promissory   19
Note, promissory   20
Note, promissory   22
Note, promissory   23
Note, promissory   28
Note, promissory   29
Note, promissory   33
Note, promissory   47
Note, promissory   53
Note, promissory   55
Note, promissory   60
Note, promissory   64
Note, promissory   65
Note, promissory   71
Note, promissory   73
Note, promissory; assignment of   44
Note, promissory; forgery of   12
Note, promissory; party bound by his   12
   acceptance of an instrument bearing
   a forgery of a signature
Note, promissory; warranty   12
   concerning genuineness of

"Of and concerning" element of tort 66
   of defamation
Parol evidence 42
Parol evidence rule 23
Parties, joinder of indispensable parties 24
Parties, joinder of necessary parties 24
Parties, necessary 32
Partnership 32
Partnership 67
Partnership 75
Party, necessary 45
Paternity proceeding 62
Payment of promissory note, 23
   as affirmative defense
Pendente lite, nihil innovetur 32
Pendente lite, purchase of land 32
Pleading, common law 54
Pleading, declaration in slander action 66
   defective because of lack of specificity
Pleading, maker of promissory note's 11
   burden of pleading
   non-occurrence of condition
   precedent to his duty
   under promissory note
Pleading, insufficiency of declaration 54
   to recover on bail bond for having
   failed to allege, with certainty,
   the entry of a judgment against
   the principal on the bail bond
Pleading, sufficiency of declaration's 53
   allegation of endorsement of
   promissory note over to plaintiff
Posse, citizen's obligation to join 13
Possession of personal property, 2
   as sufficient to permit bringing of
   action for trespass to personal property
Power of attorney 3

Power of sale, conferred by will   50
   on executor; as not authorizing
   administrator with the will annexed
   to sll land without court approval
Prairie fire, setting   63
Presumption, evidentiary; drawn from   44
   date on bearer notes, as to time
   that holder had obtained possession
   of notes
Presumption, evidentiary (that every person   4
   in Illinois is free rather than slave)
Presumption in favor of delivery of deed,   61
   in the case of gift of land to an infant
Principal, undisclosed   32
Principal, undisclosed   56
Priority, as between competing writ of   43
   execution and a distress for rent
Priority of competing interests   32
   of creditors in a debtor's land
Priority, of mechanic's lien   82
   with respect to claims of other creditors
Privilege against self-incrimination   8
Process, service of, upon necessary   45
   parties; as a prerequisite to
   circuit court's entry of judgment
Promissory note   4
Promissory note   8
Promissory note   9
Promissory note   11
Promissory note   19
Promissory note   20
Promissory note   22
Promissory note   23
Promissory note   28
Promissory note   29
Promissory note   33
Promissory note   47
Promissory note   53

Promissory note	**55**
Promissory note	**60**
Promissory note	**64**
Promissory note	**65**
Promissory note	**71**
Promissory note	**73**
Promissory note, assignment of	**44**
Public sale of land in mortgage foreclosure action	**33**
Public works, state board of	17
Publication of notice as insufficient notice to defendant in tort action	**58**
Punitive damages in action for seduction	**10**
Purchaser, bona fide	32
Purchaser *pendente lite,* as being bound by decree although not a party to the suit	32
Quantum meruit	**48**
Quarter-quarter section	55
Quitclaim deed, sufficiency of; to pass grantor's after-acquired title to grantee	**49**
Railroad	17
Ratification of wrongful sale of horse	**16**
Real estate taxes	51
Recognizance	**68**
Record on appeal	25
Record on appeal	74
Record on appeal, ambiguities worked by omissions from record on appeal resolved against the appellant	25
Recorder, County	40
Recorder's misplacing of deed delivered for recording, effect on rights of grantor named in deed	40
Recorder, State	40
Recording Act	32

Recording Act   40
Recording of mortgage, as giving   33
  constructive notice thereof
  to mortgagor's other creditors
Redemption, equity of   19
Redemption, equity of   81
Redemption from execution sale   72
Redemption money, paid to redeem land   6
  from execution sale
Redemption time   72
Relation back of attachment lien   32
  (which leads to a judgment) to the
  date of the levy
Rent, amount owed for   43
Replevin, action of   16
Replevin, action of   26
Representation of parties not joined   32
  to action, by parties who have been
  joined to action
Rescission of contract on basis   29
  of seller's fraud
Rescission of contract for one party's fraud,   64
  necessity of defrauded party's electing
  to rescind within a reasonable time
  after having learned of fraud
Res judicata   8
Res judicata   15
School Commissioners   55
Scire facias   68
Seal, necessity of; to make power of   3
  attorney valid
Secretary of State   41
Secretary of State   80
Section 16, in township;   55
  as owned by School Commissioners
Seduction, action for damages for   10
  defendant's seduction of plaintiff's
  daughter

Seduction of daughter,   **83**
   action for damages for
Self-dealing by agent   **64**
Servitude, indentured   **4**
Settlement of litigation   **39**
   as removing all matters left for trial
Set-off   **44**
Set-off   **51**
Set-off, defendant's inability to assert,   **75**
   as set-off, unliquidated damages arising
   out of claims not connected to subject
   matter of plaintiff's claim
Sheriff's bond   **6**
Sheriff's deed   **18**
Sheriff's deed   **40**
Silence of parties, not taken as consent   **63**
   to decision by a majority, rather than
   by a unanimity, or arbitrators
Slander and Libel Act   **66**
Slavery   **4**
Special bail   **32**
Specific performance   **42**
Specific performance   **55**
Specific performance, action for;   **55**
   defeated by lack of clarity in the evidence
Standing or party to bring suit   **80**
State Auditor   **80**
State Bank of Illinois, bankruptcy of   **73**
State bonds   **41**
Status quo ante, restoration of parties to; **64**
   in event of rescission of contract for fraud
Statute of limitations   **16**
Statute of limitations   **65**
Steamboat   **5**
Steers   **36**
Stipulated facts   **80**
Strict foreclosure   **19**
Strict foreclosure   **33**

Subdividing of land	11
Subdivision lots	11
Substantial performance of construction contract	38
Suggestion of death	45
Sureties on official's bond	41
Surety	19
Surety, liability of; on sheriff's bond	6
Surety on appeal bond	3
Surety on bail bond	54
Surety on bond	6
Suretyship	6
Tax anticipation warrants	51
Tax deed	18
Tax deed void because of uncertainty as to owner's payment of real estate tax on portion of land sold	18
Termination of child support obligation, of father of illegitimate child	62
Theft, of horse	2
Timber	14
Timeliness of filing, appeal bond	1
Title bond	28
Title search, failure to make	33
Title to land	18
Title to land, defective	29
Title to land, defective	33
Title to land, defective	75
Trespass, action of	59
Trespass for criminal conversation, action for	69
Trespass on the case	63
Trespass *quare clausum fregit*	52
Trespass to personal property, action of	2
Trespass *vi et arms*	83
Trial *de novo*	7
Trial *de novo*	51
Trial *de novo*	56
Trial *de novo*	65

Trial of right of personal property   39
   seized upon levy of execution

Trover, action of   2

Trust   32

Usury   9

Usury   60

Voluntary dismissal, as rendering   70
   alleged previous errors in proceeding
   unappealable by party who obtained it

Voluntary nonsuit   70

Wages, sought by farmhand   48

Waiver on appeal of defenses not raised   65
   in the trial court

Warrant, for arrest   13

Warrant, for payment of funds   80
   by State Treasurer

Witness, competence of party to testify   38
   in his own case at equity

Witness, incompetence of party to testify   38
   in his own case at law

Witness, incompetence to testify   35
   because of financial interest
   in the matter being tried

Workmanlike performance   76
   of construction work

Writ of error, motion for a rule   46
   requiring necessary parties
   to join in the proceeding in error
   before the Illinois Supreme Court

Index of Authorities cited in Lincoln's Briefs	Case and Page Numbers (Case number bolded and listed first, page number regular typeface)

1	A. K. Marsh 87	**50**
	Bacon's Abr. title Stat.	**32**, 79
1	Bac. Abr. 346-49	**26**
6	Bac. Abr., title Trespass, E 577	**2**
6	Bac. Abr. 577	**2**
6	Bac. Abr., title Trover, C 684	**2**
1	Barb. 593 par. 30	**31**
1	Barb. & Har. Dig. 591, 592, par. 17	**31**
4	Barb. & Har. Dig. 232 par. 2	**31**
6	Barn. & Cres. 671 *(Milores vs. Duncan)*	**26**
1	Bibb. 455	**31**
1	Bibb. 509 *(Henderson vs. Bradford)*	**30**
2	Bibb. 89, 93 *(Gillespie vs. Gillespie)*	**83**, 215
2	Bibb. 238	**4**
3	Bibb. 456 *(Tanner vs. Davidson)*	**30**
2	Black. Com., 177	**40**
2	Black. Com. 450	**16**
1	Blackf. 170 *(Ewing vs. French)*	**75**, 190
2	Blackf. 420 *(Kelly vs. Duignan)*	**75**, 190
1	Bouvier's Law Dic. 409	**40**
2	Burr 1012 *(Moses vs. M'Ferlan)*	**26**
2	Caines 61,66 *(Simmons vs. Catlin)*	**18**

3	Caines 325	**4**
	Calvert 5	**32**, 74
	Calvert 58	**32**, 74
	Chitty on Cont. 184	**80**, 204
1	Chit. Plead 138	**2**
1	Chit. Plead 153	**2**
	and note 2 on 153, 1541	
1	Chit. Plead. 205	**11**
1	Chit. Plead. 280, 354, 254	**11**
1	Chitty's Pl. 354	**41**
2	Chitty's P. 472	**54**
5	Coke's R. 22a	**41**
2	Comyn on Cont. 7	**80**, 204
2	Comyn. on Cont. 142	**77**
2	Cond. R. 157, 160	**75**, 190
	Const. of Ill., Art. VI (1818)	**4**
	Cooper 286, 288, head paging	**75**, 190
2	Cowen 483	**27**
5	Cowen 231	**44**
	(*Wheeler vs. Raymond*)	
5	Cowen 671	**30**
	(*Marvin vs. Vedder*)	
6	Cowen 693	**44**
	(*Johnson vs. Bridge*)	
9	Cowen 120	**32**, 81
9	Cowen 121	**32**, 79
9	Cowen 409, 419	**44**
	(*Bank of Niagara vs. Rosevelt*)	
7	Cowen 64	**31**
	(*Campbell vs. Tousey*)	
7	Cowen 177	**44**
	(*Mauran vs. Lamb*)	
6	Cranch 8, 24	**32**, 76
	Cushing's Trustee Process 25, 47, 51	**32**, 78
3	Dana 66	**83**, 215
	(*Sullivan vs. Enders*)	
1	Dana 231	**31**
	(*Vance vs. Campbell's Heirs*)	

1	Dana 481, 502	**83**, 215
	(*Gaines vs. Buford*)	
2	Dana 221	**83**, 215
	(*Allen vs. Kopman*)	
2	East 227	**32**, 77
4	East 545	**43**
	(*Payne vs. Drew*)	
7	East 5, 6, 7	**2**
8	East 80	**11**
1	Eng. Com. Law R. 136	**75**, 190
2	Eng. Com. Law R. 432	**80**, 204
	(*Robson vs. Andrade*)	
13	English Com. Law R. 293	**26**
	Gale's Stat. 44	**4**
	Gale's Stat. 711	**30**
1	Gall. 630, 635	**32**, 76
1	Gillman 15 [6 Ill. 15 (1844)]	**51**
	(*Kaskaskia Bridge Co. vs. Shannon*)	
1	Gillman 649 [6 Ill. 649 (1844)]	**51**
	(*Kelly vs. Garrett*)	
	Gould's Pl. part IV par. 12, 13	**54**
	Gould's Pl. part IV par. 26	**54**
1	Greenl. 76	**77**
4	Greenl. 391	**42**, 108
	(*Dwight vs. Pomeroy*)	
1	Greenl. Ev. par. 5	**63**
1	Greenl. Ev. 197, 199	**63**
1	Greenl. Ev. 210	**32**, 76
9	Har. 548	**77**
1	Har. and Gill 435	**18**
	(*Thomas vs. Turvey*)	
3	Har. & Johns, 57	**77**
2	Harrison's Dig. 1521	**13**
2	Hill's (N.Y.) R. 387	**52**
	(*Smith vs. Barse*)	
2	Irdell's Eq. R. 360	**61**
	(*Snider vs. Lackenou*r)	

293

2	Iredell's Law R. 388, 391	**61**
	(*Morrow vs. Alexander*)	
2	J. J. Marsh. 404	**31**
	(*Whilledge's Heirs vs. Collis*)	
3	J. J. Marsh. 332	**75**, 190
7	J. J. Marsh. 321	**83**, 215
	(*Trotter vs. Saunders*)	
1	Johns. Cas. 184	**18**
2	Johns. 260	**18**
2	Johns. 455	**12**
	(*Markle vs. Hatfield*)	
3	Johns. 146	**41**
3	Johns. 239	**27**
4	Johns. 46	**32**, 77
4	Johns. 216	**32**, 81
5	Johns. 193	**44**
	(*Eells vs. Finch*)	
6	Johns. 39	**63**
	(*Green vs. Miller*)	
7	Johns. 278	**40**
	(*Collins vs. Torrey*)	
8	Johns. 249	**77**
9	Johns. 168	**32**, 74
9	Johns. 270-277	**18**
	(*Jackson vs. Vosburgh*)	
9	Johns. 291	**75**, 190
10	Johns. 176	**27**
	(*Murray vs. Barling*)	
10	Johns. 198	**4**
10	Johns. 456	**32**, 74
13	Johns. 249	**43**
	(*Wiley vs. Hyde*)	
13	Johns. 471	**32**, 81
13	Johns. 537, 551-2	**18**
	(*Jackson vs. Delaney*)	
14	Johns. 148, 160	**35**
	(*Graves vs. Delaplaine*)	
14	Johns. 188	**4**

16	Johns. 102	32, 80
16	Johns. 226	44
	(*Gould vs. Chase*)	
18	Johns. 205	13
19	Johns. 49	44
	(*Henry vs. Brown*)	
19	Johns. 322	44
	(*Jefferson County Bank vs. Chapman*)	
19	Johns. 325	40
	(*Curtis vs. Bronson*)	
1	Johns. Ch. R. 49, 95-99	8
1	Johns. Ch. R. 348, 437	24
1	Johns. Ch. R. 565, 579	32, 76
1	Johns. Ch. R. 574	32, 76
2	Johns. Ch. R. 197	24
2	Johns. Ch. R. 197	32, 74
2	Johns. Ch. R. 441	32, 77
6	Johns. Ch. R. 360, 376, to end	30
	(*Mooers vs. White*)	
3	Johns. Dig., 575	2
1	Kent's Com. 432-3	32, 79
2	Kent's Com. 491, and note	30
4	Kent's Com. 99 to 103	40
	Kyd on Awards 106	63
15	Law Lib. 6, 9	32, 73
5	Law Reporter 55	32, 78
1	Littell 325	8
2	Littell 71	55
	(*Burnett vs. Robinson*)	
	Long on Sales 174	16
1	Lord Raym. 369	31
	(*Yard vs. Eland*)	
16	Maine (4 Shepley) 308	30
	(*Smith vs. Dutton*)	
2	Mass. 455	75, 190
4	Mass. 135	30
	(*Wallis vs. Wallis*)	

6	Mass. 182	12
	(*Young vs. Adams*)	
7	Mass. 205	13
9	Mass. 104	32, 77
9	Mass. 265, 112	32, 77
12	Mass. 11	77
14	Mass. 217	32, 77
15	Mass. 58	30
	(*Ex parte Allen*)	
15	Mass. 326	30
	(*Wellman vs. Lawrence*)	
16	Mass. 171	30
	(*Stearns vs. Stearns*)	
17	Mass. 328	42, 107
	(*Dwight vs. Pomeroy*)	
1	McLean 322	18
	(*Lessee of Dunn vs. James et. al*)	
3	Monroe 111	24
	(*Surlott vs. Beddoe*)	
7	Monroe 346	24
	Montagu on Lien 29 and note (f); Esp. N. P., 584	2
	Morehead's Par. 251, bottom of the page	70
7	Munroe 150, 170	31
	(*Chapline vs. Moore*)	
3	N. Y. Dig. 590 sec. 83	13
2	N. H. Rep. 319	2
6	New Hamp. 418	48
	(*Britton vs. Turner*)	
1	Ohio 171-2	75, 190
6 and 7	Ohio 418-21	61
	(*Lessee of Lloyd vs. Giddings*)	
	Ordinance of Congress, Art. VI (1787)	4
2	P. Wms. 500	32, 80
3	P. Wms. 244 n.	32, 76
3	Paige 23, 379	24
3	Paige 379	24
	(*Rogers vs. Rogers*)	

4	Paige 23	**24**
4	Paige 33	**24**
4	Paige 64	**31**
	(*Van Epps vs. Van Deusen*)	
4	Paige 314	**24**
3	Peters Cond. R. 624	**80**, 204
	(*Jones vs. Shore*)	
3	Peters' Dig. 154	**24**
3	Peters' Dig. 161	**24**
1	Peters 305	**24**
4	Peters 349	**18**
	(*Ronkendorf vs. Taylor's lessee*)	
5	Peters 276, 277	**42**, 108
	(*Cathcart vs. Robinson*)	
5	Peters 445	**80**, 204
	(*Buel vs. Van Ness*)	
5	Peters 580	**80**, 2O4
	(*Tiernan vs. Jackson*)	
9	Peters 607	**30**
	(*Owings vs. Hall*)	
14	Peters 322-328	**18**
1	Pick. 232	**2**
2	Pick. 567	**30**
	(*Petition of Richmond, Adm'r*)	
5	Pick. 142	**30**
	(*Heath vs. Wells*)	
11	Pick. 140	**83**, 215
	(*Tufts vs. Seabury*)	
14	Pick. 210	**26**
	(*Parish vs. Stone*)	
15	Pick. 465	**40**
	(*Tracy vs. Jenks*)	
18	Pick. 314	**40**
	(*Ames vs. Phelps*)	
22	Pick. 11	**45**
	(*Commonwealth vs. Dunham*)	
1	Powell on Con. 397 citing Dyer 17a	**41**

3	Powell on Mortgages, 1088, XIV. and note (1)	**40**
	Prin 23, 44-5, 54-5	**26**
	R. L. 57	**4**
	R. L. 87, 93	**32**, 79
	R. L. 320, 483	**8**
	R. L. 374, par. 10	**18**
	R. L. 603	**14**
	R. L. 644 par. 98, 99	**30**
3	R. L. 25, 182	**32**, 80
	Reeve's Dom. Rel. 192	**31**
	Rev. Stat. Ch. IX par. 3	**58**
	Rev. Stat. 83 par. 8	**54**
	Rev. Stat. 342 sec. 9	**71**, 178
	Roscoe's Ev. 27, 324	**14**
	S. C. 3 Peters' Cond. R. 395 notes	**41**
1	Salk. 306	**31**
	(*Wankford vs. Wankford*)	
2	Salkeld, 666	**4**
2	Saunders' Pl. & Ev. 675	**80**, 204
1	Scam. 464 [2 Ill. 462, 464 (1838)]	**75**, 190
	(*Edwards vs. Todd*)	
1	Scam. 468 [2 Ill. 468 (1838)]	**71**, 178
	(*Berry vs. Hamby*)	
1	Scam. 476 [2 Ill. 476 (1838)]	**32**, 77
1	Scam. 491 [2 Ill. 490, 491 (1838)]	**56**, 142
	(*Smith vs. Shultz*)	
1	Scam. 525 [2 Ill. 525 (1838)]	**75**, 190
	(*Covell vs. Marks*)	
1	Scam. 532 [2 Ill. 532 (1838)]	**63**
	(*Johnson vs. Moulton*)	
2	Scam. 17 [3 Ill. 17 (1839)]	**32**, 77
2	Scam. 351 [3 Ill. 351 (1840)]	**37**
	(*Harmon vs. Thornton*)	
2	Scam. 499 [3 Ill. 499 (1840)]	**32**, 74
2	Scam. 499 [3 Ill. 499 (1840)]	**32**, 81
3	Scam. 6, 7 [4 Ill. 5, 6, 7 (1841)]	**37**
	(*Rogers vs. Hall*)	

3	Scam. 18 [4 Ill. 15, 18 (1841)] *(Leigh vs. Hodges)*	**56**, 142
3	Scam. 18 [4 Ill. 15, 18 (1841)] *(Leigh vs. Hodges)*	**63**
3	Scam. 71 [4 Ill. 71 (1841)] *(Bailey vs. Cromwell)*	**11**
3	Scam. 169 [4 Ill. 168, 169 (1841)] *(Carson vs. Merle)*	**45**
3	Scam. 203 [4 Ill. 203 (1841)] *(Ballentine vs. Beall)*	**24**
3	Scam. 298 [4 Ill. 298 (1841)] *(Nichols vs. Ruckells)*	**75**, 190
3	Scam. 385 [4 Ill. 385 (1842)] *(Sappington vs. Pulliam)*	**53**
3	Scam. 487 [4 Ill. 483, 487 (1842)] *(Schlencker vs. Risley)*	**56**, 142
3	S1cam. 536 to 539 [4 Ill. 535 (1842)] *(Pettis vs. Westlake)*	**44**
3	Scam. 539 [4 Ill. 539 (1842)] *(Ryder vs. Stevenson)*	**45**
4	Scam. 30 [5 Ill. 30 (1842)] *(McKee vs. Ingalls)*	**37**
4	Scam. 460 [5 Ill. 460 (1843)] *(Rowan vs. Dosh)*	**37**
3	Stark. Ev., 1504, note 2	**2**
2	Starkie's Ev. 58	**77**
	State Recorder, R. L. 587	**32**, 80
	Story on Agency par. 266, 267	**56**, 142
	Story on Bail. 197, 204	**32**, 78
	Story on Con. par. 314	**56**, 141
	Story on Partn. 373	**32**, 80
2	Story's Eq. 179-183	**8**
	Story's Eq. Jur. 138	**32**, 74
1	Story's Eq. Jur. par. 471-2	**80**, 204
1	Story's Eq. Jur. 483	**32**, 77
2	Story's Eq. Jur. 584 par. 1355	**31**
2	Story's Eq. Jur. par. 692, 693,	**42**, 108
2	Story's Eq. Jur. par. 770	**42**, 108

2	Story's Eq. Jur. 976	**50**
2	Story's Eq. Jur. par. 1058 to 1064	**50**
	742, 750, 751, 769	
	Story's Eq. Plead. 74, par. 72	**24**
	Story's Eq. Pl. 74a par. 76c	**45**
	Story's Eq. Pl. 97, 135, 145, 414	**32, 74**
	Story's Eq. Plead. par. 75	**24**
	Story's Eq. Plead. par. 127, 139	**24**
	Story's Eq. Plead. par. 138 see par. 72	**24**
	Story's Eq. Plead., 138, sec. 140	**5**
	Story's Eq. Plead. 175 par. 189	**24**
	Story's Eq. Plead. 182, Par. 197, 199	**24**
	Story's Eq. Plead. par. 226	**24**
	Story's Eq. Plead. par. 231	**24**
2	Sug. on Ven. 254, 336	**32,74**
6	T. R. 606	**2**
5	T. R. 710	**41**
5	Taunt. 488	**12**
	(*Jones vs. Ryde*)	
1	Term R. 285	**26**
	(*Bize vs. Dickason*)	
2	Term R. 370	**26**
	(*Stratton vs. Restall et al.*)	
4	Term R. 514	**14**
	(*Barry vs. Babbington*)	
8	Term R. 167	**11**
	Toller on Executors 241, 358	**31**
1	U. S. Dig. 180 par. 424 and	**45**
	cases there cited	
	(*Brooks vs. The President &c., of Jacsonville*)	
1	U. S. Dig. 281 pr. 325	**77**
1	U. S. Dig. 283 pr. 251	**77**
1	U. S. Dig. 540. par. 66	**47**
3	U. S. Dig. 58, title "Nonsuit"	**70**
	sec. 30, 33, 34	
3	U. S. Dig 571 pr. 563-565	**83, 215**
1	Vernon 255	**31**

(*Barlow vs. Grant*)
1   Vern. 286   **32**, 76
    (*Preston vs. Tubbin*)
3   Ves. 75   **32**, 73
6   Vesey 473   **31**
    (*Walker vs. Wetherell*)
11 Ves. 4, 29   **32**, 74
13 Ves. 397, 526   **32**, 74
16 Ves. 321   **32**, 74
16 Ves. 326, 1808   **32**, 73
2   Ves. jr. 458   **32**, 76
2   Wash. Va. R. 74   **61**
    (*Currie vs. Donald*)
2   Wend. 481   **77**
3   Wend. 412   **26**
3   Wend. 418   **83**, 215
    (*Wardell vs. Hughes*)
    (*Burr vs. Veeder*)
4   Wend. 436, 442   **30**
    (*Jackson vs. Robinson*)
5   Wend. 48   **13**
6   Wend. 284   **77**
8   Wend. 112   **77**
10 Wend. 119   **27**
10 Wend. 384   **4**
12 Wend. 27   **13**
14 Wend. 76   **80**, 204
    (*Waddell vs. Morris*)
9   Wheat. 680   **41**
    (*Miller vs. Stewart*)
12 Wheat. 180   **83**, 215
    (*United States vs. Tillotson*)
2   Williams on Executors 130   **31**